SIR WILLIAM TRUMBULL
IN PARIS

Portrait of Sir William Trumbull engraved by Vertue
after Sir Godfrey Kneller

British Museum, Print Room

SIR WILLIAM TRUMBULL
IN PARIS
1685–1686

By

RUTH CLARK

CAMBRIDGE
AT THE UNIVERSITY PRESS
1938

CAMBRIDGE
UNIVERSITY PRESS

University Printing House, Cambridge CB2 8BS, United Kingdom

Cambridge University Press is part of the University of Cambridge.

It furthers the University's mission by disseminating knowledge in the pursuit of
education, learning and research at the highest international levels of excellence.

www.cambridge.org
Information on this title: www.cambridge.org/9781107464148

© Cambridge University Press 1938

First published 1938
First paperback edition 2014

A catalogue record for this publication is available from the British Library

ISBN 978-1-107-46414-8 Paperback

Contents

Plates

Preface

A "sober worthy gentleman" went to France as Envoy Extraordinary for the space of less than a year. He had his first public audience at Versailles on December 11, 1685, and his *audience de congé* on September 22, 1686. He was not brilliant; people wondered why he had been appointed; he gave displeasure to the French court; he received little support from his own King; he was unsuccessful in most of his negotiations; everyone was relieved to see him depart for Constantinople. His letters have a pedestrian quality—he could not write like Henry Savile, and still less like Matthew Prior. It may well be asked why the story of his brief mission should be told.

The period is one of unusual complications and distress. Above all, it accounts for much that was to happen. A month before Sir William Trumbull landed in France the Revocation of the Edict of Nantes was signed. The vexations and persecutions meted out to French Protestants were extended at times to English Protestants residing in France, especially to those who had some more intimate connection with the country —Englishmen who had married Frenchwomen, Englishwomen who had married Frenchmen, English parents who had children born in France, or English residents who had French servants. English captains sought to help French refugees and were imprisoned. Frenchmen naturalized in England were captured at sea. Englishmen naturalized in France protested when they met with the same treatment as French natural-born subjects. Often Sir William was called upon to intervene, and once also in behalf of a future King of England whose subjects in the little Principality of Orange had been exposed to the activities of the "booted missionaries". That King was to make Sir William one of his Secretaries of State.

The unrest, the distrust, the growing hostility to France, the growing antagonism to James II need no further proof or explanation. But if they were needed they could be found in these pages.

The materials for an account of these months in France are abundant, but as the period covered is short they are not overwhelming, and an unusual opportunity is offered to survey the work of one ambassador in detail.

Sir William wrote to Sunderland twice a week. His ninety-seven letters are at the Record Office. A letter to Lord Preston is printed in the Appendix to the *Seventh Report* of the Historical Manuscripts Commission and two letters to Dijkvelt are printed in the Appendix to the *Eighth Report*.[1] The letters received by Sir William during this period are practically all in existence, in possession of the Marquess of Downshire at Easthampstead Park, Berkshire. They form the subject of one of the reports of the Historical Manuscripts Commission. In the *Calendars of Treasury Books* one finds valuable information concerning Sir William's expenditures.

The correspondence between Louis XIV, Colbert de Croissy and Barrillon, preserved at the Archives of the Ministère des Affaires Étrangères, gives "the other side of the story". These letters were utilized by M. C. Pascal[2] in a series of three articles in the *Bulletin de la Société de l'Histoire du Protestantisme français* for 1894—"Un ambassadeur désagréable à la cour de Louis XIV, Sir William Trumball."[3]

It is a privilege to remember all those who made the writing of this book possible.

The Most Honourable the Marchioness of Downshire with unusual generosity allowed me access to Sir William Trumbull's papers at Easthampstead Park. The Right Honourable the Earl of Denbigh and Sir Fergus Graham, Bart., gave me ready permission to reprint manuscript material in their possession. For various information I am indebted to M. le Pasteur Pannier,

---

1 The letters written to Sir Richard Bulstrode in 1686, at one time in the collection of T. E. P. Lefroy, Esq. (see *Hist. MSS. Comm. 1st Report*, App., p. 56) were sold at Sothebys in 1889. I have been unable to trace them after this date.

2 M. Pascal uses French sources only.

3 The name is occasionally written this way.

Dr théol., Conservateur de la Bibliothèque du Protestantisme
français; to M. Mauricheau-Beaupré, Conservateur du Musée de
Versailles; to Mr C. T. Flower, Secretary of the Public Record
Office; to Mr S. C. Ratcliff, Secretary of the Historical Manuscripts Commission; to Major A. F. St Clair Stapleton, to Mr
Leonard Foster and to Messrs Sotheby and Co. To all I express
my gratitude.

RUTH CLARK

WELLESLEY COLLEGE
WELLESLEY, MASSACHUSETTS
1938

Abbreviations used

A.É. Angleterre. Archives du Ministère des Affaires Étrangères, correspondance politique d'Angleterre.

A.N. Archives Nationales.

B.N. Bibliothèque Nationale.

Cal. St. P., Col., A. and W.I. Calendar of State Papers, Colonial, America and West Indies.

Cal. Treas. Books. Calendar of Treasury Books.

D.N.B. Dictionary of National Biography.

H.M.C. Historical Manuscripts Commission.

H.M.C., Downshire MSS. Historical Manuscripts Commission, Report on the MSS. of the Marquess of Downshire.

N.S. New Style (dates).

O.S. Old Style (dates).

R.O. *France.* Public Record Office, State Papers, Foreign, France.

"R.P.R." "Religion prétendue réformée."

Note on dates

Unless there is some indication to the contrary, dates are given in New Style.

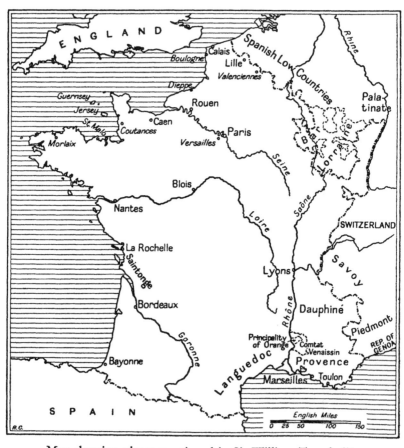

Map showing places mentioned in Sir William Trumbull's correspondence.

CHAPTER I

Sir William Trumbull

SIR WILLIAM TRUMBULL was born on August 12, 1639,[1] one year after the child who was to reign over France as Louis XIV. We can say little of Sir William's father, Mr William Trumbull, except that he was a country gentleman residing at Easthampstead Park and a justice of peace in Berkshire,[2] but his grandfathers, who both served the state, are better known. William Trumbull, his father's father, was a diplomatist, and for many years, from 1609 to 1625, and in spite of many difficulties, was resident at Brussels.[3] His mother's father, Georg Rudolph Weckherlin, was a native of Stuttgart, but after travelling in France as secretary to the ambassador of Württemberg, had settled in England. Here he became an under-secretary of state, Latin secretary to Charles I, and, passing into the service of Parliament, "secretary for foreign tongues". He was, moreover, a voluminous writer of German, French and English verse.[4]

Sir William wrote an account of the first fifty years of his own life, and one cannot do better than quote it in the outline form in which the *Gentleman's Magazine* printed it in 1790. It is brief, clear, and throws certain sidelights on the author.

1 I owe this information to Mr Leonard Forster who is preparing a Life of Weckherlin, and has examined the Weckherlin papers at Easthampstead Park. The above sketch of Sir William's life is based in great part on Mr W. P. Courtney's article in the *D.N.B.*, and on the authorities suggested there. See also the introduction to the *Report on the Downshire Manuscripts* by Mr E. K. Purnell.

2 *Gentleman's Magazine*, vol. 60, Part 1, 1790, p. 4.

3 Article on William Trumbull, the elder, *D.N.B.* He died in 1635.

4 1584–1653. *D.N.B.*, article Weckherlin, where it is said that his German biographer Fischer considers him the most important national poet of this period prior to Opitz.

Sir William Trumbull's Life annaliter

1638[1] Born at Easthampstead, Berkshire, in August.

1644 Receives early instructions in Latin and French from his Grandfather, Mr Wekerlin, Latin Secretary to Charles I.

1649 Sent to Oakingham[2] School.

1654 Admitted a Gentleman Commoner (under Mr T. Wyat) in St John's College, Oxford.

1657 Chosen Fellow of All Souls.

1659 Went out Bachelor of Laws.

1664 Went into France and Italy; lived there with Lords Sunderland, Godolphin, Sidney, and the Bishop of London (Dr Compton).

1666 Returned to College.

1667 Practises as a Civilian in the Vice-chancellor's court; appeals to the Chancellor Clarendon, and carries a point respecting the non-payment of fees for his doctor's degree; gains great credit by it, and all the business of the Vice-chancellor's court; July 6, takes the degree of LL.D.

1668 Michaelmas Term, admitted of Doctors' Commons, attends diligently the courts, and takes notes.[3]

1670 Marries a daughter of Sir Charles Cotterell; 24 Nov. £350 a year only settled upon him by his father: this sharpens his industry in his profession.

1672 Sir William Walker's death; Sir R. Wiseman's being made Judge of the Arches; Sir Lionel Jenkins, Judge of the Admiralty, etc., contribute to his advancement in business; gets about £500 per annum by his business, and the reversion of the place of Clerk of the Signet on Sir Philip Warwick's death, which happened in 1682.

His entrance into public employments

1683 Engages to go to Tangiers with Lord Dartmouth; kisses the King's hand upon his appointment of Judge Advocate of the fleet, and, Commissioner for settling the properties of the leases of houses etc. at Tangiers between the King and the inhabitants, he has occasion to remark "the great difference between the value of assistance when wanted, and after it is

---

1 According to the Weckherlin papers at Easthampstead Park he was born on August 12, 1639, as we have seen.

2 Now Wokingham.

3 He also became Chancellor of the Diocese of Rochester.

given and done with". Lord Dartmouth's commission [to evacuate Tangier] opened at Cape St Vincent's, "all surprised at it".

In September, arrived at Tangiers; he returns to Doctors' Commons in November; refuses the Secretary of War's place in Ireland.

1684 November 1, presented to the King by Lord Rochester and knighted. Made Clerk of the Deliveries of the Ordnance Stores, Feb. 1, £300 per annum.

1685 Appointed Envoy Extraordinary to France against his inclination; the King insisted upon his going; accepts a pension of £200 in lieu of his place of Clerk of the Deliveries: ...this the only pension he ever had. An account of the persecution in France: Sir William gives in memorials in behalf of the English Protestant subjects, of whom he sheltered many, and preserved their effects.

1686 He receives letters of revocation from France; and is appointed Ambassador Extraordinary to the Ottoman Porte.

1687 The Turkey Company present Sir William with a gold cup, value £60, before he embarked for Turkey, 16th April.

Here the MS. account ends.[1]

One notes his acquaintance with Latin and French at an early age;[2] his industry, tenacity, and thrift; the interesting travelling companions who also at one time included Edward Browne, the son of Sir Thomas Browne;[3] his dislike of the "Tangier business" when he accompanied the expedition that was sent to dismantle Tangier, little more than twenty years after it had been bestowed on England as part of Catherine of Braganza's dowry. With Pepys he was to adjust the claims of

1 *Gentleman's Magazine*, vol. 60, Part 1, 1790, pp. 4–5.
2 Sir William never seems to have learned German, though he learned Italian and Spanish. See *H.M.C.*, *Downshire MSS. passim.*
3 Sir Thomas Browne, *Works*, 1, pp. lxxvii, 92, 97, 99, 100, 102, 107, 110. After five months' residence in Italy (*H.M.C.*, *Downshire MSS.* 1, p. 3) Trumbull went to France and with Edward Browne he visited Nice, Antibes, Cannes, Fréjus, Vidauban, Marseilles, Aix, Salon, Arles, Avignon, Montpellier, Pézenas, Béziers, Narbonne, Carcassonne, Castelnaudary, Toulouse, Agen, Bordeaux, Blaye, Saintes, La Rochelle, Nantes, Angers, Saumur, Tours, Blois, Orléans. The Mr Trumbull on p. 107 who praises the "papists" is obviously not William Trumbull. After they parted Edward Browne wrote that he was searching for a companion with whom he might travel in Spain or in Germany, but he could never make a happy journey without Mr Trumbull. *H.M.C.*, *Downshire MSS.* 1, p. 4.

the dispossessed inhabitants. "Dr Trumbull", as he was then called, complained that he had been misinformed with regard to his mission, he regretted his fees at home, was unnerved by the prospect of possible dangers, distressed the good chaplain, Dr Ken, and provoked Pepys by his lack of spirit—"a sheepish man" said Pepys, agreeing with Lord Dartmouth. Finally Dr Trumbull returned to England before the others.[1]

We have seen that Sir William was sent to Turkey after he came back from France. Here he remained until 1691. In 1694 he was made a lord of the Treasury, and in 1695 a member of the Privy Council and Secretary of State. He resigned the seals on December 1, 1697, taking umbrage at some grievances, real or imaginary—the lords justices, he said, had treated him "more like a footman than a secretary"[2]—and now he retired from active life. He had been several times member of Parliament as well as a governor of the Turkey Company and the Hudson's Bay Company. "He was the eminentest of all our civilians", wrote Burnet, "and was by much the best pleader in these courts, and was a learned, a diligent and a virtuous man."[3]

There remained to him some happy years at Easthampstead. His second wife, daughter of the Earl of Stirling, Lady Judith Alexander, whom he married in 1706, two years after the death of his first wife, Katherine Cotterell, brought him the heir he desired, William, born in 1708.[4] Books and his garden occupied his leisure.[5] His correspondence filled many hours.[6] Men of letters interested him still. "It is rare to find such a Maecenas", Pierre Sylvestre had told Bayle.[7] And writing in the year of Sir William's retirement Dryden brought his tribute. "If the last Æneid shine among its Fellows, 'tis owing to the Commands of Sir William Trumbull, one of the Principal Secretaries of State, who recommended it, as his Favourite, to my Care, and,

---

1 Pepys, *Tangier Papers*, pp. xxvi, xxvii, xlix, 26, 38, 39, 40, 42, 44, 45.
2 *Correspondence of Charles Talbot, Duke of Shrewsbury*, London, 1821, pp. 504–5.
3 Burnett, *History of My own Time*, III, p. 276.
4 A daughter, Judith, lived for one year only, 1707–8.
5 H.M.C., *Downshire MSS.* I, Part II, *passim*.
6 In his meticulous way Sir William writes out drafts of letters informal as well as formal.
7 Gigas, *Lettres...*, vol. I, *Correspondance de Bayle*, p. 697.

for his sake particularly I have made it mine."[1] His friends did not forget him; and he made a new friend in "little Pope", as he called him.[2] The boy of sixteen and the old man rode together almost daily in Windsor Forest, and they talked of the classics dear to Sir William's heart. The youthful Pope inscribed one of the Pastorals to him, addressing him in his retirement:

> You that too wise for pride, too good for power,
> Enjoy the glory to be great no more
> And carrying with you all the world can boast
> To all the world illustriously are lost.[3]

And elsewhere:

> Happy...who to these shades retires,
> Whom nature charms and whom the muse inspires:
> Whom humbler joys of home-felt quiet please,
> Successive study, exercise and ease.[4]

Sir William urged him, and not in vain, to translate the *Iliad*, just as he had encouraged Dryden in his translation of the *Æneid*.[5]

Amicus meus humanissimus a juvenilibus annis, wrote Pope on the fly-leaf of the Elzevir Virgil where he recorded Sir William's death,[6] on December 14, 1716, and with Pope's Epitaph this brief sketch of Sir William's life may be brought to a close.

> A pleasing form; a firm, yet cautious mind;
> Sincere, tho' prudent; constant, yet resign'd:
> Honour unchang'd, a principle profest,
> Fix'd to one side, but mod'rate to the rest:
> An honest courtier, yet a patriot too;
> Just to his prince, and to his country true:
> Fill'd with the sense of age, the fire of youth,
> A scorn of wrangling, yet a zeal for truth;
> A gen'rous faith, from superstition free;
> A love to peace, and hate of tyranny;
> Such the man was; who now, from earth remov'd,
> At length enjoys that liberty he lov'd.[7]

1 Dryden, *The Works of Virgil*, III, p. 1004. Postscript to the Reader. London, 1748, 3 vols.
2 Pope, *Works*, I, p. 267.   3 *Ib.* pp. 266–7.   4 *Ib.* pp. 354–5.
5 *Ib.* p. 46.   6 *Ib.* p. ix.   7 *Ib.* IV, p. 382.

CHAPTER II

Preparations

SEPTEMBER—OCTOBER[1]

IN beginning an account of Sir William Trumbull's year in France it may be useful to give a rapid sketch of the principal characters we shall meet. The main personages of these chapters are the following:

James II, at the beginning of his short reign. A professed admirer of the grand monarch's religious zeal, but with occasional obstinate insistence on his rights. Apprehensive of the "noise" certain "violences" in France may cause in England. In a wrong position, often unable to say what he really thinks on certain subjects.[2]

Louis XIV, indomitable in his resolve to force conversion on all his Protestant subjects and on some not his subjects.

The Prince of Orange, deeply resentful of the wrong done to his little Principality of Orange, in the south.

M. Barrillon[3] (Paul Barrillon *or* de Barrillon d'Amoncourt, marquis de Branges), French ambassador to England. Level-headed, moderate, intimate with James to the point of rousing the jealousy of the other envoys,[4] his mentor in many matters, encouraging him in his devotion to the King of France, respectfully admonishing when necessary.

1 As far as possible chapters have been made to coincide with certain divisions of time, but this is possible only in an approximate way.

2 "Il n'ose s'expliquer publiquement de ce qu'il a dans le cœur." A.É. *Angleterre*, vol. 156, f. 175, Nov. 19, 1685. [Il est obligé] "de garder quelques mesures dans ses discours et de ne pas s'expliquer toujours selon ses veritables sentimens." *Ib.* vol. 158, f. 11, Jan. 7, 1686. "Il est obligé d'avoir de grands esgards pour tout ce qui l'environne, de ne se pas expliquer toujours conformement a ses veritables sentimens." *Ib.* f. 30, Jan. 17, 1686. "Le Roy...se croit obligé de ne pas abandonner ouvertement l'intérêt de M. le Prince d'Orange." *Ib.* f. 86, Feb. 11, 1686. Letters from Barrillon to Louis XIV.

3 Cf. *Recueil des Instructions...*, xxv (*Angleterre*, ii).

4 *Ib.* p. 306, *n.* 4. Barrillon's own account.

Lord Sunderland (Robert Spencer, second Earl of Sunderland), principal Secretary of State and Lord President of the Privy Council,[1] a former ambassador to France. Wily, insincere, on smooth terms with Barrillon, being on the French pay roll; a friend to Sir William Trumbull only when convenient.

M. de Croissy (Charles Colbert, marquis de Croissy), brother of the great Colbert, a former ambassador to England, Secretary of State for Foreign Affairs, a stiff, choleric man, "high in his resentments", as Sir William once remarked,[2] but not unreasonable when his temper had abated.

Occasionally we shall hear of others:

Laurence Hyde, Earl of Rochester, "My Lord Treasurer", a somewhat shadowy patron of Trumbull, his influence on the wane.

M. de Seignelay (Jean-Baptiste Colbert, marquis de Seignelay), son of the great Colbert and nephew of Colbert de Croissy, Secretary of State for the Navy, but also concerned with the affairs of the Huguenots, since his "department" further included "Paris et l'Isle de France. L'Orléanois. Le Blaisois. Les Fortifications... La Maison du Roi. Le Clergé. Le Commerce. Les Manufactures hors le Royaume. Les Galères. Les Compagnies des Indes Orientales et Occidentales...Les Haras. Les Pensions."[3] Capable, but overbearing.

M. de Bonrepaus (François d'Usson de Bonrepaus), on a mission in England, ostensibly informing himself on matters of the navy and trade, but sent over to "eye the refuged French".[4]

And finally there is Sir William Trumbull himself, honest, outspoken, insistent and persistent, punctilious and slightly pedantic, his zeal obnoxious to the court of France and unwelcome to James. In a difficult situation, arising from his own sympathy for the Prince of Orange, and the instability of James, embarrassed by his envoy's protests.

1 From Dec. 4, 1685 on.
2 See p. 188 *post*. The most closely observed portrait of Colbert de Croissy is to be found in Spanheim's *Relation*.
3 *État de la France*, 1684, quoted in Guitard, *Colbert et Seignelay*, p. 10.
4 *H.M.C., Downshire MSS.* I, p. 172. On Bonrepaus' mission see *Recueil des Instructions...*, xxv (*Angleterre*, II); and Durand, "Louis XIV et Jacques II", in *Revue d'Histoire moderne et contemporaine*, x, pp. 28–44.

"Milord Preston est retourné en France et doit bientost prendre son audience de congé de V.M.", so Barrillon wrote to Louis XIV on August 16, 1685.[1] But it was not yet known who was to be the new envoy. There had been certain rumours— that a Catholic was to be sent in Preston's place, that Preston had left for England in great anger to prevent this step, that the Protestants would now turn for protection to milord Montaigu,[2] a former ambassador, and that milord Montaigu, now absent in England, would return when the new Catholic ambassador came, in order to keep an eye on him.[3]

Three weeks later Barrillon was able to give more definite news. "Le sieur Gromstal" had been chosen, a gentleman who was said to have considerable ability—though little known at court he had been employed on divers occasions, he had undertaken several journeys to Tangier, and it was on the strength of his reports that the demolition of Tangier had been decided on[4]—a most flattering tribute to Sir William, who had played a somewhat inglorious part in the Tangier expedition and had never set eyes on the place before.

In the next letter "Gromstal" has become "le chevalier Trombal". The King of England had a high opinion of him and greatly esteemed his knowledge of civil law and the laws of other countries.[5] The decision did not create a particularly favourable impression in France. " Je n'ay rien à vous dire sur le choix que le Roy d'Angleterre a fait du chevalier Tumbal pour remplir la place du Sr Preston," wrote Louis XIV to his ambassador, "mais il me paroist que la qualité de Jurisconsulte anglois n'est pas la plus convenable, pour maintenir la bonne intelligence entre moy et le Roy d'Angleterre et qu'elle ne sert souvent qu'à trouver des difficultés où il n'y en doit point avoir."[6] A newsletter reported somewhat contemptuously

1 A.É. *Angleterre*, vol. 155, f. 463.
2 Ralph Montague, later Duke of Montague.
3 B.N. MS. fr. 7052, reports sent to the Lieutenant de Police, La Reynie, f. 367, June 18; f. 364, June 30; f. 358, July 17, 1685.
4 A.É. *Angleterre*, vol. 156, ff. 10–11, Barrillon to Louis XIV, Sept. 6, 1685.
5 *Ib.* f. 20, same to same, Sept. 10, 1685.
6 *Ib.* ff. 31–2, Louis XIV to Barrillon, Sept. 20, 1685.

that the King of England was sending nothing but "une manière de Docteur" called Franseval to be Envoy Extraordinary.[1] And now it became known that the choice had met with objections even in England—Sunderland would have preferred milord Douvre,[2] milord Renela[3] or Henry Savile[4], but Rochester had carried the day. The latter had taken pains to tell Barrillon that "le chevalier Tombal" was an able man and a great lawyer, but the courtiers did not think "Tombal" suitable for Versailles, and in secret they criticized the choice.[5] Tréval was coming only as resident, said the newsletter, "en cette qualité nos ministres ne luy céderont point la main",[6] and a little later it reported that his household was to be entirely Protestant.[7]

Trumbull himself, according to his account, accepted the appointment with reluctance,[8] but the King, who had even thought of making him Secretary of State the year before,[9] insisted on his going, and Trumbull "kissed hands on appointment" on September 2–12.[10] He was to be paid at the rate of £5 a day for his ordinary expenses with due allowance for his "extraordinaries".[11]

"Courage," wrote the Archbishop of York, Dolben, "and leave your spleen behind you at Doctors' Commons, or some other place where there is need of melancholy. The air of France, variety of business, and the most agreeable conversation of Madame l'Ambassadrice...will I hope suffer no clouds to gather about your heart."[12] The Bishop of Oxford, John Fell, also wrote wishing him success, that notwithstanding the

---

1 B.N. MS. fr. 10265, f. 65, Sept. 19, 1685.
2 Henry Jermyn who had been raised to the peerage a few months before as Lord Dover.
3 Richard Jones, first Earl of Ranelagh.
4 A former envoy to France. Brother to Halifax.
5 A.É. *Angleterre*, vol. 156, f. 26, Barrillon to Louis XIV, Sept. 13, 1685.
6 B.N. MS. fr. 10265, f. 67, Sept. 26, 1685. The writer has corrected Tréval to Trumbal in the margin.
7 *Ib.* f. 83, Nov. 14.   8 Cf. p. 3 *ante*.
9 Clarendon, *Correspondence*, I, p. 95.
10 *Cal. Treas. Books*, 1685–9, p. 674.
11 *Ib.* p. 342; see pp. 173–6 of the present work for his "extraordinaries".
12 H.M.C., *Downshire MSS.* I, p. 43.

opposition between human policy and Christian wisdom, and the difficulty to please man and be the servant of God, he might secure his eternal interests while pursuing his temporal, and return back not only in the favour of his Prince, but of Almighty God. And asking Sir William to pardon his freedom he continues: "I need not recommend to you the paying respect to religion, and giving opportunity to those who are abroad, of serving God with you: for though there be something like an instance of an Envoyé from here, who had no Chaplain, I dare say you will not imitate the example." [1]

Sir William could not but realize that he would have to face unusual difficulties. Little by little, but more especially from 1679 on, the privileges conferred on the Protestants of France by the Edict of Nantes had crumbled away. Declaration after declaration brought some new restriction, "it being made according to ye new edicts very uneasy either to live or die in France". [2] His predecessors at the court of France, Henry Savile and Lord Preston, had been obliged to come to the help of their countrymen, and ward off the forcible ministrations of an over-zealous clergy. "Priests and *curés* here are very busy in attempting upon many of the King's Protestant subjects when they are upon their deathbeds", so Lord Preston reported; "I have had many sharp contests with this court upon that subject." [3]

In Savile's day a Mrs Bickerton, "an English gentlewoman", had been visited by the *Commissaire du Châtelet* and the *curé* of Saint Sulpice, and had been asked whether or not she would die in her religion, [4] and the same *curé* had been to see Lord William Hamilton at another time, but "the young Lord, though very weake, tooke a little bell, and ringing it at his owne ease, told the curate that noise should drowne his, and hee would not hearken to what hee said". [5] Savile "discours'd

1 H.M.C., *Downshire MSS.* I, p. 44.
2 Savile, *Correspondence*, p. 270, Feb. 3 (O.S.), 1682–3.
3 H.M.C., *7th Report*, App., Part I, p. 292 [Nov.], 1683.
4 *Ib.* p. 280; Savile, *Correspondence*, p. 269.
5 Savile, *op. cit.*, pp. 204–6, July 12, 1681; cf. H.M.C., *op. cit.* pp. 280–1.

pretty warmly" with Colbert de Croissy, the Secretary for Foreign Affairs, demanding an apology from the *curé*, and though "M. de Croissy spoake of the Curates of Paris as much greater men" than Savile "took them to bee", in the end the envoy carried his point.[1] "I keep all quiet hear", he wrote, "more by a perticuler management of the curates then by any security from the Government."[2] In Marseilles Consul Lang's maid, an Englishwoman, received a "rude visit".[3] In Paris two men, one of them a priest, "rushed in with great violence" and went to the chamber of Lady Harvey's English coachman, who begged to be allowed to die in quiet.[4] He did not lack spiritual comfort since he was attended by Lord Preston's chaplain, Wake, a future Archbishop of Canterbury.[5]

At Lille an English merchant, Mr Bedford Whiting, had refused to pay the pension for his daughter who, converted to Roman Catholicism, had gone to a convent. The Intendant of the province ordered reprisals, and his order "was executed with all violence upon Mr Whiting...several of his goods and merchandizes were sold, not only for paying the pretended arrears of the pension, but also the pay of the archers who had been commanded to lye upon him for several days, all which amounted to a great sum".[6] This measure seems to have been repeated every quarter, and "poor Mr Whiting" continued to have "garrisons" put in his house, in spite of protests and memorials on the part of Lord Preston.[7]

Things were worse, if anything, now. "Messrs Graham and Walker", who seem to have been bankers in Paris, sent bad news to Lord Preston after his departure from France.

Wee have of late the saddest letters from severall English and Scotish of our Religion at Bourd^x that can be upon accompt of the bad usage they meet with at present ther. They adresse themselves to us for advyce and assistance. But his Maj. having none to represent

---

1 Savile, *loc. cit.*   2 Savile, p. 246, December 1681.   3 *Ib.*
4 *H.M.C., op. cit.* p. 285; cf. p. 331, April, 1683.
5 *Ib.* pp. 285, 292, and *D.N.B.*
6 *H.M.C., op. cit.* p. 267.
7 *Ib.* pp. 266, 267, 269, 274, 278, 279, 280, 282, 329, 330, 353, 354, 355, 357, 371.

him here in any character all wee can do is to acquaint Yo^r Lo^p with it and humbly to desyr that by your Lo^p meanes Sir William Turnbull (*sic*) may have ample and sufficient instructions to act for all his Majesties subjects in France who are in thes circumstances.[1]

A letter written by Sir David English, consul at Bordeaux, was sent to Sir William Trumbull by Sunderland. It brought further news of the doubtful security of the English Protestants in that town.

"My Lord," wrote Sir David on September 11, "May it please your Lo. to know that the most Christian King hath intimat to his Subjects by the Intendant of this province that its his will to have all of his subjects of the Reformed Religion shall renounce that heresie (as they call it) and become Romaine Catholiques, otherwaise are molested and their fortunes consumed by souldiers quartered on them and severalls of the english Marchants being advertised by some late Alderman of this Citty and other persones of quality that they hard the intendant publickly say he had order from his King to use the Subjects of his Matie of Gr. B. as he did his owne in the Matter of Religion, upon this rapport I at the Nations desire addressed my selfe to the Intendant to know if he had such order, that if soe the Merchants might address for remedie. His answer was very generall pretending that noe Gentleman traveling or other, that had not resided above a yeare would be stoped, but may go when they please but for those that had remained some 3 or 4 yeare were esteemed Regnicoles,[2] this imported as Much as was before reported for None of them are Naturalized or ever injoyd the priviledges as french, so I humbly pray yor Lordship in behalf of his Maties Subjects...and likewaise humbly beseech your Lo. to Impetrat of his Matie a Minister of the Church of England upon our charges, to indoctrine us and administer the Sacraments seeing we are now deprived of the exercise of the protestant religion and in soe Doeing Your Lo. will doe an act of piety and will oblidge those of the Nation here.[3]"

Trumbull himself heard from two Bordeaux merchant-factors, John Strang, a Scotsman, and Henry Lavie, born at Londonderry. They had settled in Bordeaux twenty years

---

1 Downshire MSS. at Easthampstead Park, vol. xxii, No. 42, Sept. 29, 1685.
2 Natives.
3 *Ib.* vol. xxiii, No. 27, Sept. 11, 1685; R.O. *France, Entry Book* 19, Sunderland to English, Oct. 17–27 (no foliation).

before, were naturalized, and now feared the worst. Lavie's son John was already imprisoned at Bayonne, where he had gone to do some business for his father. They wanted leave to remain as before, or permission to retire with their families and estates to their native countries. Mr William Popple had already abjured.[1]

English merchants at La Rochelle sent complaints[2] to Whitehall, and friends of these merchants and the Bordeaux merchants came to see Sir William,[3] who received orders to interpose that the "violences" might cease.[4]

The Dutch ambassador[5] in Paris complained that a citizen, le sieur Drevon, had been carried out of the Principality of Orange, and Sir William was instructed to consult the ambassador and apply for redress.[6] Before Dijkvelt, Dutch Envoy Extraordinary, left London he supplied Sir William with a name and an address at the Hague to which he could write more safely than to him in person.[7]

Meanwhile preparations went on apace. Sir William's credentials were made ready.[8] His instructions were issued, the customary general instructions, hardly differing from those of his predecessor or his successor, lacking the interest of those valuable documents that accompanied the French ambassadors to England.

Sir William was to maintain the good correspondence between the two crowns, to protest against the confiscation of vessels by the French governors of the West Indies and the granting of commissions to privateers; he was to obtain the admission of English consuls in France, to preserve the privileges

---

1 H.M.C., Downshire MSS. 1, p. 46, Sept. 29, 1685. Popple was Marvell's nephew, and was the first to translate Locke's Letter on Toleration from the Latin. D.N.B.
2 Mentioned in their letter to Trumbull, Jan. 8, 1686; R.O. France, vol. 148, f. 159.
3 Ib.; H.M.C., Downshire MSS. 1, pp. 50, 65. Also R.O. France, Entry Book 19, where the text of Downshire, 1, p. 50, is fuller.
4 H.M.C., Downshire MSS. 1, pp. 49, 50.
5 W. Starrenburg, Baron van Wassenaer, Recueil des Instructions, XXIII (Hollande, III), pp. 445-7.
6 H.M.C., Downshire MSS. 1, p. 50.
7 H.M.C., 8th Report, App., Part 1, p. 557.
8 R.O. France, Entry Book 19, Oct. 20-30, 1685. For the text see p. 172 post.

of the Scottish nation, to protect subjects of the crown trading in any of the territories of the Most Christian King. He was to be friendly with the minister of the Duke of Modena, to recommend the interests of the Duke of Lorraine whose estates were in the hands of France, and to do all good offices to the Elector Palatine Philip William of Neuburg, some of whose claims had been contested by Louis XIV in behalf of his sister-in-law, the Duchess of Orleans, sister of the late Elector. Finally he was to correspond constantly with the Secretary of State, observing diligently what passed at the French court; he was likewise to maintain a correspondence with the English ministers at other courts, and on his return he was to present a perfect and ample narrative of his sojourn.[1]

But if Sir William did not derive much guidance from this document he received some excellent advice from Henry Savile, Lord Preston's predecessor in France. One wishes that Sir William could have had something of Savile's lively manner.

"At your arrival at Paris", the new envoy is informed, "the first step is to send to the Master of Ceremonies to let him know you are come upon such an occasion and to learn from him when you may see the Secretary of State. Having shewed your credentials to the Secretary, you ask him when the King will receive you; the day being appointed you are carried in the King's coaches, every coachman's fee upon that occasion being two pistoles. You are to send to all foreign Ministers notice of your arrival; those of your character and below it, will thereupon come to see you; the Ambassadors will send, but I suppose with them you will meet only in third places, except such as will give you the hand in their own houses if there be any such.

As most of them are altered since my time I can only recommend you to him of Mantua,[2] who having been there these 20 years knows more than his neighbours, and upon living civilly with him, will impart to you what he knows which will perhaps be the best part of your intelligence, till acquaintances of your contracting provide better for you, and in order to this, your own seeming to distinguish

1 R.O. *France, Entry Book* 19, Sept. 21—Oct. 1, 1685. For the text see pp. 169–72 *post*.

2 Count Camillo Balliani who died in Paris in 1702 after having been for almost forty years at the French court. *Recueil des Instructions*, xv (*Savoie-Sardaigne t Mantoue*, 11), pp. 397–8.

him from the rest as the choice of your judgment will go further than any recommendation can be given you, though for an introduction you may name me to him as one I thought worthy your first friendship. Considering the difference of our circumstances probably my rules of economy will not fit you, but I thought it turned extremely to account to keep all my servants in livery at board wages of 20 sols per diem and no wages, so that without further counting they were easily dismissed in case of misdemeanour.

Your countrymen that pray with you on Sunday will expect to dine with you, I mean the better sort; one dinner more a week to such as are most deserving on one of the days you expect news from England (especially in Parliament time) will do your business as to the creditable part of your living; less hardly will. I had many spies upon me of Scotch and Irish; you will have more, especially priests; I despised and evaded them; whether that will be the best method in this conjuncture your own judgment will best tell you. Your predecessor drank with them, and perhaps it did him good, however that good was dear bought by keeping so ill company.

At Court you will meet many open faces; let yours be so too, but your mouth shut, for except very few they are given to repeat with additions, and those are the most dangerous who will by commending your own country lead you into the discourse of it.

I see not how you will get amongst the Court ladies whose tittle-tattle is sometimes informing unless you will either play or love, or give presents worth more than their acquaintance, though I must repeat some of them are informed betimes of things worth knowing.

Your business will lie most with Monsieur de Croissy [1] who upon the least dispute is very passionate, and calmed only by your moderation, after which he will be accountable to you for his own anger, which upon the whole matter is a good man to deal with, for *fortiter in re, suaviter in modo* will do your business with him.

You will have little occasion of seeing Monsieur de Louvoy; [2] if you have, you will find a pretty civil mind under a rough figure and behaviour; a short reasoner and will not hold you in suspense.

My dear friend Monsieur de Seignelay [3] will talk to you of me, and be very civil to you if you have no business, but if you have, his positiveness is not to be surmounted nor his peevishness to be supported, but this to yourself, for I love him with all my heart.

The Archbishop of Rheims [4] and the Maréchal of Bellefonds [5]

1 See p. 7 *ante*.
2 Louvois, the Secretary for War.
3 See p. 7 *ante*.
4 C. M. Le Tellier, Louvois' brother.
5 Bernardin Gigault, marquis de Bellefonds, sent to England at the time of the death of Madame.

are frequent and dangerous questioners; avoid them like the plague if you can, but you will find you cannot. The Duke d'Anguyen,[1] Duke of Villeroy,[2] and Monsieur le Grand[3] are likewise great questioners, but mean no harm. The Prince of Condé,[4] Cardinal of Bouilon,[5] and Bishop of Maux[6] are questioners too, but wiser than the last and safer than the first.

There is no degree of friendship you may not safely venture with the Marquis de Shomberg;[7] his religion as well as his honour are your security; other honourable worthy men are the Marquis de Humières, (a great lover of our King),[8] the Duke of Vendôme,[9] the Marquis de Cavoy[10] (a bosom friend of mine as well as both the Ruvigny's[11]), the Marquis de Dangeau[12] and the Chevalier de Beuvron.[13] Monsieurs[14] Court you will hardly frequent much; the Chevalier de Lorraine[15] has to his greatness a most vile reputation, but the Comte de Martan,[16] the Comte de Chastillon,[17] and the Chevalier de Nantouillet[18] (since his late marriage called, I think,

1 Henri Jules de Bourbon, son of "le grand Condé". He bore the title of duc d'Enghien until his father's death.
2 Nicolas de Neufville, duc de Villeroy (1598—Nov. 28, 1685), father of the general who fought at Ramillies.
3 Louis de Lorraine, comte d'Armagnac; grand écuyer de France, hence his title "Monsieur le Grand".
4 Louis II de Bourbon, "le grand Condé".
5 Emmanuel Théodose de la Tour d'Auvergne, cardinal de Bouillon.
6 Bossuet, bishop of Meaux.
7 Frederick Herman, later first Duke of Schomberg. He was to join William III and fall in the battle of the Boyne.
8 Louis de Crevant, marquis, and later, duc d'Humières. "...de tout temps lié d'une amitié particulière avec le roi d'Angleterre....Cette amitié avoit commencé du temps que le défunt roi d'Angleterre, le duc d'York étaient réfugiés en France..." Sourches, *Mémoires*, 1, p. 282 and *n*.
9 Louis Joseph, duc de Vendôme, the great general.
10 Louis d'Oger, marquis de Cavoie, one of the heroes of "le passage du Rhin".
11 Henri de Massué, marquis de Ruvigny, an outstanding Huguenot, three times in England as envoy or envoy extraordinary. His son, Henri de Massué, afterwards Earl of Galway.
12 Philippe de Courcillon, marquis de Dangeau, best known for his *Journal*.
13 Charles d'Harcourt, chevalier de Beuvron, capitaine des gardes de Monsieur.
14 Philippe, duc d'Orléans, the King's brother.
15 Philippe de Lorraine-Armagnac, "chevalier de Lorraine", one of Monsieur's minions.
16 Charles de Lorraine-Armagnac, comte de Marsan, younger brother of "Monsieur le Grand" and the chevalier de Lorraine.
17 Alexis Henry, chevalier, afterwards marquis de Châtillon, premier gentilhomme de la chambre de Monsieur.
18 François du Prat, comte de Barbançon, premier maître d'hôtel de Monsieur. As chevalier de Nantouillet he had distinguished himself at the "passage du Rhin".

Comte or Marquis de Barbanson) are men of honour, and the last one of the most ingenious men in both nations. I should have named La Farre [1] who is as good a man as any of them. I say nothing of the Archbishop of Paris [2] because he will come very little in your way. I found him extremely civil, and the world will have him to be the greatest dissembler in it. Perhaps you will have a mind to know some of the Long Robe; Monsieur de Courtin, [3] formerly Ambassador here, will help you in that point, being himself a civil, honest man, a great talker, but a great knower too of all the affairs in Europe in which he has been a long negociator. Such another is Monsieur de Gourvile [4] who will certainly come in your way and whose acquaintance will be every way beneficial, and in my opinion safe.

To end with the King himself, though he can be morose upon occasion, his reception of foreign Ministers is generally very affable, especially when the respectful open countenance of the speaker draws the like from him; personal flattery (not too gross) takes wonderfully with him, whenever any favour is required of him.

Other things one might trouble you with, but your own observation will soon outstrip any directions of your friends; if in mine I have erred, pray believe it from forgetfulness and the natural changes four or five years makes in men, for willingly I would not misguide you but go to the end of the world to serve you as an old kind friend who loves you with honest old English reality, and so God send you a good journey." [5]

The Bishop of Oxford renewed his exhortations:

There are always many of considerable quality of our nation in Paris, who being removed from the eyes of their friends, take unfortunate liberties; and it will be a noble charity to interpose your authority and put some stop to them who are hasting to ruin. Besides your agency for your Prince, you will have opportunity of doing good offices to his subjects, but none can be greater or more

1 Charles Auguste, marquis de La Fare, better known as a writer than a soldier.
2 François de Harlay de Champvallon. "There is not a more intriguing man in the world than the Archbishop." Lord Preston to Secretary Jenkins, Jan. 20, 1683. H.M.C., 7th Report, App., Part 1, p. 278.
3 Honoré Courtin, Ambassador Extraordinary in 1665 and again from July 1676 to Sept. 1677.
4 Jean Hérauld de Gourville, author of interesting Mémoires.
5 H.M.C., Downshire MSS. 1, pp. 88–90, 1685. In connection with this letter it is interesting to read Spanheim's Relation de la Cour de France en 1690.

acceptable to Almighty God than to reduce from vice and licentious practises.[1]

The Archbishop of York, less solemn, sent a hogshead of ale with his good wishes: "I will undertake you shall regale their Monsieurs with as good ale as ever they drank with Lord Preston",[2] and his wife sent Lady Trumbull a little pot of baked meat for her entertainment on board.[3]

Many offers of service were received. A chaplain was appointed, Mr Hayley of All Souls College.[4] Communion plate and prayer books were purchased, likewise mourning cloth for Sir William, his coach and servants.[5] A French secretary was engaged, a French *maître d'hôtel* and *valet de chambre*. In order to avoid quarrels in his household Sir William took only Protestants, "fearing difficulties if a sick Catholic servant required the Sacraments to be brought into the house", and before leaving London he wisely called together his servants and "enjoined upon them good behaviour in his service, especially in point of Religion, telling them that for any breach of his wishes on the point they would be dealt with by Law".[6] The secretary, Jacques d'Ayrolle, who had already served Lord Preston, was sent to France to find a house.[7]

When the customs officers came to Sir William's lodgings at Doctors' Commons to visit the goods that were going to France[8] they must have found a vast array of things, for Sir William's household consisted of forty people, himself, his wife, his niece Deborah—"Debby Pet", as the Archbishop of York calls her[9]—probably also the nephew who helped him as secretary,[10] and a large suite. Besides a coach, a chaise and twenty horses there were two trunks full of plate, nine boxes full of copper and pewter vessels, fifty boxes filled with pictures, mirrors, beds, tapestries, linen, cloth for liveries, and kitchen

1 *H.M.C., Downshire MSS.* 1, pp. 48–9.
2 *Ib.* pp. 46, 47, 48.   3 *Ib.* p. 48.
4 *Ib.* pp. 44, 48.   5 *Cal. Treas. Books,* 1685–9, p. 1116.
6 *H.M.C., Downshire MSS.* 1, p. 228.   7 *Ib.* p. 50.
8 *Cal. Treas. Books,* 1685–9, p. 348.
9 *H.M.C., Downshire MSS.* 1, p. 48.
10 *H.M.C., 7th Report,* App., Part 1, p. 381.

utensils, there were seven or eight dozen chairs and armchairs, twenty boxes containing tea, coffee, chocolate, wine, ale and other provisions; four large and three small cabinets; six trunks and six boxes with Sir William and Lady Trumbull's apparel; forty boxes, trunks, bales, valises, portemanteaux containing the belongings of Sir William's suite, all of which goods were to enter France without being opened before Paris.[1]

Shortly before Sir William left for Paris the King of France put his name to an act that was perhaps the most unfortunate of his reign, the edict revoking the Edict of Nantes, while Sir William's master, James II, heard with joy of the marvellous things that were being accomplished in France.[2] But the French ambassador Barrillon requested with some forethought that "le chevalier Trumball" be instructed above all not to interfere in matters concerning the "R.P.R."[3]

Jacques d'Ayrolle, the newly appointed secretary, had already reached France. Things were in a pitiful state, he wrote on October 27; the Edicts of Nantes and Nîmes were entirely suppressed. All over the kingdom troops were being sent to make Protestants into Catholics. The temple at Charenton was pulled down. He also added, not too tactfully: "When you were first nominated, it was said that the King was sending a nobody here, but since your merits are known they are singing in a new tone, and your presence will efface all unjust ideas."[4]

1 A.É. *Angleterre*, vol. 151, f. 331. A list of belongings.
2 *Ib.* vol. 156 *passim.*
3 "Religion Prétendue Réformée," *ib.* f. 152. Barrillon to Louis XIV, Nov. 12, 1685.
4 *H.M.C., Downshire MSS.* 1, pp. 50–1.

CHAPTER III

Arrival in France

NOVEMBER

ON Friday, November 17, 1685, Sir William Trumbull landed at Dieppe.[1] Pepys had put the *Katherine* yacht at his disposition,[2] and another vessel carried the horses.[3] The winds were "contrarie" and the crossing was a very long one.[4]

No sooner had Sir William set foot in France when he found himself face to face with the tragic situation of the Huguenots. "The Arch B^p of Rouën and ye Coadjutor came to Diepe with 4 Troopes of Dragoons ye Munday before I landed," he writes, "and 4 Troopes more followed them ye same weeke."[5] According to the *Gazette de France* 5000 persons were made to abjure at Dieppe at this time.[6] Sir William brought with him a message significant enough, for it proved that James II would not facilitate the escape of any Protestant. "The Govern^r of Diepe being gon into ye Countrie I communicated his Maj^ties Order (Prohibiting ye Captains of his Yatchts to receive any of ye K. of France's Subjects on board without Passeports) to Monsr le Marquis de Bevrons,[7] Lieut^t Generall of y^t Province and to Monsr Marillac,[8] Intendant du Roy, with wch they seemd very well satisfyd."[9]

From Rouen Sir William wrote that great rains having fallen for many days his progress would be slow,[10] and indeed it took

1 R.O. *France*, vol. 148, f. 118, Trumbull to Sunderland, Nov. 20, 1685.
2 *H.M.C., Downshire MSS.* 1, p. 51.
3 *Cal. Treas. Books*, 1685–9, pp. 1116–17.
4 R.O. *loc. cit.*   5 *Ib.*
6 *Gazette de France*, 1685, p. 696.
7 François d'Harcourt, marquis de Beuvron.
8 René de Marillac.
9 R.O. *loc. cit.* James himself informed Barrillon of this order. A.É. *Angleterre*, vol. 156, f. 152, Barrillon to Louis XIV, Nov. 12, 1685.
10 R.O. *loc. cit.*

him six days to go from Dieppe to Paris.[1] The ways were hardly passable[2] and there were accidents of lame horses and servants left by the way.[3] Before he reached Paris he received a letter from his secretary saying that he had taken a house, in the Faubourg Saint-Germain, called the Hôtel de Béziers, in the rue du Colombier for 30 pistoles a month, there being no alternative. The Hôtel d'Écosse—which Sir William had evidently wanted—was let. Sir William seems to have wanted a country-house also, for he was told that a small country-house on the Versailles road was difficult to find. D'Ayrolle had gone to see one at Boulogne, but if the king stayed on at Fontainebleau Sir William would not want it. Perhaps Mr de Gachon, tutor of Lord St Albans, could lend the house they had taken two leagues from Paris on the Sceaux Road.[4]

The Hôtel de Béziers in the rue du Colombier cannot have been entirely suitable, for before the end of his stay Sir William had moved to number 6 rue du Bac, Faubourg Saint-Germain,[5] a street in which lived his friend Spanheim, envoy from Brandenburg.[6]

A postscript to d'Ayrolle's letter contained a request that was doubtless the forerunner of many similar ones on the part of others. He recommended to Lady Trumbull as a waiting maid a girl of his kin. She wanted no pay—only the shelter of Sir William's house, "to avoid the violence of the Dragoons".[7]

On November 23 Sir William and his household arrived in Paris.

"I have not had any time to informe myself how matters go here", he wrote to Sunderland next day, "but I find there is little discourse except about yᵉ affaires of Religion. My Secretarie D'Ayrolle herewith sends yoʳ Loᵖ an Accᵗ of wᵗ he has been able to gett. And I shall adde yᵉ Particular Journal of what has happend in yᵉ Princi-

1 *Cal. Treas. Books*, 1685–9, p. 1116.
2 R.O. *France*, vol. 148, f. 123, Trumbull to Sutherland, Nov. 24, 1685.
3 *Ib.* vol. 150, f. 43, same to same, March 9, 1686.
4 *H.M.C., Downshire MSS.* 1, p. 55; cf. p. 50.
5 *Ib.* p. 223.
6 Pagès, *Le grand Electeur et Louis XIV*, p. 557.
7 *H.M.C., Downshire MSS.* 1, p. 55.

pality of Orange¹ since yᵉ last wᶜʰ was sent to yoʳ Loᵖ,² wherein I shall humbly beg his Majᵗⁱᵉˢ further Orders, Those wᶜʰ I received before I left England extending no further than a particular Information concerning an Insult made upon yᵉ Sieur Drevon...I shall gett my Equipage ready as soon as possibly I can, in order to my Audience; wᶜʰ I hope may be abᵗ 10 or 12 dayes hence. Whilst I am writing this, I heare there is an Envoyé Extraʳⁱᵉ coming hither from Holland about yᵉ affaires of Orenge (*sic*)." ³

In his next letter Sir William, still waiting for his audience, made bold, as he said, to send such news as came to his hands. As a rule his letters contain chiefly news concerning his negotiations. Other news is apt to be secondhand, or is conveyed in newsletters and gazettes enclosed with the dispatches. But he makes a good beginning here.

Novᵇᵉʳ 28, S.N. 1685.... The Embassadʳ of Poland⁴ had yesterday his Audience de congé att Versailles: He had att first demanded assistance against yᵉ Turks; And his Audience of Congé having been putt off for 8 days longer than he desird he flatterd himself that he should obtaine his Request in that time, att least in part; But it had no effect; For yᵉ Answer was, That yᵉ King of France had occasion to make very great Expences for yᵉ good of Religion in his Kingdome, And allso to be att Excessive charges this Yeare in Buildings and Fortifications, so that he was not able to second his owne Desires in favʳ of yᵉ Embassadʳˢ Demands.

The reason why his Audience of Congé was delayd so long, is to endeavʳ to keepe him here as long as may be; Because yᵉ very great

1 This "Journal" is probably the long newsletter, relating the incidents of Nov. 10–12, "suite de ce qui s'est passé à Orange", R.O. *Newsletters, France,* Bundle 22. It is doubtless the document to which the President de Lubières refers, "sa grande relation veritable du 14ᵉ de 9ᵇʳᵉ". Downshire MSS. at Easthampstead Park, vol. xxiii, No. 51.

2 Probably the following documents: R.O. *France,* vol. 148, ff. 100–1, "Extrait des registres de deliberaõns du conseil de cette ville d'Orange...du dimanche quatorsiesme [octobre, 1685]"; f. 102, "Extrait des registres du parlement. Arrest du parlement du 22ᵉ 8ᵇʳᵉ, 1685"; f. 103, "Exposition et Reqᵗ de Mrs les Consuls d'Orange, Extrait des Registres du parlement du 22ᵉ 8ᵇʳᵉ, 1685"; f. 104, "Proces Verbal de Mʳ le President de Lubieres du 26 d'oct. 1685"; ff. 105–6, "Proces Verbal de Mr le President de Lubieres du 28 [24] 8ᵇʳᵉ, 1685". These documents add little to the account given by Arnaud in his *Histoire des Protestants* ...*de la Principauté d'Orange,* vol. ii.

3 R.O. *France,* vol. 148, f. 123, to Sunderland, Nov. 24, 1685.

4 J. Wielopolski. His first audience was on Oct. 18, Dangeau, i, p. 234; Sourches, i, p. 316. Of his departure Dangeau merely says: "On avoit cru qu'il feroit plus de séjour en France" (i, p. 258).

hast he shewd to be gon after y° first Refusall that was made him, made his Discontent appeare very Publick, And it is desird here that y° world should beleive there is a very good Correspondence establisht betweene this Crowne and that. Yesterday att his Audience y° King invited him to make another Journey to Versailles to see y° Court and y° Buildings. It is thought he will be yet further dissatisfyd, if he does not obtaine a Request from y° Queene of Poland,[1] wch is, That her Bro^r-in-Law, Mr de Bettune [2] (who is in Poland att present) should have y° Caracter of Embassad^r.

I heare Monsr D'Avaux [3] (who made a Step hither) desird a Pension of 2000 Crowns, wch was refusd him....

The King has commanded y° Physitians to publish their Remedies.[4]

The affairs of Orange were to take up Sir William's efforts for many a week. Long before the little Principality of Orange was definitely made a part of France in 1713 by the Treaty of Utrecht it had been exposed to all kinds of vexations.[5] During the Dutch war Louis XIV had occupied it, until the Treaty of Nimeguen in 1679 had obliged him to restore it to the Prince of Orange. In 1682 he claimed the principality for the house of Longueville, and on the ground that the inhabitants had built certain fortifications, he razed the walls of the town of Orange, claimed an indemnity, and limited the privileges of the inhabitants. The Dutch envoy Heinsius could obtain nothing, nor did Charles II give the moral support expected.[6] A neighbour land to the provinces of Dauphiné, Languedoc and Provence where the Protestant element was strong, the principality served as a place of refuge and could not but prove a hindrance in the campaign to eliminate the "R.P.R." Such a

---

1 Marie Casimire de la Grange d'Arquien, wife of John Sobieski.
2 François-Gaston, marquis de Béthune.
3 French Ambassador in Holland. Dangeau mentions his arrival in France, I, p. 239.
4 R.O. *France*, vol. 148, f. 119, to Sunderland, Nov. 28, 1685.
5 Chambrun, *Les Larmes*; A, de Pontbriant, *Histoire de la Principauté d'Orange*; Arnaud, *Histoire des Protestants...de la Principauté d'Orange*, vol. II; V. Bourilly, "Les Protestants de Provence et d'Orange sous Louis XIV", *Bulletin de la Société de l'Histoire du Protestantisme*, 1927, pp. 167–200.
6 For Lord Preston's Correspondence on this subject see *H.M.C.*, *7th Report*, App., Part I, pp. 270–5, 278, 281, 282, 284, 291, 356, 357, 358, 360. See also F. A. Middlebush, *Dispatches of Plott and Chudleigh* (The Hague, 1926), pp. 149, 151–2, 157, 172, 176, 193, 202.

stumbling-block could not be tolerated. Religious uniformity was to be enforced in Orange. Dragoons entered the town under M. de Tessé on October 24, the ministers were arrested, the "temples" demolished. Other localities in the principality suffered the same fate. But for a while the dragoons had no orders to molest the inhabitants. On November 10, however, the signal arrived, and the "booted missionaries" set to work. Panic stricken, the population abjured as a whole on the 11th and the members of the *Parlement* twenty-four hours later.

"I am appointed to waite upon Monsr de Croissy tomorrow morning at Versailles", wrote Sir William on November 30, "so that I take ye Libertie to write to yor Lo^p tonight and give you ye Newes... that is come to my hands.... The Officers of ye Parlem^t and other Inhabitants of Orange surrendred their Religion upon certaine Articles, whereof I send yor Lo^p ye Copie.[1] ·Besides w^{ch}, they obtain'd a verball Promise, that in 3 Months time they should not be obligd to go into any Church of ye Catholiques, nor assist at any of their Ceremonies or Exercises. The last weeke there arrivd there a Courier from Mons^t de Louvoy (in 2 dayes and a half from Versailles) who brought an Order to ye Comte de Tessé, that ye Regim^t of ye Queenes of Dragoons (*sic*) should immediately march out; the next day another Squadron of 4 Companies, And ye last to remaine there as long as one Person should be upon ye Place that was not a Catholique."[2]

The arbitrary proceedings at Orange could not go unchallenged. Orders came to Sir William to take up the matter. His Majesty having received an account of "several violences" committed in the Principality of Orange, Trumbull was to inform himself of the matter from the Dutch ambassador, and to let the ambassador know that he had orders to interpose by acquainting the Most Christian King with the said complaints.[3]

Sir William borrowed two volumes of the Treaty of Nimeguen from "Monsieur Lilieroot", the Swedish envoy who was "very

1 These articles are printed in Arnaud, *op. cit.* II, pp. 403–4.
2 R.O. *France*, vol. 148, f. 120, to Sunderland, Nov. 30, 1685.
3 R.O. *France*, *Entry Book* 19, Sunderland to Trumbull, Nov. 9–19; cf. *H.M.C., Downshire MSS.* I, p. 53.

kind" to him,[1] and took counsel with the Dutch ambassador and the envoy of the Elector of Brandenburg, Spanheim.[2]

"J'ai sceu que le Sr Trumball a ordre de parler sur l'affaire d'Orange," reported Barrillon. "Les amb^{rs} d'Hollande l'ont demandé par un memoire de la part des Estats generaux. Sa M.^{té} Britannique ne m'en a point parlé et l'ordre qu'a le Sr Trumball n'est autant que je le puis scavoir, qu'un office en termes generaux auquel il peut estre repondu de la mesme maniere. Je verray ce que je croiray pouvoir insinuer sur cela de moy mesme a Sa M.^{té} Brit^{que} en attendant que j'aye ordre de V. M. de m'expliquer de sa part."[3]

Dijkvelt, whom Sir William had met in London as Dutch Envoy Extraordinary, wrote from the Hague hoping that he would strongly support the representations of the King of England.[4] The Prince of Orange himself appealed to Sir William. His letter follows:

La Haye, ce 22 de Novem. 1685

Monsieur,

Vous m'avez donne des asseurances si obligens de l'attachement que vous avies pour mes interests tant en la lettre que vous avez pris la piene de m'escrire que par ce que vous aves dit aus Ambassadeurs de cett Estat qui ont este en Angleterre que j'ay cru estre oblige de vous en temoigner ma recognoissance et vous prier en mesme temps comme vous estes a present en France de vouloir prendre la piene de vous emploier efficatieusement pour mes interets selon les ordres que vous en aures du Roy a qui j'ay supplie de nouveau de vous envoyer de precis et generales pour tout ce qui pouroit concerner mes interests, puisque depuis que j'en avois escrit a Sa Maj. les choses sont changees a de telles extremites que sans un promt remede je me vois entierement ruine en la Principaute d'Orange, des particularites je ne vous en informeres pas pour le present puisque vous en aures d'autre part toutte les informations necessaires, j'espere que la puissante intercession de sa Maj^{te} pourra apporte quelque soulage-ment a ce povre paiis, et que je seres a couvert pour l'avenir de telles insultes, je vous prie d'y travallie de vostre possible, et d'estre

1 H.M.C., MSS of the Marquis of Bath, III, p. 121.
2 "Je scay que vous avez conféré avec M. l'amb. de Hol. et avec M. l'Envoyé Extraord^{re} d'Angleterre. [Lubières, President of the Parlement d'Orange] to Spanheim, Dec. 14. R.O. France, vol. 148, f. 138.
3 A.É. Angleterre, vol. 156, f. 175, to Louis XIV, Nov. 19, 1685.
4 H.M.C., Downshire MSS. I, p. 53, Nov. 22, 1685.

persuade que je vous en aures une tres grande obligation que je
tacheres de recognoistre en tous les occasions ou je vous poures
temoigne combien je suis

Monsieur

Vostre tres affectione

a vous servir

G. Prince d'Orange [1]

From the town of Orange came letters from the President of
the *Parlement*, M. de Lubières,[2] begging for the English envoy's
aid, that he and his family might get passports to be gone. He
might be described as an officer or a servant of the King of
England in his passport, but he would never be a burden or
request any aid. All the hopes of the principality were stayed
on the King of England.

On recourt à l'Intercession de M^r l'Envoyé, parce que M^r de
Schulembourg, Secret^{re} de M. le P. d'Orenge vient d'écrire aud.
President que S.A. le renvoye pour avoir secours et remede aux
maux presens à l'Intercession de sa Ma^{té} Britannique. Quelque
grands qu'ils puissent étre, si sa ditte Majesté vouloit y faire remedier,
Elle en viendroit a bout surtout pour faire *rétablir Orenge en l'état qu'il
étoit avant le 25 d'8bre dernier*.[3]

C'est d'Elle que ceux d'Orenge attendent toutes choses, et de La
Haye on les renvoye à S.M.B. et à son Intercession pour toutes
choses, de quoy on écrit meme aud^t President qu'on attend un succez
favorable.[4]

It was to be a vain hope.

The "violences" committed at Orange were not the only
matter of that kind to be taken up by Sir William. Letters from
various parts of France brought him word of the harsh treatment to which English Protestants were exposed. A letter

---

1 Downshire MSS. at Easthampstead Park, vol. xxiii, No. 146 (*holograph*).
(English résumé in *H.M.C., Downshire MSS.* i, p. 55.)

2 R.O. *Newsletters, France*, Bundle 22, endorsed in a modern hand "Nov. 30–
Dec. 10", but is rather Nov. 14 (N.S.); Downshire MSS. at Easthampstead Park,
vol. xxiii, No. 75, Nov. 23–27, 1685. (English résumé in *H.M.C., Downshire
MSS.* i, pp. 53–4.)

3 October 25 was the date of the entry of the dragoons.

4 Downshire MSS. at Easthampstead Park, vol. xxiii, No. 51, December 3,
1685. (English résumé in *H.M.C., Downshire MSS.* i, pp. 65–6.)

written from Caen by an English merchant, William Daniel, to a friend in England was forwarded to Sir William.

Caen ce 8ᵉ Novemb. 1685

Mr Harbert Aylevin and honored frende

...Wee are here in a most sad condition expecting soldiers every day wᶜʰ hath already caused many of this Citty to change and more changeth dayly. I have been summoned to yᵉ Townhouse to do yᵉ like and have beene several times beefore yᵉ Intendent on yᵉ same accompte I have told them all yᵗ I am borne a subject to yᵉ King of England and never Naturallised and yᵗ I was of yᵉ Church of England wᶜʰ his Majesty hath promissed to protect in wᶜʰ beeleefe I did hope by God's Assistance to live and Dye, all yᵉ Answer I coulde have from yᵉ Intendant was yᵗ if 20 troupers were not enuf to make mee change, I should have 40. I answered yᵗ my house was full of goods for yᵉ accᵗ of several frends in England wᶜʰ would demande satisfaction, if my house was plundred and yᵗ it was verry hard yᵗ I could not receive yᵉ same protection yᵗ others of any Nation had and all other Strangers in this Kingdom. Tomorrow I [intend?] not wᵗʰ standing to present him my requeste.... If hee will not grant mee yᵉ same protection yᵗ other strangers have at Rouen and Bourdeaux, I am resolved to venter body and goods to save the soole. My wife, I bles God, is of the same opinion. Dieu nous fasse la grace de combattre jusqu'à la fin pour obtenir la couronne de gloire... I doubt not but yᵒ have hard wᵗ hath past att Rouen, many personns have abandonned the howses and are fled, as to Trade all is att a stand heere and no vessel is lading at present.[1]

Daniel's eldest daughter had fled with some French friends.[2]

In Rouen, John de Grave, "natural subject of the King of England", as he declared, had so many soldiers quartered upon him that the charge amounted to more than 20 crowns a day. He would gladly give 200 pistoles for a pass or would pay for his wife and children to live in some private chamber in Sir William's house.[3] It should be added, however, that John de Grave had been naturalized French. Like some others who had the same status he imagined, poor man, he could still enjoy the protection of England.

At La Rochelle also troops were quartered on English

[1] *Ib.* No. 65.   [2] *Ib.*
[3] H.M.C., *Downshire MSS.* I, pp. 57, 61, 62, Nov. 24–28.

merchants.[1] The consul at Bordeaux, Sir David English, wrote
again. Some of His Majesty's subjects who had married
Frenchwomen feared to be forced to abjure their faith, and
could not obtain passports for themselves and their families.
Those who were naturalized only for some benefit of trade
were in prison till they abjured.[2] And indeed Henry Lavie and
John Strang, who had already told Sir William of their fears,
now wrote from their place of confinement. Coming from their
business they had been seized.[3]

In Nantes a certain William Gray and his children were
detained forcibly.[4] A Scotsman living in Nantes, James Bruce,
cousin of Sir William Bruce of Balcashie, hailed Sir William's
coming in biblical language.

I hope this may find you happily arrived in our land of Gozen
hoping the Eternal may have pitched on your person to be the Moses
of our age and that by the character He has clothed your person with
may procure us the poor children of Israel upon whom He hath put
His mark liberty to pass through these Red Seas to serve our God in
spirit and in truth even in a desert if it be His holy will and pleasure
till he bring us to that eternal Cannane which we in the end of our
miserable and dangerous passage of Jordain pray for.

Any money necessary would be thankfully supplied as well
as a tun of the best white wine this river—the Loire—could
afford for Sir William's use.[5]

The affair of Orange excepted, Sir William Trumbull did
little during his early months in France but interpose for English
Protestants. The echoes of their complaints continue sad and
monotonous through his correspondence. The volume of
other business done is insignificant in comparison with his
efforts to secure redress for them.

But in all justice to France several points should be made.
Englishmen naturalized as French expected, not altogether

1 R.O. *France*, vol. 148, f. 140, Sir William Trumbull's Memorial, Dec. 15.
2 *H.M.C.*, *loc. cit.* p. 40, undated.
3 *Ib.* p. 57, Nov. 24.
4 *Ib.* pp. 54, 56, Nov.–Dec. See also R.O. *France*, *Entry Book* 19, Nov. 23
   (O.S.) which reads "children", not "child".
5 *Ib.* pp. 61–2, Nov. 27.

reasonably, that some difference should be made between them and natural-born subjects of France. In those days there seemed no hard and fast line between naturalized subjects and those foreigners who were not. It was felt that an Englishman who had lived for some years in France, whether he was naturalized or not, should be treated differently from his countrymen who were not established there. The Intendant at Bordeaux declared, as we have seen, that those who had remained some three or four years were esteemed *régnicoles*.[1] Of an English merchant at Lille it was said: "Altho not naturalized...his actual abode at Lille...for now almost 20 years maketh him to be regarded as upon the same foot with the native subjects."[2] M. de Croissy, in speaking of a native of Canterbury—of French origin, it is true,—asserted that "having establisht himself for 20 years and married himself and driven a Trade in France he was to be looked upon as naturalized".[3] There was uncertainty about the nationality of married women. Orders were indeed given to exempt non-naturalized Englishmen from vexatious measures, but the Intendants did not always carry out these orders, whether from ignorance or not, one cannot say. Some of Sir William's English correspondents wrote to him in French, as if that language were more familiar to them; and it is quite likely that in their towns they were considered as more or less French.

1 See p. 12, *ante.*
2 *H.M.C.*, *7th Report*, App., Part 1, p. 278, Lord Preston's correspondence.
3 *R.O. France*, vol. 150, f. 93, Trumbull to Sunderland, June 26, 1686.

CHAPTER IV

First audiences

DECEMBER

ABOUT a week after he arrived in Paris Sir William Trumbull made his first official appearance. He was not yet to be received by the King, but went first to call upon the Secretary for Foreign Affairs, already armed with one of those "memorials" that the French court was to find so irritating.

"On Sat^rday last", he writes to Sunderland on December 5, 1685, "I made my first visit to Monsr de Croissy, who receivd me very civilly, and has appointed Tuesday next for my Publick Audience. According to my Orders (that as soon as might be after my Arrivall here I should complain of ye Quartring of Troopes upon his Maj^ties Subjects trading in these Kingdomes) I presented to him a Memoriall,[1] ye Copie whereof I here send inclos'd: W^ch I drew in generall Termes, that it might not onely serve ye Petitioners, but comp^rhend ye rest of ye English Merchants that are in severall Places under ye like Circumstances, according as my following Instructions did import. Monsr de Croissy entred into a long discourse to shew ye Reasonablenesse of Strangers being equally subject to all Burthens of this Countrie with ye rest of ye Kings Subjects: But when I insisted upon ye Treaties between ye two Crowns relating to ye Merchants Trading and coming hither for their Commerce, He sayd He would represent ye matter to ye King and that I should have an Answer."[2]

Always cautious, Sir William asked Sunderland for further instructions.

"I have receivd Letters from very many of ye English Merchants" he continues, "full of Complaints of ye like kind. Some of them are Naturalizd and others are not. They generally desire nothing but Passeports to withdraw their Effects and be gon. Wherein, because

---

1 See pp. 182–3, *post.*
2 R.O. *France,* vol. 148, f. 128, to Sunderland, Dec. 5, 1685.

I apprehend great Prejudice may follow to his Maj^{ties} Interest, as well as to his said Subjects, ye Merchants, I would humbly beg to receive further and particular Directions." [1]

After the English merchants it was the turn of the affair of Orange, and Sir William learned from M. de Croissy that it was all the fault of the Prince of Orange.

I have communicated ye Affaire of ye Principality of Orenge (*sic*) to ye Dutch Embassad^r and receivd an Acc^t from him of ye severall Instances he has made from time to time to this Court; but without any Effect. The same day I entred into that matter with Monsr de Croissy [2]; who told me, that ye most Chris^n King had sent Orders to Monsr Barillon to speake with his Ma^ty about it: That he could give me no other Answ^r, than what he had often given to ye Dutch Ambassad^r and others, wch was, That ye King acknowledgd no Souveraignty there, That although he had left ye Prince of Orenge for some time in Quiet, so long as his Conduct might deserve it, yet now having opposd his most Christ^n Maj^ty so openly, he did not thinke fitt to keepe any longer ye same Measures; And that all was now don there, his Troopes being come away. When I urgd ye Treatie of Nimeguen, by wch ye Prince of Orenge was restord to his said Principality, with all ye Rights and in ye same Condition and ye same Manner that he had Enjoyd before; And that I desird ye most Christ^n King to consider further ye neare Allyance between his Maj^ty and ye Prince of Orenge obligd his Maj^ty to interpose in a Matter of such Consequence; He replyd, That he would speake to ye King of it and represent what I had said. [3]

So much for the first encounter with M. de Croissy. If Sir William had known what message had been sent to Barrillon he would not have expected any great results from M. de Croissy's intervention.

"Comme il ne s'est rien passé dans la principauté d'Orange que je ne sois pas en droit de faire", Louis XIV had written to his ambassador in London, "et que les esgards que mes predecesseurs et moy avons eu pour les pere et ayeul du prince d'Orange ne peuvent

---

1 *Ib.*

2 M. de Croissy, it would appear, was at first surprised, even shocked, when Spanheim informed him of the "violences" committed at Orange, but, "il n'en étoit pas le maître, mais M. de Louvois". Spanheim, *Relation*, pp. 406–8.

3 R.O. *loc. cit.* The passage referring to Orange is printed in Dalrymple, II, p. 159.

nuire a la souveraineté qui a tousjours apartenu et apartient encore
incontestablem^t a ma couronne j'ay sujet de croire que le Roy
d'Ang^{re} ne s'engagera pas bien avant dans cette affaire d'autant plus
que le bien de notre religion ne permettoit pas de laisser plus longtemps cette ville dans l'heresie. Vous pouvez...faire connoitre que
j'ay assez de confiance dans l'amitié du Roy d'Ang^{re} pour croire qu'il
abandonnera entierement cette solicitañon." [1]

There was one more matter that troubled Sir William, and he
took it up in this letter to Sunderland. Now that all Protestant
cemeteries were done away with, where were Protestant
foreigners to be buried? Some weeks before a letter from
Marseilles had hinted at certain difficulties: "Our late Consul
Mr Lang was buried yesterday evening wth all ye decencie y^e
tymes would admitt." [2] The envoys of other courts had already
protested. [3] The death of two English subjects raised the
issue.

"The last weeke", writes Sir William, "there dyd in this Towne
Sr Anthony Thorold and an English Gentlewoman; Their friends
sent to me, That I would acquaint Monsr de la Renie, Lieuten^t de la
Police de Paris, with it and desire a Burying Place for y^m; He sent
word, That there was no Publick Place appointed, And that all
Strangers might bury their dead friends in ye Feilds or Gardins, as
they thought fitt. Now in regard ye Dutch Embassad^r, and severall
others of ye Publick Ministers here have already made their Instances,
and are in some short time intending to presse for an Answ^r, And
because his Maj^{ty} has usually many of his Subjects in this Towne, I
would humbly intreate that I might receive some Directions, whether
I should joyne with y^m in endeavouring to obtaine a Permission for a
Place to Burie ye Dead." [4]

"There are a great number of Missionaires sent into severall
parts of these Provinces", Sir William continues, " to supply y^e
Defects of ye Ignorant Curés, and to prevent ye Inconveniencies

1 A.É. *Angleterre*, vol. 156, f. 181, Nov. 29, 1685.
2 R.O. *France*, vol. 148, f. 110, Francis Hill to Sunderland, Oct. 29, 1685.
3 "Les ministres des princes étrangers huguenots faisoient alors de grandes
plaintes de ce que le Roi avoit fait détruire le cimetière où l'on enterroit dans Paris
les étrangers qui n'étoient pas catholiques. Et M. de Meyerkrôn, envoyé extraordinaire de Danemark, disoit publiquement dans Versailles que c'étoit une
cruauté inouïe et qui étoit directement contraire au droit des gens." Sourches,
Mémoires, I, p. 337.
4 R.O. *France*, vol. 148, f. 128 (still the letter of Dec. 5).

that might happen from thence, in respect of ye new Converts. Y^e King has given full Power to ye Bishops to Deprive all such of their Benefices; And because many of them (especially in ye Diocess of Rouën) were beginning to make their Defences Par des Appels comme d'Abus, ye King sent a Lettre de Cachet to ye Parliam^t of Rouën, forbidding y^m to receive any such Appeales upon that Subject." [1]

Sir William's "Memoriall" in behalf of the merchants protested, as we have seen, against the quartering of troops in the houses of English subjects. Messages of distress continued to reach Sir William from all sides. From Rouen an Englishman not naturalized, a certain Burrish, asked for protection, and sent with his letter a loin of veal and a box of eight pots of walnuts.[2] Henry Lavie [3] wrote from Bordeaux that he had been detained seven days in prison, but by means of friends he had obtained a month from the Intendant to produce a pass from the King to stay or be gone without being molested in religion. Without this he must return to prison or suffer soldiers in his house or change. Mr John Strang was still in prison, and Lavie's son was threatened with the galleys.[4]

Orders in Council directed Sir William to interpose in behalf of John de Grave of Rouen[5] and William Gray of Nantes.[6] And from Nantes James Bruce, who had hailed Sir William as "the Moses" of his age, sent an account of his lamentable plight, for he too had devils, as he said, lodging in his house.

Nantes, ye 7 December 1685

Right honorable,

I hope yor ho/may have received myne of ye 27th past giving you in part accompt of our miseries, which since have much augmented, for on the 4th ther aryved two Companies of Dragoons, no I may say Divels, when aryved they sent to my house by order of Monsr le Duc de Chauen governor of this province per the Major and

---

1 *Ib.* f. 129. The same letter.
2 *H.M.C., Downshire MSS.* 1, p. 68, Dec. 5.
3 Cf. p. 28, *ante.*
4 *H.M.C., op. cit.* 1, p. 65, Dec. 1.
5 *Ib.* p. 61, Nov. 27 (O.S.), p. 69, Dec. 7 (O.S.).
6 *Ib.* pp. 54, 56 and R.O. *France, Entry Book* 19, Nov. 23—Dec. 3.

Echevins of this City eight Dragoons and horses and a Mareshal de logis, besydes as many more they called into my house to eat and drink at discretion, and they each one [demanded?] a louis d'or on ther assiete befor they began supper, 20 Crownes in confitures besydes wyn and pardridges, turkies, cappons and all other things necessary. After Supper they putt me out of my house betwixt 9 and 10 a clock at night, keeped my wife in torment till the morning wher after having obliged her to give them what money she had or could borrow they went to rest. She being free of ther torment was by ther torments forced to absent wher they wer,[1] after putting me and her abroad, they wer Masters of my household goods, which I esteem 2000 *ll*,[2] which they have burned, sold and hacked in pieces, that sold they have retained the money, opened my study, have diverted my papers, some of them opened my Cash and what was in it nothing left. I cannot now particularly condescend on the Summe; it may alwyse be within ye Summe of 8000*ll*. I have essayed to make a proces verbal of the dommadge they have done, but neither Judge, Advocat, procureur, nottary or Sergeant darre doe it. Enfin it is a truth I and my wife are ever since absent, because I had rather abandon all my temporall then to losse my spirituall. When they had eat all was in my house they were putt into ye taverne at 3*ll* a day. You see dear S^r what a consternation I am in, and if I could goe away I wold, but can not without a passeport. Yo^r honor sees how our King of Englands Subjects are exposed to pillage contrary to all manner of human law and treaty of commerce. You see I may be totally ruined in a short tyme, however I hope alwyse you may send me speedy deliverance. I have been recommended to yor honor with old Mr Gray, but he has changed and will stay here, but for me my wife and child for Gods sake procure us liberty to depart if it be possible, if not that I may with my family live at liberty without being molested.... All I can say more is that I can not tell you the half of ye evill of what they doe, so as I hope yor honor will have me in consideration of yor brother in law,[3] Sr William Bruce of Balcashie[4] and Sr Andrew Foster[5].... I hope and intreats yor honor may likewise procure my dedomagement, besydes the losse of my

---

1 Thus in text. Perhaps there is some omission.
2 *Livres tournois.* Sir William counts 1230 livres tournois to 100*l*. *Cal. Treas. Books,* 1685–9, p. 1117.
3 M. Saumarets of Jersey, cf. *H.M.C., Downshire MSS.* 1, p. 62.
4 Architect in Scotland to Charles II, better known as Sir William Bruce of Kinross. *D.N.B.*
5 Or Forester, "Conjunct Secretary for Scotland", *H.M.C., Downshire MSS. loc. cit.*

Credit and tyme, having sold my goods publickly in y⁰ Street, and keeps the money, and must tell yoʳ honor I owe nothing to no man in France, so that my being delt with in such a maner has spoilled my Credit, besydes the losse of my goods.[1]

But to return to Sir William and his "public audience". On Tuesday, December 11, the envoy was received for the first time by the King of France. A newsletter tells us that he was attended by a large number of Englishmen, so that the number of tables prepared for their reception had to be doubled.[2] In the *Gazette de France* we read:

Le 11ᵉ, le Chevalier Trumball Envoyé Extraordinaire du Roy de la Grande Bretagne, eut sa premiere audience publique du Roy, de Madame la Dauphine, de Monseigneur le Duc de Bourgogne, de Monseigneur le Duc d'Anjou, de Monsieur et de Madame. Il estoit accompagné d'un grand nombre de Gentilshommes Anglois et il avoit esté amené par le Sieur de Bonneuil, Introducteur des Ambassadeurs, qui avoit esté le prendre dans les Carrosses du Roy et de Mme la Dauphine.[3]

The *Mercure galant* reported that his harangue gave great satisfaction: "Il fit un Discours qui charma tous ceux qui l'entendirent. Sa Majesté en fut extremément satisfaite et dit qu'Elle n'avoit point oüy d'homme qui parlast mieux."[4] In Sir William's bills of extraordinaries one finds the following items[5]:

	livres	sols
For my expences the first day I had my audience at Versailles	118	
Given according to custom to the Guardes des Portes, the coachmen of the King and Mad. la Dauphine, the Servants of Monsieur de Croissy, the Introducteur and his Lieutenants	290	
For the expence of making my mourning equipage, for myself, coaches and servants	1033	13

No affairs of any kind were discussed at this ceremony, but

---

1 R.O. *France*, vol. 148, f. 150 (copy); cf. *H.M.C., Downshire MSS.* 1, pp. 69–70.
2 B.N. MS. fr. 10265, f. 91. Dangeau also mentions the audience, 1, p. 265.
3 *Gazette de France*, 1685, pp. 719–20.
4 *Mercure galant*, Dec. 1685, pp. 134–5.
5 *Cal. Treas. Books*, 1685–9, p. 1116.

Sir William did not miss the opportunity of seeing M. de Croissy afterwards.

"I had my Publick Audience yesterday", he writes on December 12, "and was receivd with very great Civility; the King assuring me of his Desire and readinesse to entertain ye good Correspondence between ye 2 Crowns, And to shew his good Affections and Respects to his Maj^{tie} upon all occasions; with ye Returns of ye usuall Complements to her Maj^{tie} and ye Princesse of Denmarke.

After ye other Ceremonies (Except onely to Monseign^r le Dauphin, who was gon a Hunting) I waited on Monsr de Croissy, in order to obtaine another Audience, wch is appointed me on Saturday morning; And to desire an Answer to my Memorial about his Maj^{ties} Subjects, And ye Affaire of Orenge.

He told me, That as to such of ye English as were in France, not Naturaliz'd the King had given Orders to free them from any Trouble, And that they should receive no Molestation upon ye Account of Religion in any fashion whatsoever.

And if it happned, That any particular person had notwithstanding this any Cause of Complaint, if I would give an Account of it, there should be care taken immediately for Redresse.

As to those that were Naturaliz'd, he sayd, the King lookd upon them in all Respects as his own Subjects, And by Reason of ye Present Commotion in his Kingdom upon ye Account of Religion (which had made so many desirous to be gon) ye King thought fitt, at this Time, to grant no Passeports, though perhaps a Month or two hence it might be obtaind. That which gave him occasion to say this, was, That severall English Merchants Naturalizd had gon themselves and presented their Placets to him, Alleadging (among other things) That they had Estates left y^m in England, which of Necessitie requird their Presence. And that their Letters of Naturalizaõn being given not onely upon Condition of enjoying ye Libertie of their Religion, but allso of their Dwelling and Residing in France, their Affaires now calling them away, they were to be lookt upon onely as Temporary Subjects (that is, so long onely as they did Abide here) And therefore they desird to Renounce their said Letters of Naturalizaõn, to deliver them up, and be gon."

Sir William listened in silence.

"I did not interpose herein in his Maj^{ties} Name," he remarks, "having no Orders to that Purpose, Except onely in ye Case of Strang and two or three others particularly Nam'd; So that I humbly submitt the Consideration hereof to his Maj^{ties} Pleasure, And to such further Directions and Commands as may be thought fitt to be given herein." [1]

M. de Croissy then spoke of some other affairs of state. The relations between France and Spain were somewhat strained at this time in spite of the Truce of Ratisbon which, signed in August of the year preceding, was supposed to have patched things up for the next twenty years, but it was hard to forget that the Spanish Low Countries had been cruelly ravaged. [2] There had been trouble between the Spanish garrison at Fuenterrabia and the French inhabitants of Hendaye; and because the government of Corunna had confiscated the cargo of two French ships [3] Louis XIV had retaliated by confiscating the revenues of certain Spanish subjects residing in his dominions. [4] According to M. de Croissy the question of peace was entirely dependent on the good intentions of Spain.

"He assurd me further", relates Sir William, "That this King was extreamly desirous of ye Peace and Quiet of Christendom; That in case ye Spaniards would contribute anything on their part, there could be no Doubt of a happy issue; And that, as to ye late Difference about ye Ship taken at Courogne, and ye Seizure following in ye Low Countries, things were in a good disposition to make an Amicable end," [5]

The question of the Palatinate was still pending. The late Elector, Charles of Simmern, had died childless on May 26 of that year, and Louis XIV was claiming part of the succession for his sister-in-law, Madame, wife of the Duke of Orleans and sister of the late Elector.

"He entered into ye Discourse of ye Palatinat," continues Sir William, still speaking of M. de Croissy , "And sayd that ye King had referrd this matter to ye Decision of ye Pope, which was no new

---

1 R.O. *France*, vol. 148, ff. 136, 137, to Sunderland, Dec. 12, 1685.

2 See H. Lonchay, *La Rivalité de la France et de l'Espagne aux Pays Bas* (1635–1700); Pirenne, *Histoire de la Belgique*, vol. v.

3 The *Marie* and the *Nostre Dame de Lombardie*, A.É. *Angleterre*, vol. 156, f. 103. Sir William mentions one ship only.

4 Cf. A.É. *Angleterre*, vol. 156, ff. 103, 116, 120, 136, 147, 148, 150, 165. Correspondence between Louis XIV and Barrillon on this subject, Nov. 1685, vol. 158, f. 169; Barrillon to Louis XIV, March 28, 1686.

5 R.O. *loc. cit.*

thing, For there were multitudes of Presidents, where in Differences happning even between yᵉ Princes of yᵉ Empire they had been sometimes referrd to yᵉ King of France, sometimes to other Princes; yᵉ Emperour (by reason of some particular Interest) being not lookt upon as a Judge, in such Cases, Competent; And that this offer was judg'd so Reasonable by most of yᵉ Princes of yᵉ Empire, That although some few did oppose it yet he doubted not but that it would be Accepted and have a happy Conclusion."

And what about the unhappy Principality of Orange?

As to yᵉ affaire of Orenge, He sayd This King could give me no other Answer than to yᵉ same purpose he had given me before; That all was now don there, and yᵉ Troopes come away; That this King resolving to have but one Religion in his Countrie thought himself oblig'd in Conscience and Justice to take Order for their Conversions in that Place, as he had don in others; which being don, yᵉ Temporall Jurisdiction there was left in yᵉ same Condition it was before; That he hopd the King my Master would be satisfyd with this Answer And not interpose in a thing wherein he had no Interest, but leave this King free to do as he thought fitt in his own Dominions.

This was yᵉ Substance of his Answer, together with some Repetition of what I sent yoᵣ Loᵖ before, vizt: That yᵉ Right of Souveraignty did not belong to yᵉ Prince of Orenge, but to yᵉ House of Longueville, wᶜʰ yᵉ King had taken care to putt into a Course of Triall before a competent Judicature, and would be determind in due Time.[1]

Thus ended the second interview with M. de Croissy, at the close of the public audience. And now Sir William was getting ready for the second audience with the King, to be given on the coming Saturday, an audience which was to be more than mere outward show. He continues,

Concerning yᵉ Company of Hudsons Bay, The Ships taken by yᵉ Privateers in yᵉ West Indies, And yᵉ other Particulars I have in my Instructions, I am preparing my Memorials for Saturday, and hope to have most of yᵐ ready; And in particular to make my Instances (after I have presented both their Majesties Letters) in behalf of yᵉ Dutchesse of Mazarine.[2]

1 R.O. *loc. cit.* The passages referring to Orange are printed in Dalrymple, II, p. 160.

2 R.O. *loc. cit.* Cf. *H.M.C., Downshire MSS.* I, p. 53: "...letter...to desire the King to interpose his authority with the Duke of Mazarin to restore her pension to the Duchess." Sunderland to Trumbull, Nov. 9–19.

Finally Sir William adds some news:

I am informd this morning, That y⁰ Court of Spaine has given Orders for Restitution of y⁰ Ship and Lading taken at Courogne; Though ye Count del Val (y⁰ Spanish Envoyé here) pretends to know nothing of it; And was very much Dissatisfyd with y⁰ Answer given him by Monsʳ de Croissy, That he would entertain no Discourse with him upon any Affaire whatever, till that of Courogne were fully Accommodated. The same Spanish Minister made an Agreement yesterday with Monsʳ de Louvoy about y⁰ Extraordinary Couriers of Spaine that passe through France; wᶜʰ was, That y⁰ Post Master here should give a Note, according to an Exact Account to be deliverd in to him, of y⁰ Number of all their Pacquets; And y⁰ same thing to be don there of all y⁰ French Pacquets that should passe through y⁰ Dominions of y⁰ Catholique King: which is to hinder them from carrying any letters, but those onely for y⁰ Service of their Respective Masters.

"I have waited upon y⁰ Dutchesse of Portsmouth",[1] he concludes, "and deliverd his Majᵗⁱᵉˢ Letter, to wᶜʰ y⁰ Inclos'd is an Answr."[2]

On the day of the public audience the unhappy Bruce had written again from Nantes, recounting all the tribulations the dragoons had inflicted upon him.

"Having done all the mischief they could on the 7ᵗʰ," he reports, "they lockt my house doors and delyvered the Keyes to the Major of y⁰ City, who has them in possession ever since; and I have not a mynd to enter my house till yoʳ honor advyse me, My wife ever since absent they threatten terrible things against her unlesse she change if found and imprisonement to me if I find her not, which makes me keep out of y⁰ way till I hear from yoʳ honor how to act. I can not send you either ane attestation or a proces verbal of what doeings I have met with, being none dare doe it. God of his mercy have mercy on us and by yoʳ meanes send us a speedy deliverance."[3]

He had gone to complain to the Governor and magistrates, but they told him they could do nothing for him except his wife change her religion.[4]

---

1 Louise de Kéroualle, mistress of Charles II, mother of the Duke of Richmond.
2 R.O. *loc. cit.*
3 *Ib.* f. 150, Dec. 11, 1685 (copy).
4 *Ib.* His wife was the daughter of a Scotsman, but born at Nantes. *H.M.C., Downshire MSS.* I, p. 98.

It was known that Sir William was to interpose in the matter of Orange. The English envoy at the Hague, Bevil Skelton, wrote that the Prince heard Trumbull had orders to intercede about the business of his Principality of Orange. What hope had Trumbull of success?[1] Wassenaer, the Dutch ambassador at Paris, desired to know whether, on the preceding Tuesday, anything had passed between Sir William and M. de Croissy about affairs at Orange, and Sir William had to admit reluctantly that M. de Croissy had given him the same answer at the second interview as at the first. He wished he had something else to relate, for he took no less interest in the affairs of the Prince of Orange, he assured the Dutch ambassador, than did the ambassador himself.[2]

Sir William also sent a lengthy account of his two conversations with M. de Croissy to Dijkvelt who, as Envoy Extraordinary in London, had recommended the Prince's interests to him.

"A la première visite que j'ay rendu à Monsr de Croissy quoy qu'on n'y attendoit que des complimens," he writes a little complacently, "je n'avois garde pourtant de la laisser eschapper sans lui ouvrir les ordres du Roy mon maitre sur cette affaire, et l'interest particulier qu'il y prenoit, et de luy faire sçavoir l'estime et le cas que mon maitre faisoit de S. A. [the Prince of Orange] et de l'alliance prochaine qui est entre eux. La dessus il disoit que le Roi son maitre avoit escrit sur cette affaire à Monsr Barillon, et qu'il ne doutoit point que ce qu'il en communiqueroit au Roi mon maitre ne luy satisfait de la sorte qu'il n'y prist aucun interet dorenavant."

Was this the only answer Sir William was to give his King?

Mais comme je luy demandois si c'estoit la response que j'envoyerois au Roy mon m're il repartit que non, et ensuite reprit la parole et me dit qu'il avoit souvent parlé sur cette affaire tant à Monsr l'Embassad^r d'Hollande qu'à Monsr l'Envoyé de Brandenbourg, et qu'il ne pouvoit pas dire autre chose que ce qu'il leur avoit deja dit, cet a sçavoir que le Roy son m're ne reconnoissoit point la souveraineté d'Orenge, et qu'ayant pris la resolution d'abolir la religion P.R. dans son royaume, et Dieu ayant beni ses soins—here M. de Croissy halted his discourse, for he realized that Sir William could

---

1 *H.M.C., Downshire MSS.* 1, p. 74, Dec. 14.   2 *Ib.* p. 67, Dec. 14.

scarcely be expected to appreciate this language—(il faut, dit-il, que je vous parle de la manière, quoy que je sçache que vous ayez des sentimens tous contraires).

Then he continued to point out that the King his master being blessed in his undertaking, felt obliged to extend his efforts to Orange as well: "Il se croyoit obligé en conscience et justice de faire la meme chose pour convertir les habitans de la ville d'Orenge qu'ailleurs en son royaume."

Sir William, who was a great reasoner, could not let this occasion go.

"Mais comme je l'interrompois pour raisonner," he tells Dijkvelt, "tant sur les contraventions qu'on avoit fait en cet egard a beaucoup des traittés, que particulierem^t a celuy de Nimegue (dont le Roy mon m're estoit le guarand) il repondit que le dit traitté de Nimegue ne laissoit a Monsr le P. d'O. que les mesmes droits qu'il avoit auparavant, et que s'il n'avoit pas aucun droit auparavant (comme, dit-il, il n'en avoit point, mais que ce droit estoit incontestablement à la maison de Longueville) ce traitté ne luy en donnoit point."

This could not go unchallenged.

Je ne pouvois pas m'empesche de luy repliquer brusquement que non obstant tout cela le dit traitté de Nimegue porte formèllement que le P. d'O. seroit remis dans la possession de la dite principauté au meme etat et en la meme manière dont il jouissoit auparavant, et que c'etoit cette possession la qu'on luy avoit ostée à cette heure et qu'on avoit manifestement violée. Il ne me repondit autre chose la-dessus, si non qu'il en parleroit au Roy. Apres cela je n'ay pas manqué d'escrire en Angleterre, non seulement le detail de tout ce discours et une lettre en particulier au Roy,[1] mais aussy les nouvelles de tout ce qui s'est passe en Orenge depuis l'enlevement du Sieur Drevon jusques à present dont Monsr Langy Mont-Miral[2] m'a fait part toutes les fois qu'il les avoit receues.

Et comme j'ay pris la hardiesse de supplier tres humblement le Roy mon m're de me vouloir donner de temps en temps des ordres necessaires pour cette affaire, je les attends de jour en jour avec beaucoup d'impatience.

Finally Sir William described his second conversation with M. de Croissy.

---

1 This letter is not at the R.O.
2 M. de Langes Montmiral, or Montmirail, was brother to M. de Lubières, President of the Parlement d'Orange.

Mardy passé j'eus ma première audience, et le meme jour je fus encore chez M. de Croissy à demander la reponce que j'eus à mander au Roy mon m're sur cette affaire. Il me dit qu'il avoit representé mes instances au Roy son m're, mais qu'il me faloit repondre de la meme manière qu'auparavant, et que le Roy avoit tout fait en Orange à cette heure; que ses troupes en etoient sorties; que se croyant obligé en justice de pourvoir au salut des habitans de cette ville, tout ce qu'il avoit fait c'etoit a l'egard du spirituel, mais a l'egard du temporel il n'y avoit point du changement, mais tout y etoit demeuré comme auparavant; qu'il croyoit que cela satisfit au Roy mon m'tre, et qu'il n'y prist pas aucun interest mais qu'il laissast le Roy son m're en toute sorte de liberté de faire ce qu'il jugeroit à propos dans son Royaume.

In a postscript Sir William alluded to certain dangers attending their correspondence.

Je ne vous envoye pas celle cy par le pacquet de Monsr l'Embassad^r d'Hollande pour des certaines raisons dont je vous ferai part une autre fois; mais je me sert de l'address que vous mavies donné à Londres pour Mon^r Jean Frederic Molwat etc. Faites moy la grace de m'advertir si celle-cy n'ait point été ouverte.[1]

The persecutions at Orange were making a "noise" in England. Thus the representatives of certain foreign states condemned the violences committed, drawing their information, so it was said, from the envoy of the Great Elector at the court of France. "The public Ministers aggravate the cruelties there, and publish privately a detail of them which I believe comes from Mr Spanheim", wrote Owen Wynne to Sir William. "You will have much ado to wipe off the odium that some will endeavour to throw upon the King."[2]

As for the French ambassador in England, he was instructed to make James understand the disadvantages that would accrue to him if he asked for favours that could not be granted.[3] And no favours could be shown the Principality of Orange.

1 H.M.C., 8th Report, App., Part I, pp. 556–7, Dec. 14, 1685. Reprinted by permission of the Right Honourable the Earl of Denbigh.
2 H.M.C., Downshire MSS. 1, p. 59, Nov. 29—Dec. 6, 1685.
3 A.É. Angleterre, vol. 156, f. 269, Louis XIV to Barrillon, Dec. 14, 1685. The King adds: "J'ay veu par vos lettres que le Sr Trumball sera seulement chargé de me faire de simples offices, mais il ne faut pas douter que le Prince d'Orange n'en tire toujours quelque avantage."

CHAPTER V

Memorials and Petitions

DECEMBER

AFTER the "publick" audience came the "particular" audience. The first audience at Versailles had been limited to a pleasant exchange of compliments and civilities, but on Saturday, December 15, the King received Sir William Trumbull in private, yet not without a certain amount of ceremonial. As Lord Preston once wrote from France: "The circumstances of an English minister in this Court are much different from those of a French one in England, for tho we have access to the King at all times, and may discourse him upon indifferent things, we cannot mention business to him without all the formality of an introducteur and of an audience." [1] Sir William was again presented by M. de Bonneuil, Introducteur des Ambassadeurs, and was also received by the Dauphin on this occasion. [2] Dangeau notes the event and speculates upon the subject of discourse. "Le chevalier Trumbal eut une grande audience particulière du roi, où il fut parlé à ce qu'on prétend, des huguenots sortis du royaume pour passer en Angleterre." [3]

"On Saturday last," writes Sir William, "I had my Particular Audience, and Represented to yᵉ King at large, How much his Majᵗʸ was concerned that yᵉ Peace of Christendom should be Preservd; (According as that Article of my Instructions commanded me) And tooke that occasion to mention yᵉ late Pretensions of yᵉ French in yᵉ Spanish Netherlands, And that his Majᵗʸ desird they might be amicably determind, according to yᵉ Methods Prescribd by yᵉ Treatie of Nimeguen, To which he Answd, That he was very ready

1 H.M.C., 7th Report, App., Part I, p. 271.
2 Gazette de France, 1685, p. 735.
3 Dangeau, Journal, 1, p. 266.

to Joyne in Contributing to yᵉ Generall Peace and Quiet of Christendom, And as he had already, so for yᵉ future he would not be wanting to give all Assurances on his Part to that Purpose. As to what had happned in yᵉ Spanish Netherlands, he sayd, That it was occasiond by yᵉ Fault of yᵉ Spaniards, who had been yᵉ Aggressors, by seizing on yᵉ Ship att Courogne, And after by yᵉ Insult upon yᵉ Marquis de Bouflers in Fontarabie; That in this latter Case They had sent a Courier to let him know how much yᵉ K. of Spaine disapproovd of this Insolence, and to offer all Satisfaction; And that assoon as he had Justice don him for yᵉ Ship taken at Courogne... there would be an End of yᵉ Seizures in those Countries, But till that were don, he would continue yᵉ Seizures as they were. And for yᵉ other Differences in yᵉ Païs d'Haynault,[1] about yᵉ Propositions of yᵉ Rents and Contributions, It was a matter wherein he had no Participation, relating onely to Particular Persons who were to be Subject to yᵉ Lawes, and that Justice should be don yᵐ, according to what yᵉ Courts should there determine."[2]

And not unlike the lion in one of La Fontaine's fables he touched lightly on his own commendable moderation.

He added, That alltho it was given out, That He [had?] a Mind to possess himself of yᵉ Low Countries, yet as his Conduct yᵉ last Yeare [shewed?] (when yᵉ Spaniards were not in a Condition to have Resisted his Forces) so for yᵉ Time to come He would make it sufficiently Evident, That he had no such Thoughts, And that it should be yᵉ Fault of yᵉ Spaniards, and not His, if all things did not continue in Quiet and Peace."[3]

Sir William now raised the question of the Duchess Mazarin,[4] one of the Cardinal's beautiful nieces who had separated from her strange husband and was living in London, unable to regain the riches she had brought him.[5] The pension that the Duke was supposed to pay her had stopped some years ago, on the ground that she had lodged at Whitehall.[6] The Duchess

---

1 Cf. A.É. *Angleterre*, vol. 156, f. 116 and f. 120, Louis XIV to Barrillon, Nov. 6 and 8, 1685.
2 R.O. *France*, vol. 148, f. 146, to Sunderland, Dec. 19, 1685.
3 R.O. *loc. cit.*
4 Cf. p. 38, *ante*.
5 Cf. Renée, *Les Nièces de Mazarin*.
6 On Nov. 8, 1685, Barrillon mentions the granting of certain lodgings at Whitehall to the Duchess. A.É. *Angleterre*, vol. 156, f. 138, to Louis XIV.

had written recently to James, asking him to use his influence.[1]

"After this", continues Sir William, "I presented both their Maj^{ties} Letters in behalf of ye Dutchess of Mazarine, and Acquainted him with ye great Interest they tooke in this Request and ye particular Satisfaction they would receive by ye Granting of it; And with ye Justice and Equitie of ye Pension being payd, in respect of her Qualitie and ye great Fortune she brought her Husband; And therefore I could not but hope, That as by his Gracious Interposition it had been payd formerly, So that ye same thing might be don for ye future. To this he sayd, That having been often importund by a Multitude of Creditors, who had Pretensions upon ye Duke of Mazarines Estate, He had made a Resolution to leave them to ye Law, and to meddle no more in his affaires; That he could not but do ye same thing in this Case; For althô, as he had Power to make ye Lawes, so he could allso repeale them, yet whilst they stood in Force, he must be Just, and leave ye Dutchess to ye determinaõn of those Lawes; And (in Conclusion) sayd, That he would not faile to

[1] "Sire, ie supplie tres humblement V.M. de vouloir adiouter une grace a toutes celles que ien ai receues, cest davoir la bonte de semploier fortement dans les conionctures presentes pour obliger le Roi de France a me faire faire iustice par Mr Mazarin qui na seu trouver dautres preteste pour me faire oster ma pantion que parce que iestois logee a Wital il y a quelques annee. Comme est fait Mr Mazarin et comme il est connu generalement cest une chose impossible que ie puisse me racommoder avec lui, ie parlere avec beaucoup de discretion et ie dis seulement que son esprit son humeur son naturel lont randu incapable de pouvoir vivre avec personne et dans cette impossibilite nesse pas la derniere des iniustices quil soit maitre de tous les milions que ie lui ay aportes sans que ien tire la moindre chose du monde.

"Le Roi de France mauoit fait donner une pantion de veint quattre mille franc donnee avec toute sorte de iustice et ostee depuis six ans sans en scavoir une bonne raison, de ce retranchement Sire est venue la necessite de mes affaires. Dans la iuste consideration que la france comme le reste de leurope doit auoir pour V.M. ie ne doute point quon ne puisse obtenir ce quon ne me peut refuser que tres iniustement, le Roy de France dire peutestre quil ne se mesle point des affaires des particuliers mais cest lui mesme qui mauoit fait auoir ma pantion de sa seule autorite et qui peut faire auiordui tout ce quil voudra pour moi plus facilement encore quen ce tems la." R.O. *France*, vol. 148, ff. 116, 117. Endorsed, "Oct.–85. Dutchesse of Mazarin to his Ma^{ty}."

Sir William notes the Duke's eccentricity on another occasion. "The Duke de Mazarin continues very much displeasd with his Son by reason of his Marriage and declares he will endeavour to dissolve it. I âm told that ye Duke himself will receive an Order to Interdict him from Wasting his Estate, he having lately bestow'd a Farme of between 5 and 6000 livres of Rent upon a poor man, on Condition that he shall every day say so many Masses and performe severall other such exercises of Devotion as are express'd in ye Instrument of Donation." R.O. *France*, vol. 150, f. 57, to Sunderland, Feb. 20, 1686.

returne an Answer himself.[1] And in discourse afterwards with Monsr de Croissy, I found, That this Request will hardly be obtaind, unlesse by further Letters from their Maj^{ties}."[2]

Sir William's interview with M. de Croissy after the "particular" audience was evidently a brief one—he left some more memorials with him and returned to Paris.

In the meantime complaints continued to come. Poor Bruce wrote again from Nantes:

My goods have been taken from me with as much injustice as to robe a man in a desert and wher thers no justice to be had except I change with my wife our R. which God preserve me from! When the dragoons had done all the mischief they could they locked my house doors, sent the Keyes to ye Major who has them in possession ever since, and since have not entred my house nor will I till I have yor honors advyce how to cary myself therin. I walk up and down the streets every day without being molested, but my wife dare not appear, they threatten if she change not to put her in a convent if found and to take my child from me. So that yor ho/ sees what hard dealling I have met with. I have this day receaved the copy of a petition presented to his Ma/ of Great Britain in privy councill which was read and expedited for Wm Gray and three daughter and James Bruces wife and child and the 23 expedited by the right honorable the E/ of Sunderland Secretary of State, which I hope may have come safely to yor hands; But must tell you that Mr Gray and daughter have all changed ther Religion, and I believe intends nay am certain will not leave this Kingdom, wherfor for them yor ho/ needs not much trouble yo^rself only for me James Bruce native of Edinburgh in Scotland and my wife Magdelen Gray daughter to a scotchman not naturalized with my son James Bruce 9 moneths old, pray procure us a passeport or liberty to go away to England wher now my affaires call me.[3]

An Englishwoman living in Caen, Elizabeth Dennis, "widow to William de la Mare", besought Sir William to obtain the King's permission for her to sell her house which was all her estate, and would soon be eaten up by the soldiers therein. "The Intendant threatens me to send 10 more soldiers

1 Cf. A.É. *Angleterre*, vol. 151, f. 357, Louis XIV to James II, Dec. 19, 1685, and vol. 156, ff. 229, 230, Louis XIV to Barrillon, Dec. 21, 1685.
2 R.O. *France*, vol. 148, f. 146, to Sunderland, Dec. 19, 1685.
3 *Ib*. f. 151, Dec. 15, 1685 (copy).

today because I will not forsake my religion." She would be ruined for ever if he did not obtain for her permission to return to her native kingdom.[1]

In Orange things were no better. Sir William received news of further incidents—the comte de Tessé had come back and compelled the officers of the *Parlement* to attend mass in their red gowns, in spite of a promise that attendance at mass would not be enforced for some months. It was said that the dragoons were to remain there till Easter.[2]

Two or three days after the "particular" audience the indefatigable Sir William was back at Versailles to see M. de Croissy. When Sir William had handed in a memorial he was in the habit of calling weekly to find out whether there was an answer. M. de Croissy received foreign envoys very regularly on Tuesdays, "le jour des étrangers". A waiting-room was reserved for them in the palace, on the ground floor near the Chambre du Conseil d'État. They also frequently ate at the palace at a special table, "la table du grand Chambellan", but they never spent the night there. Their business was always exclusively with M. de Croissy, who transmitted their requests and protests to the other ministers, an arrangement not without inconvenience, since it deprived them of the possibility of stating their own case to the secretary of state in question.[3]

The memorials which had been presented on the day of the "particular" audience concerned shipping and colonial affairs chiefly. Like his predecessor, Lord Preston, like his succcessor, Skelton, Trumbull was directed to complain against the violences committed at Hudson's Bay. It was claimed that the French had invaded Port Nelson in July 1683 and September 1684, and, to crown it all, one of the Hudson's Bay Company's ships coming from England with provisions had been captured in July 1685.[4]

1 *H.M.C., Downshire MSS.* 1, p. 75, Dec. 17, 1685. We do not know whether her husband was naturalized or not.

2 R.O. *France*, vol. 148, ff. 138–9, [le Président de Lubières?] to Spanheim, Dec. 14, 1685. Cf. *H.M.C., Downshire MSS.* 1, pp. 67–8, probably one of those copies which the President's brother used to supply to Sir William.

3 Spanheim, *Relation*, pp. 285–6, 352.

4 For the text of Sir William's Memorial see pp. 183–5 *post*.

The French Governors of the West Indies, so Sir William had been instructed, said that they had orders from the Most Christian King to confiscate the vessels that anchored in their roads;[1] also they had seized some fishing vessels on the coast of Nova Scotia.[2] Finally these Governors granted commissions to privateers in time of peace.[3] A ship called the *St George* belonging to a certain John Banks had been confiscated by the Governor of Petit Goave, a settlement of Hispaniola.[4] The captain of a French privateer, *la Dauphine*, Captain Yankey, "le capitaine Janquais"—his real name was John Williams [5]— had seized "the *James* shallop, John Thorpe master, and carried her into Petit Guave where she was condemned without the least colour of reason".[6]

1 Cf. "Memorial concerning the French in the West Indies", and "Memorial to French Ambassador concerning the French in the West Indies." *Cal. St. P. Col., A. and W. I.* 1685-8, pp. 134, 147.   2 *Ib.* pp. 66, 141, 626.

3 See p. 169 *post*. Instructions for Sir William Trumbull. "Le Roy d'Ang^re parle souvent avec aigreur de ces pirates....Il m'a dit que le Gouverneur du petit Guave les favorise." A.É. *Angleterre*, vol. 156, f. 15, Barrillon to Louis XIV, Sept. 10, 1685. Later Bonrepaus, on a mission in England, asked for instructions: "Je vous supplie de me faire scavoir ce qu'il y aura a dire au sujet de ces flibustiers qui courent les mers, sans commission, et qui se retirent dans les ports de la domination du Roy." *Ib.* vol. 160, f. 58, to Seignelay, Jan. 31, 1686.

4 R.O. *France*, vol. 148, f. 144, Trumbull to Sunderland, Dec. 15, 1685; *Entry Book* 19, Sunderland to Trumbull, Nov. 30—Dec. 10, 1685; *H.M.C.*, *7th Report*, App., Part I, pp. 306, 308, 332, 370; *H.M.C., Downshire MSS.* 1, p. 64; *Cal. St. P. Col., A. and W. I.* 1685-8, p. 87. The Governor in question was M. de Fransquenay, a temporary Governor. The confiscation of this boat went back to the time of Lord Preston's embassy. In answer to his complaints Preston had been informed by M. de Seignelay that "it had been a custom, and established by the laws, to seize all stranger ships trading within the Isles of America; and that so the Governor of Petites Guaves had with justice seized that English vessel having found it actually trafficking". "My Secretary," continues Lord Preston, "desiring Monsr de Seignelay to observe that it was proved by the certificate annexed to my memorial, that the master of the pincke had put into the Bay of Meriguana with a design of only taking in fresh water, he answered that that was the same thing, nothing being so easy for a vessel to lie by under the pretence of watering and then to traffic privately with her chaloupe," *H.M.C., 7th Report*, App., Part I, p. 307, July 1684. M. de Seignelay's reply was not considered satisfactory, and Preston was ordered to renew instances in behalf of the owner John Banks, R.O. *France, Entry Book* 19, Oct. 14, 1684. *H.M.C., op. cit.* p. 318. See also A.É. *Angleterre*, vol. 160, f. 44, Bonrepaus to Seignelay on this subject, Jan. 21, 1686.

5 Haring, *The Buccaneers in the West Indies*, pp. 235, 254n, 274.

6 R.O. *France, Entry Book* 19, Sunderland to Skelton, March 14-24, 1686-7. Cf. *Cal. St. P. Col., A. and W. I.* 1685-8, pp. 60, 87, 255; A.É. *Angleterre*, vol. 151, ff. 224, 228: "L'état et détail de l'afaire...de la Chaloupe appellée Jacques."

Genoa had been bombarded in May 1684, to teach the Republic "to behave respectfully in the future".[1] The strained relations between France and Genoa had incidentally involved English shipping, and a London merchant, John Mascall by name, wanted some damask that had been sent to him from Genoa, but had been taken to Toulon.[2]

All these matters had been laid before M. de Croissy only a few days before, but Sir William thought optimistically that a reply would be ready.

"I was againe at Versailles yesterday", he writes on December 19, "to desire of Monsr de Croissy an Acc^t of the following Memorials wch I had given. (1) Concerning ye Company of Hudsons Bay.[3] (2) the Confiscation of ye Ships that come to Anchor in ye Roades, And to know if ye King had given any such Orders to his Govern^{rs} in those Parts, and concerning ye Commissions said to be granted to Privateers.[4] (3) In behalf of John Banks, John Thorpe[5] and others for their Ships taken and confiscated at Petit-Guaves. (4) For Restitution of ye Damask belonging to Mascal taken and brought to Toulon. To all which he sayd, That he had putt y^m into ye Hands of Monsr de Seignelay, and that I should have particular Answers as soon as they were informd of ye severall Facts and ye Proofes to justify y^m."[6]

No discussion of these affairs being possible the subject of the English Protestants was taken up again.

"After that, He repeated to me ye former assurances he had given, That all his Maj^{ties} Subjects residing in France, not Naturaliz'd, should be freed from any Trouble, and that Orders were sent to all Places to that Purpose. But when he added...That allthô in Justice all Strangers in this Kingdom were lyable to ye same Burthens that ye French Subjects were; Yet out of particular Respect and Friends^p to ye King my Master he had given those Orders before mention"— Sir William was not going to receive as a favour what he considered a right—"I thought myself obligd to say", he continues, "That I

1 H.M.C., *7th Report*, App., Part 1, p. 331.
2 *Ib.* pp. 329, 333; *Downshire MSS.* 1, p. 64; R.O. *France*, vol. 148, f. 144, Trumbull to Sunderland, Dec. 15, 1685.
3 For the text see pp. 183–5, *post*.
4 For the text see pp. 185–6, *post*.
5 For the text see A.É. *Angleterre*, vol. 160, ff. 94, 96.
6 R.O. *France*, vol. 148, f. 146, to Sunderland, Dec. 19, 1685.

doubted not but any marke of y⁰ most Christian King's Friendsᴾ would be allwayes wellcome to y⁰ King, my Mʳ, Yet in this Case there was nothing but Justice pursuant to y⁰ Treaties stipulated between y⁰ 2 Crownes, wᶜʰ his Majᵗʸ on his Part had most strictly observd in respect of y⁰ French subjects in all Parts of his Dominions, And therefore I could not but be of opinion, That there was y⁰ same Justice for such of y⁰ English as were in France; The Consequence whereof was, That they ought allso to receive satisfaction for their Losses sustaind, Some of them being totally Ruin'd, their Papers taken away and their Goods and Houses destroyd (Particularly in the case of one Bruce, not Naturalized, a Merchant at Nantes), according as I had represented by my Memorial given in. To this Part, I have yet receivd no Answer; And therefore humbly beg I may know his Majᵗⁱᵉˢ Pleasure, How farr He will have me insist upon it.

I have given in another Memorial, concerning y⁰ Child at Rouën, which Mrs Betterton Petitiond his Majᵗʸ might be deliverd to such Person as her Parents should appoint to convey her into Engᵈ; To wᶜʰ he answᵈ, That he would send to y⁰ Intendant at Rouën to be inform'd of y⁰ Fact and to give Orders accordingly. But 2 dayes ago I receivd a Letter, which they had caus'd y⁰ Child to write, By which she excuses herself from taking such a Journey in y⁰ Winter; And (in a word) shewes her unwillingness and refusall to returne into England." ¹

Sir William had also been instructed to take up the case of Sir William Douglas who had married a French Protestant— he was to obtain leave that she might dispose of her land and estate, and come to England with her husband.² He continues therefore:

"I acquainted him allso with Sʳ Willᵐ Douglas' Petition for Leave for his Wife and Child to go into England with him: But this he told me plainly the King had refus'd; For allthô y⁰ Husband being not Naturalizd, might go if he pleasd, Yet y⁰ Wife and Child were Subjects of France, and should not have that Permission.

1 R.O. *loc. cit.* f. 147; cf. *H.M.C., Downshire MSS.* 1, pp. 52, 73, 95. The girl's name was Watson. Cf. A.É. *Angleterre*, vol. 158, f. 80, Louis XIV to Barrillon, Feb. 15, 1686.

2 *H.M.C., Downshire MSS.* 1, p. 52. Lady Douglas' maiden name was Anne de Bey de Batilly, "she had brought her husband an Estate in Alsace", Agnew, *Protestant Exiles,* 11, p. 229, where her epitaph in St James', Westminster, is quoted "...daughter of Anthony de Bey of Batilly (Major General to Louis XIII and Louis XIV) and of the Lady Susanne de Pas, the daughter of the Marquis of Feuquières...was married to Sir William Douglas, Major General of Her Majesty's force." *Ib.* pp. 229–30.

It happned That at ye same time I requested Leave for one Mrs Wilkins to sell her Estate at Rouën and to returne to her Huband into England, whose case was this. Humphry Wilkins had been for many Yeares a Merchant at Rouën, But falling into Troubles, His Wife obtaind a Sentence of Separation D'Habitation et des Biens from him, and so he went to London. Monsr de Croissy told me, That ye King would not grant her any Leave, as she desird; But because her Husband had been Naturaliz'd, he lookt upon her as His Subject. So that", concludes Sir William testily, displeased by this lack of logic, "in ye Case of Sr Wm Douglas they separate Man and Wife; And in this, they joyne them that were separated by ye Sentence of their own Judges.[1]

Monsr de Croissy gave me allso this generall Answ^r Yesterday, That ye King was resolvd, That all Persons Naturalizd should have no Passeports; So that Mr John Strang and others of his Maj^ties Subjects, either such as are in Prison, as such as have ye Dragoons quarterd upon them till they change their Religion, have no more Hopes of obtaining Releif, or Leave to go away; Allthô severall of ye Merchants have urgent occasions to take a voyage to looke after their Trade and Commerce."[2]

Frequently Sir William encloses copies of newsletters sent to him.[3] In his bills of "extraordinaries" the expenses for "gazettes, prints and intelligence" are not inconsiderable items,[4] and in this letter he raises the question of extra pay for his secretary employed as transcriber. "I would humbly intreate ye fav^r of yor Lo^p to lett me know yor Pleasure what Allowance I shall make to D'Ayrolle for writing ye Gazettes á la Main; yor Lo^p gave me encouragem^t to hope, That if he gave Satisfaction, he should receive ye same Allowance, which Godet[5] had formerly."[6]

Two letters came from England about this time. In one of them Sir William heard that the King approved of what he had

---

1 R.O. *loc. cit.*; cf. *H.M.C., Downshire MSS.* 1, p. 73. H. Wilkins "prays God that his Wife and family may by Sir William's favour obtain their freedom out of this cruel land."
2 R.O. *loc. cit.*
3 Curiously enough there are hardly any newsletters of Trumbull's period preserved at the R.O.
4 Cf. pp. 173–6, *post.*
5 Secretary to Lord Preston.
6 R.O. *loc. cit.*

done concerning Orange.[1] But what did this same King tell the French ambassador? That is what the other letter relates.

"Le Roy d'Ang^re m'a dit", writes Barrillon, "qu'il n'avoit pu refuser aux instances du Prince d'Orange de s'interposer auprez de V.M. pour remettre les affaires d'Orange en l'estat ou elles doivent estre par un article exprez du traitté de Nimegue." In a long conversation Barrillon reminded James that this matter had been fully discussed in the time of Charles II, that he probably still remembered the trouble "Mr Van Beuning"[2] had made when the walls of Orange had been demolished, that the Treaty of Nimeguen conferred no more rights on the Prince of Orange than he had had before, and that the sovereignty of Orange belonged indubitably to the crown of France. Moreover a place of retreat for Huguenots could not be maintained in the heart of the kingdom.

James replied that he could not refuse the Prince's request without giving legitimate cause for complaint, and that would make a great noise in England—what had happened in Orange was making stir enough. And then, characteristically, he turned away to dally with a question of doctrine—he showed Barrillon the copy of the capitulation of the magistrates of Orange that Sir William had sent, the conditions they had made—did Barrillon think that Rome would approve of them? Barrillon hastened to reassure him—one could indeed make all kinds of concessions to facilitate the return of heretics.

James then asked him to believe that he did not wish to oppose any of the designs of the King of France in favour of the Catholic religion, but the Principality of Orange had been reputed a sovereignty. Barrillon suggested respectfully that if he would examine the books treating that subject he would find that this pretended sovereignty was entirely dependent on the crown of France.

"Je ne scais point la question de la souveraineté d'Orange a fonds," said James, "mais ce qui se passe a Orange fait grand bruit

---

1 H.M.C., *Downshire MSS.* 1, p. 66, Dec. 3–13, 1685.
2 Conrad Van Beuninghen, Dutch diplomat, at one time Dutch ambassador in London.

ici et en Hollande. C'est a quoy je souhaiterois qu'on pust remedier et qu'il s'y pust trouver quelque temperament. Vous connaissez cependant le fonds de mes intentions pour le Roy vostre maistre et pour l'avantage de la religion Catholique."

To this Barrillon adds: " Je croy que le Roy d'Ang^re ne se met pas beaucoup en peine de ce qui se passe a Orange, mais il a crû devoir en parler comme il a fait pour pouvoir se disculper envers le Prince d'Orange et quelques uns de ses Ministres." Doubtless James would bring up the question again—if not, Barrillon would, having many things to say to him about the Prince of Orange which would not come amiss in the present state of affairs.[1]

To go back to the letter received by Sir William—His Majesty "approved very well" of what he had already performed in the affair of Orange and in that of his subjects molested upon account of their religion. He was to continue his offices in their behalf and also to desire a burial place for English Protestants. The same letter from Sunderland acquainted Sir William with two new incidents of which more will be said presently, in fact one of them, at least, was to occupy Sir William for many a day.[2]

"At present," wrote Sir William in reply, on December 22, "by reason of ye Holy-dayes next weeke, there is nothing to be_ don; Monsr de Croissy being come from Versailles, and ye rest of ye Ministers retird from businesse for that time.

I crave leave to observe, That in ye Order now sent, wherein his Maj^ty commands me to insist, That his Subjects may enjoy ye Liberties stipulated to them by ye Treaties, without being Molested upon the Account of their Religion, or otherwise, There is no Difference made between such of his Subjects as are Naturalizd here, and such as are not... I adde my humble Request, That I may know his Maj^ties Pleasure, How farr I should insist to demand ye same Right may be don to such of his Subjects as have married French-women here, and have Children, in respect of their Wifes and Children."[3]

1 A.É. *Angleterre*, vol. 156, ff. 231–4, Barrillon to Louis XIV, Dec. 17, 1685.
2 H.M.C., *Downshire MSS*. 1, p. 66, from Sunderland, Dec. 3–13, 1685.
3 R.O. *France*, vol. 148, f. 148, Dec. 22, 1685.

Two days later, on December 24, M. de Croissy came to call on Sir William Trumbull in Paris. In this season of "Holy-dayes" M. de Croissy had probably no intention of discussing any public affairs, but his host was not the man to let an opportunity go by. The last letter from Sunderland—to which some allusion has already been made—had brought news of two "insults".

His Maj^{ty} having received an Account that two Dunkirke Frigatts have lately visited the English Pacquet boats, coming from Newport, and taken out of them eighteen Passengers,[1] and that some other French Frigatts have taken and carryed away some Fishermen inhabitants of Rye from the road there, his Maj^{ty} has commanded me to acquaint Monsieur Barillon therewith and would have you also complain of the matter to the most Christian King...that the offenders may be exemplarily punished for these violences.[2]

With this letter had come a document from Rye that had been read in Council—a sworn deposition by some witnesses "they saw a French man of war seize 3 vessels belonging respectively to Stephen Boucher, John Bouchett and Francis Bridon, French Protestants of Rye and take them to Calais or Dunkirk".[3] These fishermen, it should be noted, were all naturalized English subjects.[4]

Let us hear Sir William's account of M. de Croissy's call.

This morning Monsr de Croissy giving me ye Hon^r of a Visitt, I tooke ye opportunity (wch I did not expect so soon) of acquainting him with ye Orders I had receivd to complaine of ye Dunkirke Frigatts that had searchd ye Pacquet Boates, And ye others that had carried away some Fishermen of Rye.

M. de Croissy was not very desirous of entering into an argument with Sir William.

1 Cf. B.N. MS. fr. 10265, f. 93: "Le pacquebot de nieuport passant en Ang^{re} a esté arrêté par un Batiment françois et on a enlevé 12 Religionnaires avec tous leurs effets qui s'y estoient cachez." Newsletter, Dec. 22. Evelyn writes on Dec. 4–14: "Persecution in France raging, the French insolently visit our vessels and take away the fugitive Protestants." *Diary*, III, p. 192 (London, 1906, 3 vols.).

2 R.O. *France, Entry Book* 19, Dec. 3–13, 1685; cf. *H.M.C., Downshire MSS.* I, p. 66.

3 *H.M.C., Downshire MSS.* I, p. 57, Rye, Nov. 24—Dec. 4, 1685.

4 Agnew, *Protestant Exiles*, III, p. 28. They had been naturalized in 1682.

Portrait of Charles Colbert, Marquis de Croissy, engraved by
Edelinck after Rigaud

British Museum, Print Room

He answerd, That yᵉ King had receivd an Account of this from Monsʳ Barrillon, That he had sent an Answer into England to his Majᵗʸ, wᶜʰ he doubted not but would give full satisfaction, And therefore he thought it needelesse to enter into a large debate with me about it. However he sayd, That yᵉ King intending to prevent any Inconveniencies that might arise from His designs of hindring his Subjects to go out of his Kingdome into other Countries had commanded Monʳ de Seignelay to send effectuall orders to hinder anything of this Kind; And that such orders were sent, but they came too late; And therefore there would be care taken, that nothing should happen, wᶜʰ should give yᵉ King my Master any yᵉ like Trouble or Disquiet.

Sir William was not, however, willing to drop the subject.

When I repeated to him yᵉ other businesse of yᵉ Fishermen of Rye, He pretended att first, That they were not of Rye, but onely some French-men who had endeavourd to escape, and so were justly seizd upon. But when I insisted upon yᵉ words of my order, That they were Inhabitants of Rye, he promis'd me yᵉ Fact should be examind, And in case it proovd to be so, there should be forthwith given all Satisfaction.

Now in regard yᵉ Conference I had with him was very short, And that he referrd this Matter to yᵉ Answer sent from hence into England and yᵉ Satisfaction he assurd me His Majᵗʸ would receive thereupon I thought it my Duty to write this Evening (by a Courier sent expresse by yᵉ Count de Grammont) to desire that yoʳ Loᴾ would be pleasd to let me know His Majᵗⁱᵉˢ pleasure, whether and to what point I shall make any further Instances in this Affaire and pursue my Order herein, or Desist, in case his Majᵗʸ is contented with yᵉ Answer given.

I crave leave to advise yoʳ Loᴾ of an Information I have receivd, That Monsʳ Bonrepos [1] has had Orders during a month last past to be ready to go expresse into England upon this occasion. [2]

From Nantes poor Bruce was lifting up his voice again.

By Mʳˢ Grahame and Walkers letters I perceave...the diligence and care yoʳ honor has been pleased out of yoʳ infinit bounty to have for me in particuler who indeed may say boldly that I am the Subject of England in all France that has been worst treated, however hopes by yoʳ care and diligence begunn in the continuation

1 See p. 7 *ante.*
2 R.O. *France,* vol. 148, f. 152, to Sunderland, Dec. 24, 1685.

thereof quickly to be delivered from the great and sensible menaces of my totall ruin every day by some piege or other that I am affrayed with any subject they may make for me, being they beginn one and all to say that I am the only opiniastre in this place because I nor my wife will not change my Religion.... Since yᵉ Dragoons putt me out of my house I have not gon into it...I live alwyse in fear every moment to be putt in prison till my wife appear whom they menace to putt in a convent, and lykewise to take my child of 8 moneths from me, Nay I can not tell your ho/ all that they menasse me with, however I say nothing but reclaimes the protection of my God and my Prince and yoʳ honors care to give me a quick delyverance: I lykwyse must intreat yoʳ ho/ to see performed what Monsʳ De Croissy promises, for Statesmens promises and actions are sometymes quyt different.... For Gods sake consider me as a most afflicted subject.[1]

A letter from Sunderland directed Sir William to insist for an answer in the matter of Orange. M. de Croissy's answer concerning such of His Majesty's subjects as were not naturalized seemed satisfactory. As for the English who were naturalized the King desired a copy of one of their letters of naturalization, that he might send Sir William further orders. In the meantime he was to see that they were not molested for their religion, and he was to interpose in behalf of John de Grave at Rouen.[2]

---

1 R.O. *France*, vol. 148, f. 151, Dec. 22, 1685.

2 *H.M.C., Downshire MSS.* I, pp. 68–9, Dec. 7–17; cf. p. 61. Barrillon reports: "J'ay sceu que le Sʳ Trumball a ecrit touchant les sujets de Sa Majesté Britannique establis en France. On est satisfait icy de la réponse qui a esté faite de la part de V.M. que les Anglois qui ne sont pas naturalisez en France auront toute sorte de liberté. On a formé une difficulté que je crois sans fondement sur ceux qui sont naturalisez. On suppose que la naturalisation qu'ils ont obtenue est conditionnée et qu'ils ont toujours la liberté de s'en servir ou de s'en departir. C'est une question de fait et qui dépend des termes auxquels les lettres de naturalité sont conceues." A.É. *Angleterre*, vol. 156, f. 235, to Louis XIV, Dec. 17, 1685.

CHAPTER VI

Sir William gives annoyance

JANUARY

"Yo^r Lo^{ps} of y^e $\frac{7}{17}$ Instant came not to my hands till y^e $\frac{17}{27}$," writes
Sir William on December 29, 1685, "And the other Letters of y^e $\frac{10}{20}$
(wherein I had none from yor Lo^p) not till yesterday.[1] Both y^e
Pacquets had been opend, And y^e former was brought to me all in
peices, ty'd onely together with some pack thread.

I here send yor Lo^p inclos'd a Copie of y^e Letters of Naturalization
of y^e same Mr John de Grave for whome I receivd his Majesties
Order in Council: The others which I have seen are (in Substance)
ye same. I make bold allso to transmitt herewith ye State of ye Case
thereupon, which I had drawn up to have some discourse with some
of ye most eminent Advocates here upon it. I humbly beg Pardon
for sending it in French, having not time by this Post to get it
Translated and Copied. When his Maj^{tie} shall consult his Counsell
(both of ye Civill and Common Law) upon this Matter, if it shall be
thought fitt to give any Orders hereupon, I presume to hint that all
convenient Speed is requisite, Because all such of his Maj^{ties} Subjects
as are Naturaliz'd, are either actually in Prison or have so many
Dragoons Quarterd upon them, that it is impossible to beleive they
can long resist so great Force. This I meane of such as do yet refuse
to change their Religion, For many of them, in severall of ye Port
Towns, have already sign'd their Abjuration.

According to his Maj^{ties} Orders, That I should continue my
Instances in behalf of such of his Subjects as are molested upon
Account of their Religion, and presse that effectuall Orders should
be given therein according to Justice and his Maj^{ties} Desires, I had
an Occasion to write to Monsr de Croissy yesterday in behalf of one
Bruce, a Merchant of Nantes, not Naturaliz'd.

I had before receivd severall Letters from him,"—here Sir William
gives an account of these letters—"...upon my first Application
about this Affaire to Monsr de Croissy, I had ye Answer, wch I sent
yor Lo^p, That Orders were given by ye most Christian King to free

---

[1] Cf. *H.M.C., Downshire MSS.* i, p. 72.

such of his Maj^{ties} Subjects as were not Naturaliz'd from ye Souldiers, And they should not be molested in any Kind for ye future. But now, hearing from severall Places That there was no effect, And especially from this poor Man...that there were 3 Ships come into ye Rode at Nantes from his Correspondents in Eng^d, whose effects would suffer very much if he were not sett att Liberty to looke after y^m.... I sent my Secretarie with my Letter, yesterday to Monsr de Croissy att Versailles, with an Account of this Complaint, desiring Redresse in his Maj^{ties} Name, and taking Notice, That I had orders to renew my Instances in these Cases, Requesting that ye most Christian King would be pleasd to give some Declaration in writing that might secure ye King my Master's Subjects Trading in these Countries, and prevent ye like Violences for ye future." [1]

From his predecessor Henry Savile Sir William had heard that M. de Croissy was "very passionate" in the least dispute; [2] he was now to discover this for himself.

Monsr de Croissy having began to read my Letter threw it away in great Passion, saying, That ye thing was false, That there was no such occasion of Complaint, That there was no Treatie to exempt ye English from being subject to Souldiers, And taking so great Exception to ye word, Violences, that he said he would write to Monsr Barillon to complaine of this to his Maj^{tie}; And that he would give no Answ^r to my Letter, saying further, That at Nantes all ye English had rendred themselves Catholiques (which I have heard is true in part, many of them, but not all, having submitted to ye Dragoons). I have taken ye Libertie to report ye whole Matter, That I might ye better cleare my self (in case of any Complaint) to his Maj^{ty}, submitting all most humbly to his Judgem^t and further Directions; Hoping I have don nothing that may deserve Censure; Having written with great Respect, and using no other Termes (such as might be according to ye Merit of the Proceedings), but what were pursuant to ye very Letter of my Instructions.

Having spoken to Monsr de Croissy formerly concerning ye Prince of Orange's Affaire, without any effect, as I gave yor Lo^p a full Account, I shall now give in a Memorial by ye first opportunity, and desire an Answer, according to ye last Order yor Lo^p sent of ye 7th Instant. I shall allso make my Request in behalf of Mr John de Graves; though he being Naturaliz'd, I have already receivd an expresse Denyall in ye like Cases; So that I cannot hope to obtaine anything

1 R.O. *France*, vol. 148, f. 153, to Sunderland, Dec. 29, 1685.
2 See p. 15 *ante.*

for him, till his Maj^{ty} shall be pleas'd (upon Consideration of this Matter) to interpose herein effectually.[1]

M. de Croissy was as good as his word. The very next day a letter went to Barrillon. The envoy's paper was enclosed. "Sous un faux exposé de quelques Anglois chagrins de ce qui se fait pour la conversion des sujets du Roy de la R.P.R. ce ministre prend feu." He was asking the King of France to give orders in writing, orders that could not be granted, the foreigners in the kingdom having been only too ready to take advantage of the consideration shown them—they had helped the King's subjects to flee and had harboured their goods. As for the incident at Nantes, after certain inhabitants had abjured they were relieved of the garrisons quartered in their houses, and it had been necessary to lodge these troops in the other citizens' houses, whether they were foreigners or not— foreigners could not claim greater privileges than the King's subjects. Bruce was exaggerating the hardships suffered, since all the officers at Nantes assured that there had been no disorder.

M. de Croissy had given Sir William's secretary to understand that Sir William was not serving his master by lending a ready ear to all kinds of unfounded complaints. "Et a vous dire le vray, Monsieur," he concludes, "ce ministre-cy commence a s'embarrasser de tant de sortes d'affaires et les sollicite si pressamment que je crains bien qu'il ne soit plus propre a brouiller qu'a adoucir les matieres." Barrillon was to warn the ministers to whom Sir William might carry his complaints, and Sir William should receive orders to behave with more moderation. A postscript however added that Barrillon was not to lodge any formal complaint of Sir William's behaviour—the latter had entered upon his office with an harangue that had given the King pleasure, only he should be told not to espouse the cause of private individuals with so much heat.[2]

January 1, 1686. Sir William celebrated the New Year by going to Versailles. He distributed money to the "officers at

---

[1] R.O. *loc. cit.* ff. 153-4.
[2] A.É. *Angleterre*, vol. 156, ff. 242-3, Colbert de Croissy to Barrillon, Dec. 27, 1685; cf. f. 249, Louis XIV to Barrillon, Jan. 1, 1686.

court and the servants of the Introducteurs",[1] and doubtless he brought M. de Croissy the compliments of the season. But again he wanted answers to the memorials he had delivered on the day of his "particular" audience, and he presented him with fresh memorials, including one on the Principality of Orange, in which he informed the King of France point blank that he could not claim any rights over the Principality.[2] "He had orders to put in memorials complaining of the invasion of the principality of Orange which he did in so high a strain", Burnet remembers, "that the last of them was like a denunciation of war."[3]

Barrillon had written again from London in the meantime saying that he had once more taken up the question of Orange with the King of England. He had also shown him that the Prince of Orange deserved the treatment that was being meted out to him—it was therefore quite unlikely that Trumbull would have any further orders to protest. If he did so, it would be in pursuance of his first orders.[4] The matter had seemed almost closed when Sir William arrived with his harsh declaration.

"I was yesterday att Versailles", writes Sir William on January 2, "to desire an Answer to those several Memorials I had presented, whereof I gave yor Lo^p an Account in my former Letters: But ye onely one I had (and that in Writing) I here send yor Lo^p inclos'd[5] together with my Memorial, Expecting his Maj^{ties} further Pleasure. I earnestly press'd for a positive Answer, Whether or no ye most Christian King had given such Orders as his Govern^{rs} in those Parts did pretend to have, for Confiscating o^r Shipps that came onely to Anchor in ye Road; But I could not obtaine it; Monsr de Croissy saying, He thought there were no other Orders than those Mentiond in ye Answer to my said Memorial, For though ye persons pretend

---

1 *Cal. Treas. Books*, 1685–9, p. 1117.   2 See pp. 180–2 *post.*
3 Burnet, *History of My own Time*, III, pp. 276–7. As a matter of fact it was this first memorial that was so outspoken.
4 A.É. *Angleterre*, vol. 156, ff. 238–9, Barrillon to Louis XIV, Dec. 20, 1685.
5 R.O. *France*, vol. 148, f. 155. Endorsed: "Copie of y^e said Memorial given me by Monsr de Croissy, 1 Jan. 168$\frac{5}{6}$." The Memorial concerns eight boats confiscated off the coast of Nova Scotia. Two were set free, the other six fishing without permission the confiscation was maintained.

they come onely to an Anchor for Water or other necessarie Provisions, yet they made use of that to Trade and to Fish, which was ye reason of ye Confiscation.

I have not yet had any Answer concerning ye Company of Hudsons Bay, though I have often desird it; I am promised I shall have it next weeke.

I gave in yesterday severall other Memorials; That concerning ye Prince of Orange, he seem'd extreamely to ressent, That his Maj^{ty} should againe interpose in a matter, w^{ch} (he said) did not att all concern him." [1]

Sir William then went on to the question of the Rye fishermen and the passengers removed from the packet boat. The two incidents, it should be added, had created a great deal of ill feeling in England.[2] James was annoyed, but principally, thought Barrillon, because of the outcry raised.[3] Skelton wrote from the Hague that the searching of the packet boat was making a great noise—"people are impatient to see how our Master will resent it".[4] The emissary Bonrepaus on his way to England was obliged to change his plans, and instead of taking the French boat provided for him at Calais he thought it wiser to cross by an English boat.[5] News had now been received in England that two of the three fishing boats had been sent back

---

1 R.O. *loc. cit.* f. 157, to Sunderland, Jan. 2, 1686. The passage referring to Orange is printed in Dalrymple, *Memoirs*, II, p. 160.

2 Cf. Sourches, *Mémoires*, I, p. 348.

3 "Le Roy d'Ang^{re} me dist hier qu'il etoit arrivé une chose dont il etoit fort fasché principalement a cause du bruit que cela faisoit icy, c'est qu'une fregate de Dunkerque a pris sur un Paquet booth anglois plusieurs françois qui s'estoient embarquez a Ostende. Ce Prince m'a chargé d'en ecrire a V.M. et de faire toutes les instances possibles de sa part pour eviter qu'une pareille chose n'arrivast a l'avenir, et que V.M. ordonne quelque reparation de ce qui s'est passé, comme contraire a tous les traittez. Milord Sonderland est chargé de m'informer plus particulierement du fait et aussy de ce qui est arrivé auprez de la Rye ou quatre pescheurs françois establis depuis quelques années en Ang^{re} ont esté enlevez. J'ay desja repondu de mon chef sur les Pescheurs enlevez auprez de la Rye que V.M. est en droit de reprendre ses sujets quand ils sont trouvez hors des lieux soumis a l'obeissance d'un autre Prince." A.É. *Angleterre*, vol. 156, f. 294, Dec. 13, 1685.

4 *H.M.C., Downshire MSS.* I, p. 83, Dec. 25, 1685.

5 "Le bruit que l'enlevement des batteaux a fait a la côte d'Angleterre m'oblige ...a ne me point fournir de la barque longue du Roy pour y passer. Il se trouve icy un yack du Roy d'Ang^{re} dont je me sers et je parts dans ce moment." A.É. *Angleterre*, vol. 157, f. 14, Bonrepaus to Seignelay, Calais, Dec. 27, 1685.

to Rye, but the third one having been forced by storms to put into Calais, the boat and the crew had been seized again.[1]

M. de Croissy replied to Sir William's memorial on this subject.

"To that concerning y⁰ Fisher-man's Boate detaind at Calais, he said, Orders had been given to release those that had been taken, and that he knew nothing of this Detention; But for Y⁰ Men taken both there and out of y⁰ Pacquet Boat, He declard y⁰ King had Right to take his own Subjects wherever he found them, And that these Fisher-men, though they had liv'd at Rye severall yeares, yet still remain'd Subjects of France:"—we have seen that they were naturalized English subjects—"And when I insisted upon y⁰ Marine Treaty between y⁰ two Crowns, to wᶜʰ these Procedures are a manifest Contravention, And desird to know whether y⁰ Answer he had given me were that which I should send to y⁰ King my Master, He said He would speake to y⁰ King further of it.

In this Affaire, which is of so great Consequence, I shall humbly expect to receive his Majᵗⁱᵉˢ Directions, Because they pretend here (as I wrott to yoʳ Loᴾ on y⁰ $\frac{14}{24}$ of y⁰ last Month by y⁰ Courier of Monsʳ de Grammont) That full Satisfaction is given to his Majᵗʸ, And that Monsʳ de Bonrepos went expresse into England to this Purpose, and to prevent any y⁰ like mis-understandings for y⁰ future.

I deliverd allso my Request in his Majᵗⁱᵉˢ Name for a Buryall Place; But I expect no Satisfaction; For he told me, That y⁰ King had already refus'd it to others, And that they might Bury in y⁰ Feilds or Gardens, as their friends thought fitt.[2] I represented to him y⁰ Hardship of this usage, not onely in respect of y⁰ Libertie this Kings Subjects had in England, and y⁰ Lawes of Nations in all other Places, but allso gave an Example of what had lately happned here to a Gentlewoman of y⁰ Lady Montagues,[3] who being privately putt in y⁰ Church-yard of Charenton by night, was taken up againe, and her body strippd naked and draggd about y⁰ Streetes of this towne,

1 R.O. *France, Entry Book* 19: "Memorand. the following Note was inclosd in the last letter to Sʳ Wᵐ Trumbull." (Enclosed with letter from Sunderland, Dec. 14-24.) English text of note printed in *H.M.C., Downshire MSS.* 1, p. 58, where the note is erroneously attributed to Louis XIV instead of James II.

2 "J'ai parlé au Roi de la demande qui vous a été faite de la part de l'envoyé d'Angleterre du lieu où pourra être enterré un homme mort chez lui. Sa Majesté m'ordonne de vous expliquer encore qu'elle ne veut point du tout permettre aux étrangers d'avoir aucun lieu particulier pour enterrer leurs morts." A.N. Oᴵ 29, f. 537, Seignelay to La Reynie, Dec. 5, 1685.

3 Cf. *H.M.C., Downshire MSS.* 1, p. 96.

with such shamefull Inhumanities and Barbarities as are not fitt to be Mention'd.

I gave in allso a Memorial (according to his Maj^{ties} Order in Council) in behalf of Mr John de Graves; But there is nothing to be expected for those that are Naturaliz'd; unlesse his Maj^{tie} shall be pleas'd...to interpose herein effectually.

...The Holy-dayes have been very barren of Newes: Those accounts I have been able to procure; I here send yor Lo^p."[1]

Some trouble had arisen at Valenciennes. "We are much alarmed", wrote Dr Owen Wynne from London, "to hear that some English ladies sojourning about Valenciennes were detained and pressed to change their religion."[2] A letter came from Utrecht from an Englishman who called himself Normanton[3]—his wife, on her way from France to join him with their two children and her woman, had been stopped at Valenciennes and put into prison on pretence that the children were French born, though they were born in the parish of St Giles in the Fields, London—he himself was ill and could not go to Valenciennes. Here at least Sir William was able to help.[4]

In Caen, William Daniel, an Englishman not naturalized, was still struggling with the authorities. The Intendant asked him why he had not abjured. He replied that the King of France had three times assured Sir William Trumbull that he had no intention of troubling British subjects nor of quartering soldiers upon them for their religion. In view of renewed threats Daniel asked for further protection.[5]

John de Grave wrote from Rouen begging that his effects might not be sold, or that he might have liberty to be gone with his two small children.[6] But as we have seen, he was naturalized and could not hope for any redress.

"Not withstanding ye repeated assurances from Monsr de Croissy", complains Sir William on January 5, "That Orders were sent for ye freeing his Maj^{ties} Subjects, not Naturaliz'd, from ye Quartring of any Souldiers upon y^m, I still receive Complaints from Bourdeaux,

1 R.O. *France*, vol. 148, f. 157, to Sunderland, Jan. 2, 1686.
2 *H.M.C.*, *Downshire MSS*. 1, p. 79.
3 His real name was Cox, *ib*. p. 81.
4 *Ib*. pp. 73, 74, 81, 94.
5 *Ib*. p. 92.   6 *Ib*. p. 93

Nantes and Caen, that they remaine in y° same condition they were in before, and that y° Intendants of the severall Towns threaten them still with more Souldiers, in case they do not speedily abjure.... I here send yo' Lo'' inclos'd an Extract of y° Letters that came to Mons' Spanheim, containing y° Particulars of what is don att Orange." 1

About this time Sir William wrote again to Dijkvelt. Had he received the long account concerning the affairs of the Prince of Orange, addressed to Monsieur Jean Frederick Molwat at the Hague? How were letters to be sent in the future? "Je vous supplie de me faire sçavoir par quel voye vous souhaitteries que je vous fasse tenir les miennes à l'avenir, puisque dans la presente conjoncture on ne pourroit pas prendre trop de precautions." 2

A long letter also went to his predecessor Lord Preston. Perhaps Lord Preston could throw light on Bonrepaus' mission in England?

The extremity that things are in here, in relation to the poor Protestants, and the resolution that is taken to go on in the same way makes a cessation of all other news, of commerce and of all kind of liberty in conversation and acquaintance. I would beg your lordship to give me a particular account of Mons' Bon-repos' negotiation in England. I know it is given out here that he went to our Court in order to settle some matters relating to commerce, and to regulate some differences upon that subject between England and France and also the Dutch, and that he is thereupon to pass into Holland. But I am well assured that his business is to give an account of the 18 passengers that were taken out of the Nieuport pacquet boat, and the other fishermen (belonging to Rye) which were seized and brought into France. I have not been able (what instances soever I have repeated) to obtain a satisfactory answer of this matter from England, and am still in the dark what steps I ought to make, having been assured by Mons' de Croissy that the King my master is fully satisfied in this business. In the affair of the principality of Orange, after the utmost violences committed by the dragoons, I find they are resolved here not to give the least satisfaction. It is to no purpose to insist upon the Treaty of Nimeguen (to which all these proceedings are the

1 R.O. *France*, vol. 148, f. 158, to Sunderland, Jan. 5, 1686.
2 *H.M.C.*, *8th Report*, App., Part 1, p. 557, Jan. 4, 1686 (MSS. of the Earl of Denbigh).

clearest contraventions imaginable), for Monsr de Croissy says that the King has now done all that he thought himself obliged to do in justice and conscience for the salvation of the inhabitants of that town, and so the business is at an end. Only I must acquaint your lordship with an extraordinary distinction he made to me: That in regard of the spiritual, the King had indeed taken care to reduce them all into the bosom of the church; but as to the temporal there was no innovation at all, but all things were left in the same condition they were before. And on Tuesday last when I gave in another memorial about this matter, he said he wondered the King my master would trouble himself about a thing in which he had no interest at all, but that he ought to leave this King to do what he thought good in his dominions, as he would leave our King to do in his. I cannot conclude this trouble without my very particular acknowledgements for your giving Monsr D'Ayrolle to me...he is so diligent and useful to me, that altogether with the help of my nephew (who serves to copy and translate into French any ordinary things), and my own long custom of drudging at business, I make a shift to be without any other secretary, and think I shall be able to hold out, at least as well I have begun.[1]

In reply to Sir William's dispatches from Paris Sunderland wrote directing him to obtain satisfaction for Mr Bruce of Nantes and Mrs Wilkins of Rouen. With regard to the English who were naturalized he was to do all the good services he could. "But as for Sir Wm Douglas's case, and others who have married French wives, his Majesty cannot well apprehend how leave can be refused to wives and children of such marriages to go away with their husbands and fathers." Sunderland also enclosed a copy of Barrillon's answer concerning the visiting of the packet boat by some Dunkirk frigates—Louis XIV had given orders to the commanders of his frigates to do nothing that could give ground for complaint to the King of Great Britain, but his orders had arrived too late to prevent the incident. The episode was closed therewith—Sir William was only to remind M. de Croissy that strict orders were to be given that nothing of the like nature might happen in the future—but

---

1 *H.M.C.*, *7th Report*, App., Part I, p. 381 [1686]. Reprinted by the kind permission of Sir Fergus Graham, Bart.

there remained that other one of the Rye boat detained at Calais; here he was to continue his instances.[1]

Mr Wilkins also wrote from London in behalf of his wife at Rouen. A present of "six jars of Seville wine" accompanied his request.[2] On Tuesday, January 8, M. de Croissy's next reception day, Sir William paid another fruitless visit to Versailles.

"I here send yor Lo^p", he writes to Sunderland on the 9th, "ye Answer given me yesterday by Monsr de Croissy concerning ye Company of Hudsons Bay,[3] And allso ye other Ships confiscated at Petit-Guaves.[4] I insisted againe to have a direct Answer, Whether

---

1 R.O. *France, Entry Book* 19, Dec. 21–31, 1685; cf. *H.M.C., Downshire MSS.* I, p. 58 ("I had already...") and p. 77; A.É. *Angleterre*, vol. 156, f. 229, Louis XIV to Barrillon, Dec. 21, 1685; f. 255, Barrillon to Louis XIV, Dec. 31.

2 *H.M.C., Downshire MSS.* I, p. 50, where the date is erroneously given as October instead of December. The original MS. reads "X^{bre}".

3 A.É. *Angleterre*, vol. 151, f. 360 *et seq.* (cf. f. 340): "Memoire pour servir de responce." The answer denied any undue violence at Port Nelson. As for the ship captured inquiry would be made. ("But instead of that", complained the H.B. Company two years later, "several of the crew were kept prisoners at Quebec on bread and water for eleven months and then sent slaves to Martinique." *Cal. St. P. Col., A. and W. I.* 1685–8, pp. 368–9.)
The matter of the H.B. Company was to be taken up by Barrillon and Bonrepaus presently. See *Recueil des Instructions...*, xxv (*Angleterre*, II), *passim*, and especially Durand, "Louis XIV et Jacques II...Les trois missions de Bonrepaus". *Rev. d'Hist. mod. et contemp.*, vol. x, "La première mission", pp. 28–44.
In the meantime Bonrepaus reported to Seignelay that the King of England had seen the two answers, one with regard to the boats confiscated off the coast of Nova Scotia (cf. p. 605 *ante*), the other concerning the H.B. Company. He approved of the first—"pour la forme seulement on demanderait aux marchands interessez s'ils n'avoient rien a repliquer". As for the second, they would await the results of inquiries to be made in Canada. A.É. *Angleterre*, vol. 157, f. 32, Bonrepaus to Seignelay, Jan. 17, 1686.
A number of the points brought up by Sir William are discussed in a document "Memoire des plaintes et demandes des Anglois remis le 1er avril 1686". A.É. *Angleterre*, vol. 158, ff. 175–7.

4 The *St George* seized at Petit Goave was said to have been rightfully condemned. The captain had been informed of orders forbidding him to trade, but far from obeying had gone to another port of the coast to push his trade. As for the *James* captured by Captain Yankey inquiry would be made. In 1687 Trumbull's successor Skelton was directed to renew instances in behalf of this boat. *Cal. St. P. Col., A. and W. I.* 1685–8, p. 157; A.É. *Angleterre*, vol. 151, ff. 360–1, "Memoire pour servir de response" (the date of the capture of the *St George* has been confused with the date of the capture of the *James*); f. 226, Memoir presented by Skelton; f.340, "Extraict des memoires pntez par l'Envoyé extraord^{re} d'Angleterre".

or no ye most Christian King did own those Orders, wch his Gover^{rs} in those Parts pretended to have, vizt. To confiscate all Shipps that come to Anchor in ye Rode: (Because yor Lo^p will find the Order mentiond in this Paper to extend no further than to those that actually trade) To wch he replyd, That he did beleive (att least by Consequence) there were such Orders, But at present he could give me no precise Answer till ye next weeke.

Concerning ye Fisher-boate of Rye and ye men that are still detaind (whereof I had demanded Satisfaction and Punishm^t for ye Insulte committed, by a memoriall given ye weeke before) His Answer was, That two of ye said Boates, belonging to ye English, were releasd; But this other which is detain'd at Calais, belonging to French subjects, and ye men belonging to it (as well as those taken out of ye Pacquet Boate and ye 2 other Boates of Rye) being French, this King did order that no Restitution should be made either of ye men or vessel: And since care was taken that so speedy Satisfaction should be given of all that was just to be Restor'd, And that what was don was according to ye Command given to ye Captains of this Kings Fregates to seize upon all his Fugitive Subjects wherever they could find them, He sayd, This ought to suffice, and that ye Takers ought not to be Punishd. When I insisted upon this Proceeding as a direct Violation of ye Marine Treatie between ye 2 Crowns, He replyd, It was an Extraord^{ie} Case in this present Conjuncture about Religion, and that such Accidents relating to particular persons of this Kind could not sometimes be avoided, But that Orders were given prevent any thing of ye like Nature for ye future.

This is ye particular detail of what he deliverd to me: by wch yor Lo^p will find, That they are fully resolvd to detaine ye other Boate and ye Men that are taken. I had ye Hon^r of receiving yor Lo^{ps} of ye 27th of ye last Month S.V. yesterday at my returne from Versailles. I shall not faile to make further Demands for ye Restitution of ye said Boate and men according to his Maj^{ties} Commands therein signifyd.

I had no better Effect of ye Memoriall given about ye Buriall Place for such of his Maj^{ties} Subjects as should happen to dye in this Countrie, which Monsr de Croissy told me this King did absolutely refuse to grant, Although I represented not onely ye Lawes and Practise of all nations and ye Common Sentiments of Humanity in ye same Case, But allso ye Libertie all wayes allow'd to ye French in England and ye great Inconveniencies and barbarous usage that had lately happned for want of this Permission." [1]

1 R.O. *France*, vol. 148, f. 161, to Sunderland, Jan. 9, 1686.

Far from obtaining any satisfaction on this point, Sir William
was obliged to bury one of his pages in his garden for want of
a better place.[1] The memorial presented on New Year's Day
concerning Mr John de Grave of Rouen was also fruitless.

In Answer to Mr de Grave's Request I had nothing but what I
expected upon ye generall Orders made concerning all such as are
Naturaliz'd who are every where in this Kingdome equally involv'd
with ye Naturall Subjects, and have ye Dragoons and all other
Penalties upon y^m till they Change . And having grounded, by order
of Council, my Memorial upon ye Liberty he desird to continue his
Trade, that he might dispose of such Effects as he had in his Hands
belonging to his Correspondents Subjects of ye King my Master,
He sayd, Those Effects might be reclaimd by ye Proprietors: But
for Himself, this King would not alter his Resolution; And I beleive
(according to ye last Account I had) that by this time all his Goods
are seizd upon and sold and he is clappt up (if they have found him)
in Prison.[2]

The sharp memorial concerning the affairs of Orange had
produced no result[3] except to irritate M. de Croissy.

The Answer I receivd yesterday about ye Principality of Orange
is in all respects ye same I had before, whereof having given yor
Lo^p an Account at large, I need not repeate any part of it. The Kings
Troopes are come againe into that Towne (as yor Lo^p will find by y^e
Extract I sent ye last Post) and ye Ministers still detaind in Prison:
which Proceeding is more rigorous, than ye others receivd here, All
ye Ministers being orderd to go out of ye Kingdom; which is what
those of Orange desire.[4]
I spoke yesterday againe about Mrs Wilkins: But ye Answer is

---

1 H.M.C., *Downshire MSS.* I, p. 223.
2 R.O. *loc. cit.*
3 A newsletter comments on Sir William's intervention: "Le chevalier
Trumball a fait office icy de la part du Roy d'Ang^{re} pour le prince d'Orange afin
qu'on lui restitue sa principauté avec les mesmes droits et dans l'estat qu'elle
estoit avant qu'elle fut saisie: ce qui ne peut avoir aucun effet, tant parce que ce
seroit une retraite pour tous les Religionnaires et mecontents que parce que
cette principauté est disputée par la maison de Longueville veritables heritiers
des Princes d'Orange de la maison de Châlons, dont l'Instance est pendante au
grand conseil." B.N. MS. fr. 10265, f. 103, Jan. 26, 1686.
4 The paragraph referring to Orange is printed in Dalrymple, *Memoirs,* II,
p. 160.

deferrd till next weeke, As it is allso concerning Mr Mascals re-claiming ye Damaske and ye Corn that is stoppd at Marseilles.[1]

Bonrepaus, whose mission in England was puzzling Sir William, had now arrived in London. He had no definite diplomatic title, but had been instructed to seek out those French subjects who "par un caprice de religion" had retired to England, and he was to persuade them to return to France. He was also to investigate certain commercial, maritime and colonial questions.[2] James received him cordially and assured him that he regarded all Protestants as republicans, especially those who had fled from France; however, since the reports of the "violences" inflicted on these Protestants produced an ill effect in England, and gave rise to the saying that he would do the same one day to his subjects, he wished that the thing could be done with more moderation.[3]

Was it true, Sunderland had asked of Bonrepaus, that troops had again been sent to Orange? The King wanted to know. No, said Bonrepaus, he did not think so, besides everyone there was *catholique de bonne volonté*. Had Sunderland orders to protest against the rumoured return of the dragoons? Sunderland laughed. "Non, en vérité, ce n'est qu'une simple curiosité." [4] Bonrepaus had already sent word to France that if the King of England intervened concerning Orange it was because he could not help himself. A few polite words on the matter were all that was necessary.[5]

Barrillon had now received the first account of Sir William's unnecessary zeal concerning the Nantes incident, and he had seen Sunderland at once. It was of the utmost importance to

---

1 R.O. *loc. cit.* The corn and the damask had both been confiscated during the troubles between France and Genoa. The damask was at Toulon (cf. p. 49 *ante*). The corn which belonged to some English merchants of London and Genoa had been seized on the *Essex*, which had been taken to Marseilles in Feb. 1684. *H.M.C., Downshire MSS.* 1, pp. 61, 66, 105.

2 *Recueil des Instructions*, xxv, (*Angleterre*, 11), p. 324. For this first mission of Bonrepaus see pp. 323–45 and the article by Durand already mentioned ("Louis XIV et Jacques II...La première mission de Bonrepaus", *Rev. d'Hist. mod. et cont.* x, pp. 28–44).

3 A.É. *Angleterre*, vol. 160, f. 3, Bonrepaus to Seignelay, Jan. 3, 1686.

4 *Ib.* f. 37, Bonrepaus to Seignelay, Jan. 17, 1686.

5 *Ib.* f. 20, Bonrepaus to Seignelay, Jan. 10, 1686.

the King of England, replied Sunderland, that his subjects not
naturalized should be without cause for complaint, nevertheless
the envoy would be instructed to behave with more moderation
and restraint in the future.[1] But a very mild letter went to Sir
William—His Majesty was well satisfied with his proceedings,
only he was to make sure complaints were well grounded before
he intervened.[2]

Sir William was in the meantime trying to get more legal
information on the status of naturalized subjects. "I have
consulted Sir R. Lloyd and the civilians upon the case of the
King's naturalized subjects in France," his correspondent
William Bridgeman writes from London, "they have not yet
returned their opinion in form to the King, but I find they incline
in favour of the said persons, that they ought to have passports
to come away."[3] At the Hague the case of "his Majesty's
Protestant subjects naturalized in France" was to be communicated to the "skilfulest" lawyers.[4]

Dispatches from France did not praise Trumbull. The King
wrote a testy letter—he had understood from Barrillon that the
King of Great Britain was satisfied with what had been said
concerning the "fugitives" taken from the packet boat and
from the vicinity of Rye—"vers la Rie", yet here was the envoy
continuing to interpose, not only in behalf of these people, but
also in behalf of numbers of private individuals who could
have recourse to common law—they carried their complaints
to him in order to disturb the good understanding that reigned
between the two crowns. "Le sieur Trumball" must be told to
behave with more restraint—he should confine himself to
essential matters only.[5]

Louis XIV was mistaken in thinking that James considered
the Rye incident closed, for Sunderland had just written to
Sir William again on this subject a letter which had not
reached him yet.

1 A.É. *Angleterre*, vol. 158, f. 4, Barrillon to Colbert de Croissy, Jan. 3, 1686.
2 H.M.C., *Downshire MSS.* 1, pp. 81-2, Sunderland to Trumbull, Dec. 24—
Jan. 3, 1686.
3 *Ib.* p. 85.   4 *Ib.* p. 96.
5 A.É. *Angleterre*, vol. 158, f. 7, Louis XIV to Barrillon, Jan. 11, 1686.

Monsieur de Bonrepos is here and says he is fully instructed to all matters in the West Indies and is preparing a memorial of what he has to offer. But as to the Fisherboate detained at Calais, and the complaints of his Maj^ties unnaturalised subjects in France I do not finde he concerns himselfe therewith, and you are to pursue your instructions in these matters.[1]

Sir William having now received his first mild reprimand ventured to justify himself.

"I will not faile to take all possible Care", he writes on January 12, "not to make any Complaints that are not well grounded. I know I may rely on yor Lo^Pa goodnesse to me, that you will beleive I have taken what Precautions I could: However I make bold to send yor Lo^P some few copies of those many Letters I receivd from that Bruce of Nantes which was ye occasion of all ye Heat. If yor Lo^P will take ye pains to read them, you will find reason enough of Complaint: Yet I did not altogether rely upon these Letters (knowing how querulous men are in their own Concerns) till I had receivd Testimonies of his hard usage from other Hands. And att this hour I have Letters, of ye like Treatment, from others of his Maj^ties Subjects not naturaliz'd; Particularly from Caën, where ye Dragoons are att this time quarterd upon them.

However, if my Intelligence be true, (which I had from Versailles ye night before Yesterday) I hope these Complaints will be att an End; For I heard there were Orders given att Council that Morning that there should be a Declaration Publish'd to free all Strangers. I had several times made my Instances to obtaine this, And now wish it may be effectuall; But I cannot yet learne how farr it will extend...."[2]

M. de Croissy had also been investigating the Nantes affair—there had been no wholesale quartering of troops upon the inhabitants, he found—ten or twelve of the soldiers of the château only had been employed to coerce some of the most obstinate of the "R.P.R."[3] Barrillon carried his letter to Sunderland, together with the copy of the letter that Sir William had written to M. de Croissy, and "milord Sonderland" agreed that Mr "Trumbal's" letter was not couched in proper language.[4]

1 R.O. *France, Entry Book* 19, Dec. 31—Jan. 10; cf. *H.M.C., Downshire MSS.* I, p. 84, where "naturalised" should read "unnaturalised".
2 R.O. *France*, vol. 150, f. 3, to Sunderland, Jan. 12, 1686.
3 A.É. *Angleterre*, vol. 156, f. 250, Jan. 1, 1686.
4 *Ib.* vol. 158, f. 18, Barrillon to Louis XIV, Jan. 10, 1686.

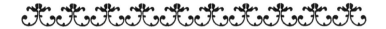

CHAPTER VII

Sir William does not mend his ways

JANUARY—FEBRUARY

ON Tuesday, January 15, Sir William went to Versailles, armed with two more memorials, one with regard to the Rye fishermen, the other with regard to the French wives of English subjects.[1] M. de Croissy, exasperated by his insistent reiteration of complaints, would scarcely listen to him. An answer might be given, an incident considered closed, but on the following Tuesday Sir William would reappear and argue anew about the matter. It was true that he claimed to have orders for these renewed interventions, but M. de Croissy knew from the ambassador in London that some of these at least were not intended to be taken very seriously.

> Yesterday I had opportunity to renew my Instances (according to his Maj^ties Commands) about ye men and Fisher-boate detain'd at Calais; But Monsr de Croissy told me in short, That he had acquainted me already with ye Kings Pleasure, and that he would not speake to him any more about it. He did further expressely assure me, That Leave is denyd to ye Wives and Children of such of his Maj^ties Subjects not Naturaliz'd, as have married French-women and have Children, to remaine here in Libertie, or to have Passeports to be gon. All which I most humbly submitt to his Maj^ties Consideration.[2]

And in the meantime other requests reached Sir William. Sir Philip Lloyd wrote in behalf of a kinsman, Mr Marsh, who had married a French Protestant of some fortune. Two months later he was still appealing—"If you should find it impossible

---

1 These two mèmorials were sent to Barrillon that he might complain of Sir William's disrespect. There seem to be no copies.

2 R.O. *France*, vol. 150, f. 4, to Sunderland, Jan. 16, 1686.

to accomplish his desires in your public capacity for God's sake assist him with your advice how he may best extricate himself from his misfortunes." [1]

Sunderland had sent Sir William a copy of M. de Croissy's letter, "upon occasion of the Letter you writ to him concerning the treatment of his Maj^{ties} subjects". [2] Sir William replies:

By what I have already written to your Lo^p, I hope it will fully appeare to his Matie, That I have been very farre from Exaggerating the Complaints of Bruce of Nantes, or indeed any other. It is now own'd (though att first denyd) by Monsr de Croissy, That he had Souldiers quarter'd in his House, though not upon his Account, but his wife's, who, he said, was a French-woman, And (by their Consequence) ye Children allso French: And yet this prooves quite otherwise, For his wife is a Scottish Woman, and was never naturaliz'd.

I shall not inlarge any further upon this matter, But onely beg leave to hint to yor Lo^p, what ye Effect may be of this Proceeding towards such of his Maj^{ties} subjects, not Naturaliz'd (which are farr ye greatest part) as have married Frenchwomen: who will be equally ruin'd in their Commerce, whether ye Souldiers be Quarterd upon them on ye Account of their Wives and Children, or on their own Account.... I take ye Libertie of adding to ye Inclos'd a Letter I receivd from ye English Merchants att Rochell. Yo^r Lo^p will find, That being not permitted to stay here in Quiet, They desire onely Passeports to be gon. [3]

"For seeing the publicq Exersise of our protestant religion is taken from us", wrote the La Rochelle merchants, "wee all beginn to looke homeward for England our deere and native country whence we came and where we desire againe to bee, to serve God without feare or danger which in this country wee cannot doe.... We know not on what ground wee stand, menaced with threatnings every moment." [4]

---

1 H.M.C., *Downshire MSS.* i, pp. 92, 131.
2 R.O. *France, Entry Book* 19, Sunderland to Trumbull, Dec. 31—Jan. 10, 1686; cf. H.M.C., *Downshire MSS.* i, pp. 81, 84.
3 R.O. *France*, vol. 150, *loc. cit.*
4 *Ib.* vol. 148, f. 159, Jan. 8, 1686. Signed by Andrew Stuckey, sen. (in behalf of himself, his wife, a child and servant). Andrew Stuckey, jun. (with a wife and five children), Robert Mckerrell (with a wife and three children), Adam Newman, Sampson Trevāhar, Francis Band and Edward Moore. None of them naturalized.

Three days later, on January 19, Sir William wrote again enclosing the "Declaration concerning Strangers".[1]

"I receivd last Night a Letter", he adds, "from Mr Daniel of Caën, an English Merchant not Naturaliz'd, by wch he acquaints me, That on Munday ye Intendant sent his Coach for him to come and Signe his Abjuration; W^ch he refusing to do, he sent ten Musqueteers to carrie him to Prison and ordered 50 Souldiers more to be Quarterd in his House; upon which He immediately sign'd."[2]

From London Barrillon sent reassuring information to the French court. The King of England was well aware that "le Sr Tumball" had complained rashly about the Nantes incident. The King did not care in the least what happened to the French Protestants, nay he rejoiced in the astonishing success with which God was blessing the efforts of the King of France. But his envoy had to look after the English established in France; the state of affairs in England made it essential that the English in France should not seem to be lacking protection. As for the Orange affair, Trumbull had reported the last answer received from M. de Croissy, and this answer being so definite it did not seem likely that he would get further orders to protest.[3]

The two new memorials, concerning the Rye fishermen and the French wives of English subjects, had incensed M. de Croissy and offended his royal master. They were dispatched the next day to Barrillon to be shown to Sunderland—nothing

1 This Declaration can be read in Pilatte, *Édits*, pp. 270–1: "Arrest du Conseil du 11 janvier 1686. En faveur des Etrangers Protestans, de quelque Religion qu'ils soient." (Benoist accuses the Jesuits of adding the clause "de quelque Religion qu'ils soient" in order to stress the "variations" of Protestantism.) *Histoire de l'Édit de Nantes*, v, p. 877; cf. pp. 191–2 at the end of the volume.

In England Bonrepaus distributed copies of the Declaration, in particular to the Postmaster-General who promised to have the Declaration translated and sent to all towns. "[Il] a un fort grand interest que le commerce soit libre partout a cause du revenu des ports des lettres que cela augmente." But the merchants in England objected to the phrase "ils ne pourront faire aucun exercice de leur religion" and wanted the word "public" added. A.É. *Angleterre*, vol. 160, f. 74, Bonrepaus to Seignelay, Feb. 7, 1686. See also f. 78, Seignelay to Bonrepaus, Feb. 22, f. 125, Bonrepaus to Seignelay, Feb. 28; vol. 158, f. 34, Louis XIV to Barrillon, Jan. 25; f. 60, Barrillon to Louis XIV, Feb. 4; *Mémoires et Documents, France*, vol. 302, ff. 121–2.

2 R.O. *France*, vol. 150, f. 5, to Sunderland; cf. *H.M.C., Downshire MSS.* 1, p. 99.

3 A.É. *Angleterre*, vol. 158, ff. 25–6, Barrillon to Louis XIV, Jan. 14, 1686.

but the consideration the King of France entertained for the King of Great Britain allowed him to put up with this envoy and his insulting threats. If the envoy continued to act as he did it would be doing the King a service to have him replaced by a more agreeable successor.

Le Roy m'ordonne de vous envoyer les deux memoires que le Sr Trumball presenta hyer, vous verrez combien le stil en est dur, esloigné du respect qu'on doit a un grand Roy, et mesme peu conforme a la maniere dont en ont usé, ceux qui l'ont precedé, enfin, Monsieur, c'est un homme fort propre a brouiller, mais peu capable d'entretenir la bonne intelligence qui n'est pas moins utile aux interests du Roy son Maistre qu'a ceux de la France. Vous communiquerez s'il vous plaist lesd. memoires au Comte Sunderlandt, et vous luy ferez connoistre qu'il n'y a que la consideration qu'a sa Ma^té pour le Roy de la Grande Bretagne qui puisse faire souffrir ce ministre et des demandes aussy menaceantes et injurieuses que sont les siennes, et pour vous expliquer les intentions du Roy sur ce qu'elles contiennent sa Ma^té ne pretend pas oster aux sujets du Roy d'Angleterre non naturalisez la liberté d'entrer et sortir de son Royaume comme bon leur semblera, mais a l'esgard des femmes françoises qu'ils ont epouzé, des Enfans qui en sont nez et des biens qu'elles possedent dans ses Estats ils ne sont pas moins dependans de la souveraineté de sa Ma^té que ses autres sujets, Et c'est une maxime sy generale et sy bien establie qu'elle ne pretend pas de s'en departir pour quelque raison que ce puisse estre. Pour ce qui est du Bastiment qui est a Calais, il appartient a des sujets de sa Ma^té et ne peut estre reclamé par led. Envoyé.

C'est, Monsieur, tout ce que vous aurez a dire sur ces deux matieres mais au fonds sy ce ministre continue a parler et escrire comme il a fait on n'aura pas grande conference avec luy et vous rendriez un bon service a sa Ma^té de luy faire donner au plustost un successeur plus commode.[1]

Barrillon had already approached Sunderland on the subject of the envoy's behaviour, and Sunderland had explained that he had all the zeal and the passion of a newcomer to office who

---

1 A.É. *Angleterre*, vol. 158, f. 21, Colbert de Croissy to Barrillon, Jan. 17, 1686; cf. f. 34, where Louis XIV reaffirms his decision: "A l'egard de quelques anglois...habituez depuis longtemps dans mon Royaume et qui s'y sont mariez il est incontestable que leurs femmes et enfans sont toujours au nombre de mes sujets et ne peuvent sortir de mes Estats sans mon consentement", Jan. 25, 1686. Cf. *H.M.C.*, *Downshire MSS.* 1, p. 106.

thinks he must intervene in any affair brought to his notice.[1] Barrillon also laid the matter before James and had pointed out to him that it was advisable for a foreign minister to abstain from interfering in the affairs of individuals who could go to law about them; otherwise he ran the risk of seeing his requests refused which was exactly what these people wanted, in their desire to disturb the good intelligence that reigned between the two Kings. James, impressed, promised to give Trumbull adequate orders, and Sunderland added that he had already written, but would write again to Trumbull, so that his conduct might be "rectified".[2] Now when the memorials arrived Barrillon showed them to Sunderland, who readily admitted that the language was extraordinary and disrespectful. He promised to see James about them that very day,[3] and James assented to the condemnation of the terms used. Sir William was to be severely reprimanded.[4]

Barrillon did not at once take up the hint of providing "le Sr Trumball" with a more easy-going successor, but Bonrepaus was interested and had some suggestions to offer privately to Seignelay. There were great obstacles in the way. "M. Trombal" was a relative and a creature of "milord Rochester", who would at once support him, as soon as the change was proposed through "milord Sunderland", the only channel open to M. de Barrillon. The two ministers, Sunderland and Rochester, so Bonrepaus explained, were entirely opposed to each other, and Rochester, "Milord tresorier", regarded M. de Barrillon as the intimate friend of his enemy. But let "M. Savel"[5] be proposed, he would be delighted to return to France, and being a great friend of milord Rochester he could easily obtain the office. M. Savel did not, however, want to propose himself, for fear that the King of England in granting him this post would withdraw a pension recently granted. He had therefore asked

1 A.É. *Angleterre*, vol. 158, f. 28, Barrillon to Louis XIV, Jan. 17, 1686.
2 *Ib*. f. 37, Barrillon to Louis XIV, Jan. 21, 1686.
3 *Ib*. f. 42, Barrillon to C. de Croissy, Jan. 24, 1686.
4 *Ib*. f. 50, Barrillon to C. de Croissy, Jan. 28, 1686; cf. f. 44 and f. 52, Louis XIV to Barrillon, Jan. 31 and Feb. 7, 1686.
5 Henry Savile.

Bonrepaus to write to Seignelay, who was to take up the matter with M. de Croissy, and then, if the King of France thought Savel more acceptable than another, letters could be written to Barrillon and to Bonrepaus, so that the one approaching milord Sunderland and the other approaching milord Rochester the office could be secured for Savel. As for "Trombal", he was a lawyer, an outsider, who imagined he gave great pleasure to his patron by an indiscreet zeal which earned him no thanks from anyone.[1]

A few days later Bonrepaus also reported that a severe reprimand was to be given to "Trombal". He added that M. de Barrillon had not yet dared to propose his revocation, for the reasons indicated, but Bonrepaus still believed that he himself could succeed, and by means of the very man whom Barrillon thought the great obstacle.[2]

Sir William was quite unaware of the storm that was brewing. His memorial concerning the Principality of Orange had impressed others, even if the answer obtained was disappointing. The Prince of Orange had sent his grateful thanks.[3] Sir Gabriel Sylvius, a native of Orange, but English envoy at Copenhagen, had learned with exultation from the *Haarlem Gazette* and other letters that Sir William had spoken to the King of France on the subject of the affairs of Orange "in a way that this King was never accustomed to hear".[4] "Your Memorial about Orange is variously dispersed", wrote Dr Owen Wynne from Whitehall, "and the answer to it as diversely reported. The Dutch Gazette is our best author."[5] "Our latest greatest news here," announced Sir Peter Wyche from Hamburg, "hath been the Memorial which was sent me from the Hague printed in French and Low Dutch, given about the Restitution of the Principality of Orange."[6] Other echoes came from Ratisbon. "Your

---

1 *Ib.* vol. 160, ff. 46–7, Bonrepaus to Seignelay, Jan. 24, 1686.
2 *Ib.* f. 53, same to same, Jan. 28, 1686.
3 H.M.C., *Downshire MSS.* I, p. 97, Jan. 10, 1886.
4 *Ib.* p. 98, Jan. 14, 1686. For Sir Gabriel Sylvius see *Nieuw Nederlandsch Biografisch Woordenboek*, I, p. 1493.
5 H.M.C., *Downshire MSS.* I, p. 100, Jan. 18–28, 1686; cf. *Hollandse Mercurius* (Haerlem), 1686, pp. 127–8.
6 H.M.C., *loc. cit.* p. 101, Jan. 28, 1686.

Memorial was printed here and made a great noise all over the Empire", said Sir George Etherege.[1] Sir William could not but feel he had achieved something. Kramprich, the Imperial envoy at the Hague, had the memorial copied,[2] and the French envoy at the Hague, M. d'Avaux, sent a copy of one of the French prints to his master, who doubtless considered it one more reason for having its author recalled.[3]

The memorial incidentally brought James some renown. "Your memorial has given no small reputation to our King," Sir William learned.[4] Every one concluded that it was in the King's own words, said a second,[5] and yet another spoke of the universal adoration in which his great Master's courage and intrepidity were held.[6] And in the meantime Barrillon reported confidentially that James did not care in the least about the fate of Orange!

The Prince of Orange was naturally aggrieved by the reply given Sir William's memorial. "I have had yours of the 18th," wrote James with an outward show of sympathy, "and you may easily believe I am sorry Sir William Trumbul has had no better answer to the memorial he gave in concerning the affair of Orange; I shall still continue doing my part in pressing it."[7]

The news from Orange showed no improvement. "The Letters from Orange say," reported Sir William, "That Monsr de Louvoy wrott to ye Count de Tessé (who is still there with his Regiment of Dragoons) to acquaint him, That ye King has united that Principalitie to ye Governt of Provence."[8] To this rumour Louis XIV made a contemptuous answer. "Monsieur Barrillon...quoyqu'il n'y ayt pas eu jusqu'a present reunion faite de la Principauté d'Orange a la Provence neantmoins vous ne devez entrer dans aucune justiffication sur ce point et vous

1 H.M.C. Downshire MSS. I, p. 114, Feb. 12, 1686.
2 Klopp, Fall des Hauses Stuart, III, p. 151.
3 A.É. Angleterre, vol. 160, f. 297, endorsed: "receu le 21 janr 1686. D'Avaux."
4 H.M.C., Downshire MSS. I, p. 98, Sir G. Sylvius.
5 Ib. p. 100, O. Wynne.
6 Ib. p. 101, Sir P. Wyche.
7 Dalrymple, Memoirs, II, p. 166, Jan. 15-25, 1686.
8 R.O. France, vol. 150, f. 13, to Sunderland, Feb. 2, 1686.

n'avez qu'a laisser croire la cour ou vous estes ce qui bon luy semblera." [1]

Meanwhile James Bruce was still writing. He could not obtain the keys of his house and no merchants would deal with him.[2] And a week later: "All I desayre of your honnour in ye world is to proceure me, my Waife and Child a pasport to retire myself to Ingland or Scotland...for god sack procure me, my Waif and Cheild the pasport I demand for I can not nor will not at all stay any more in this Kingdom if possible to get out of it." And in a postscript: "For god sack again obtain me my pasport."[3]

"Poor Mr Whiting", as Lord Preston used to call him, sent word that the "booted missionairs" were expected at Lille, and there was talk as if he must lie under the same lash as the French Huguenots, though both he and his wife were English— all his children however were born at Lille.[4]

An Englishman by the name of Allen who had lived in Morlaix for twenty years, a trader "going backwards and forwards to England," had married a French wife. An attempt was being made to put her into a convent or a prison, but she maintained she was a subject of the same prince as her husband.[5]

Another Englishman, Thomas Arundell, wanted to leave Bordeaux after having lived there for fifty years and asked for a passport.[6] "I am sure your Honnor will easily judge what oblidgeth us hereunto, I suppose it will not be denied for myself, but not granted for my wife, for that she is a native of this Kingdom, altho methinks that a man and his wife are but one person."[7]

One letter must have given Sir William pain at this time, for never was accusation more untrue.

1 A.É. *Angleterre,* vol. 158, f. 96, Feb. 21, 1686; cf. f. 86, Barrillon to Louis XIV, Feb. 11, 1686.
2 *H.M.C., Downshire MSS.* 1, p. 96, Jan. 8, 1686; cf. p. 84.
3 Downshire MSS. at Easthampstead Park, vol. xxiii, No. 7; cf. *H.M.C., Downshire MSS.* 1, pp. 98–9, Jan. 15, 1686.
4 *Ib.* p. 105, Jan, 24, 1686.
5 *Ib.* pp. 96–7, Jan. 8, 1686.
6 *Ib.* p. 96, Jan. 8, 1686.
7 R.O. *France,* vol. 150, ff. 8–9, Jan. 29, 1686.

"I will not conceal from you," wrote his friend Dr Owen Wynne, "that some merchants have reported it up and down this city that several English merchants residing in the seaport towns of France who have been tormented by the French Dragoons, had hastened up to Paris and applied themselves to your Honour, but could not obtain any other relief or advice than that they must hasten back again and become Roman Catholics; this seemed to be a piece of malice, as such it was listened to by those who know you." [1]

"Le Sr Trumball" was not more moderate in his requests, remarked Louis XIV, on January 25, but as he had not appeared at Versailles in person that week, and had merely sent his secretary to inquire what answers had been given his memorials, there was reason to believe that he had been instructed to be more reserved in the future. [2] Sir William had not yet, however, received the "severe reprimand".

"I had ye Hon^r of yor Lo^{ps} of ye 11th Instant S.V.", he writes on January 30, still unaware of his disgrace, "And shall not fail to use my uttmost Indeavours (according to his Maj^{ties} Commands) in behalf of his Subjects not Naturaliz'd: Onely I crave leave againe to observe, That most of these being married to French Women, are as much disturb'd in their Commerce upon Account of their Wives, as if they were Naturaliz'd, ye Souldiers being Quarterd upon them till their Wives do Abjure, or else their Wives and Children taken away and either putt in prison or into Convents."

A French boat from St Malo had been seized at Jersey.

"The inclosed Paper about ye Chaloup and Men seizd at Jersey", continues Sir William, "Monsr de Croissy gave me yesterday, desiring me to send it to yor Lo^p, That it may be referr'd to his Maj^{ties} Consideration. The Common discourse here is, That this is don, as it were by Reprisalls, for ye Ship and men detaind at Calais. [3]

Monsr Lilieroot, ye Envoyé from Sweden, deliverd yesterday a Memorial about ye Lutherans in Alsace and ye Countries thereabouts, who have ye Dragoons allso Quarterd upon them, Desiring they

1 *H.M.C.*, *Downshire MSS.* 1, p. 96, Jan. 7-17, 1686.
2 A.É. *Angleterre*, vol. 158, f. 33, Louis XIV to Barrillon, Jan. 25, 1686.
3 Cf. A.É. *Angleterre*, vol. 158, f. 84: "J'ay donné un memoire pour faire relascher les sujets de V.M. qui ont esté arrestes a Gerzay dans une barque de St Malo. Milord Sonderland m'a dit qu'il avoit desja escrit a Gerzay pour estre informé de la verité du fait et je ne doute pas que ceux qui ont esté arrestez ne soient incessament relaschez." Barrillon to Louis XIV, Feb. 11, 1686. Cf. *H.M.C.*, *Downshire MSS.* 1, p. 106.

might enjoy y⁰ Libertie of their Religion Stipulated to yᵐ by y⁰ Treatie of Westphaly, whereof y⁰ King of Sweden was Guarand. It is referrd to this Kings Answer y⁰ next weeke."[1]

From London Barrillon reported that the question of the French wives of English subjects would probably be settled as Louis XIV desired—Sunderland believed that his master would not insist any further. But the affair of the Rye fishermen was meeting with more opposition, and yet Barrillon thought that this was the one that should meet with the least, for the King of France unquestionably never lost his rights over his subjects unless he himself had renounced his claims. Trumbull would not be told to desist from his protests until the matter had been taken up in Council, but Sunderland had thought it best not to produce Sir William's memorials at this coming occasion, so that no one might know of his rudeness, a rudeness which would not displease everybody. James had approved of this design.[2]

A day or two later James took up the question of his envoy's behaviour. He told Barrillon he considered his misdemeanour great, and would punish him severely if ever he relapsed. But he had not really meant to offend—it was merely that he was a lawyer accustomed to the clamour of a law court: "Son manquement venoit d'avoir passé toute sa vie dans une Cour de justice et parmy des gens de loy qui sont accoustumez a parler avec vehemence et sans garder de mesures."

Barrillon replied with dignity. A man might not have been brought up at court, yet he should know he could not use expressions to a King that would be insulting even if addressed to private individuals. He hoped that steps would be taken to obviate any further cause for complaint.

"Ne vous mettez en peine," replied James, "c'est mon affaire." Then, turning to the Rye affair he went on apologetically. Explanation followed explanation. Barrillon must realize that James did not wish to favour the "pretendus reformez", he had no greater enemies—they had always been

---

1 R.O. *France*, vol. 150, f. 10, to Sunderland, Jan. 30, 1686.
2 A.É. *Angleterre*, vol. 158, f. 50, Barrillon to C. de Croissy, Jan. 28, 1686.

the enemies of the King his father and the King his brother. But he had to observe some kind of measure and not abandon those who were in a way under his protection, not being naturalized French. He would do all he could to give the King of France satisfaction, but the affair of the Rye fishermen was making a great stir. Barrillon must know how susceptible people were in England in anything that concerned the sea, and how detrimental the least slackness on his part would prove. He was sure that the King of France would not willingly, for a matter of such slight consequence, give the English occasion to censure the conduct of their King. Barrillon knew his feelings—"le fond de son cœur"—with regard to the King of France, how he shared with his Most Christian Majesty one chief object, the furthering of Catholicism, and could not hope to succeed in his own projects without his royal brother's assistance.

From Sunderland Barrillon learned that the affair had not yet been taken up in Council, but that the King his master was most anxious to have the matters contained in Sir William's memorials hushed up as quickly as possible.[1]

The reprimand that had gone to Sir William Trumbull was not very severe. After recommending the case of James Bruce of Nantes and desiring Trumbull's good offices for the un-naturalized English whose wives and children were born in France, Sunderland continues:

His Maj^ty...commands me also to let you know that great exceptions have been taken in that Court at those expressions *que ce procedé est si contraire aux droits des gens et aux loix du Christianisme* which are in your Memoriall concerning the Wives and Children of the unnaturalized English; and also at the words *conformement a la justice, au droit des gens et aux Traittez* which are in your Memoriall about the Fisherboate and men detained at Calais, and his Maj^y thinks there has been some cause for the exception taken, and chiefly at those in the former Memoriall because the same thing might have been said in more decent terms, and therefore his Maj^y would have you very cautious for the future how you express your selfe, and particularly when you make use of his name.[2]

1 A.É. *loc. cit.* ff. 56-8, Barrillon to Louis XIV, Jan. 31, 1686.
2 R.O. *France, Entry Book* 19, Jan. 18-28, 1685-6; cf. *H.M.C., Downshire MSS.* I, p. 102.

Sir William accepted the reprimand quietly, but pointed out that in both of his memorials he had used expressions taken from Sunderland's own letters. Before turning to this matter however he wrote for the last time about Bruce.

As to Mr Bruce of Nantes, I receivd lately a Letter from him, wherein he sayes He is contented to sitt downe by ye Losses he has sustain'd; Desiring me to make no further Instances here for any Reparation, Least it should proove an Obstacle to his Designe of coming away for England. I thinke my self happy, that in this case His Maj^{ty} is graciously pleas'd to be of Opinion That I did not exaggerate ye Complaint.[1]

In his letter Bruce had written that he had gone to see the Governor of the province, the duc de Chaulnes, and the Governor had explained to him that everything had been done because his wife was French.[2] Mrs Bruce was the daughter of a Scotsman, but since she was born at Nantes,[3] one can to a certain extent follow the reasoning of the authorities.

"I receive with all Submission", continues Sir William, "ye Notice yor Lo^p is pleas'd to give me of ye Exceptions taken att those Expressions in my Memorialls; And shall for ye future, not onely in these matters, but all others, endeav^r to conforme myself to His Maj^{ties} Pleasure and ye Significations thereof, which yor Lo^p shall impart to me.

I crave Leave onely to lay before yor Lo^{ps} Candor how easie it is for one of my little Experience and Capacity to mistake, and to be liable very often to Censure, if every word is to be scann'd. Besides, I was ye more easily led into that Expression in that Memoriall about ye Wives and Children of ye Un-Naturaliz'd English, by that part of yor Lo^{ps} Letter of ye 21 Decemb^r, which says, That for Sr Wm Douglas's Case and those of His other Subjects, who have married French Wives, his Maj^{ty} cannot well apprehend how Leave can be refus'd to ye Wives and Children of such Marriages to go away with their Husbands and Fathers, *The Laws of Nations and ye Law of all Countries in Europe having constantly allowd it*.[4]

And I confesse, my Lord, this Proceeding did appeare ye more Extraordinarie to me, in that it is Contrary to their own Decrees in

---

1 R.O. *France*, vol. 150, f. 14, to Sunderland, Feb. 6, 1686.
2 *H.M.C., Downshire MSS.* 1, p. 107.   3 *Ib.* p. 98.
4 For the text of this letter see R.O. *France, Entry Book* 19, Sunderland to Trumbull, Dec. 21–31, 1685.

ye Supreme Courts of France and the opinion of ye most Eminent Lawyers, As I could shew by multitudes of Examples from their own Authors.

As to ye Pacquet-Boate, I receivd these words in French inclos'd in yor Lo^{ps} of ye 14th of ye same Month, vizt. Sa Ma^{té} espere que le Roy T. Ch. donnera les Ordres necessaires pour la Mainlevée de ladite Saisie et detention Et pour la punition exemplaire des personnes qui ont commises cet Insulte *si contraire au Droit des Gens et des Traittez entre les deux Couronnes.*[1]

I am sorry I have troubled yor Lo^p with so long an Apology; which I would not have don, But that I am desirous, above all things, to keepe his Maj^{ties} good Opinion, And not onely to Obey his Orders, but to Execute them with all Respect and Decency to ye most Christian King and his Ministers."[2]

The next letter from Sunderland brought Sir William more business. His Majesty saw no reason to depart from his former orders concerning the Rye fishermen detained at Calais, and Sir William was to insist for their release. M. de Croissy was also to be told that the answers concerning the proceedings at Orange were not satisfactory and His Majesty hoped that the King of France would upon further consideration have more regard for his instances in behalf of the just pretensions of the Prince of Orange. But as for the French wives and children of the unnaturalized English in France, James, who had so recently declared that he could not "well apprehend" how leave could be refused to them to accompany their husbands and fathers, now "acquiesced" meekly in the last answer sent by Louis XIV, namely that such women and children were his subjects "et c'est une maxime si générale et si bien établie que sa Majesté n'estime pas s'en devoir départir".[3]

Heinsius, who had come to England on other business, had brought Sunderland a letter from the Prince of Orange concerning the proceedings in his principality. A copy of the passage of the letter just mentioned, directing Sir William

1 For the text of this French note see *ib*. "Memorand. the following Note was inclosed..."

2 R.O. *France*, vol. 150, f. 14, to Sunderland, Feb. 6, 1686.

3 R.O. *France, Entry Book* 19, Sunderland to Trumbull, Jan. 25—Feb. 4; cf. *H.M.C., Downshire MSS*. 1, p. 106; see also A.É. *Angleterre*, vol. 158, f. 63, Barrillon to Louis XIV, Feb. 4, 1686.

Trumbull to intervene once more, was therefore sent to the Prince of Orange with a discouraging comment from Sunderland. "This the King commanded me to write as being fit, though he does not expect much fruit."[1] To Heinsius Sunderland remarked that the King had done everything he could, except to declare war on France, which was not his intention.[2] The Prince of Orange who had begun to realize James's indifference was disheartened, even embittered.[3]

The report of the new intervention was received with pleasure in Holland.

"On escrit icy de Withal que le Roy vous a envoyé un ordre pour declarer hautement au Roy de France que sa Maj[té] n'est pas satisfaite de la response pour votre premier memoire touchant l'affaire d'Orange", wrote Dijkvelt to Sir William, "tous les honnestes gens, Monsieur, ont bien de la joye....Il importe...au bien et a l'union dans nostre estat que le Roy fasse paroistre que c'est tout de bon qu'il s'interesse et qu'il s'employe pour Mr le Prince."

The Prince of Orange, to whom Dijkvelt had delivered a letter from Sir William, sent him his warm thanks for his application.[4]

Sir William therefore drew up a second memorial concerning Orange, but less violent than the first, and took coach for Versailles.

"I was yesterday att Versailles," he writes on February 13, "but found Mons[r] de Croissy in bed very much afflicted with y[e] Gout; So that I thought it not convenient to trouble him long. However I represented to him y[e] Orders I had lately receivd from his Maj[ty] in yo[r] Lo[ps] of the 25th of last Month, S.V., concerning y[e] Fisherboate and Men detaind att Calais. He gave me att first y[e] same Answ[r] I had formerly receivd, viz[t]. That it was a French Boate and y[e] Men were Subjects of France, and that y[e] King had Right to take his Subjects wherever he found them. But when I insisted on their being Inhabitants of Rye, and that they had a Passeport from his late Maj[ty], a Certificat from ye Magistrates of that Towne, and were Fishing upon our Coasts; He told me, They were att Sea upon a Design of

1 Dalrymple, *Memoirs*, II, pp. 158-9, Jan. 25—Feb. 4, 1686.
2 A.É. *Angleterre*, vol. 160, ff. 89-90, Bonrepaus to Seignelay, Feb. 11, 1686.
3 Clarendon, *Correspondence*, I, p. 168.
4 Downshire MSS. at Easthampstead Park, vol. 24, No. 85, Dijkvelt to Trumbull, Feb. 20, 1686.

receiving this Kings Fugitive Subjects, and therefore were justly seizd and detaind."[1]

Sir William's legal mind did not accept this argument.

This I confesse was as new to me, as (with humble Submission) I thought it to have no great Weight in it; For I crav'd leave to say, That supposing they had been att Sea upon such a Design, yet having not don anything, nor putt this Design in Execution, they were not punishable; And yet further, in case they had actually taken some French on Boord, yet no Confiscation of ye Vessel could follow, but onely ye taking away those persons they had receivd. I shall go againe, as soon as he is well enough to speak of businesse, and desire an Answer to send to yor Lo^p.

I left allso with him this little Memoriall[2] concerning ye Affaires of Orange; where there continues still a Company of Dragoons: I have taken ye confidence to trouble yor Lo^p with a Copie of it to prevent (as much as in me lys) any Mis-representation. He told me he would speake to ye King of it.

This King is now pretty well recoverd of ye Tumour, wch was in a very inconvenient Place....

The Elector Palatin has given a long Memorial to ye Diett att Ratisbon, containing several Complaints against ye French Officers in ye Frontiers, and that they had given Orders to pursue ye French Huguenots into his Territories and take them away from thence.[3]

But if James had sent orders to his envoy to take up the Orange affair again, he also let it be known that it was little more than a formality. Sunderland told Barrillon that Trumbull had been instructed to interpose, because the King of England could not openly abandon the interests of the Prince of Orange and had from time to time to give some evidence of his concern. He did not, however, care what happened and saw no objection to the King of France doing what he liked in Orange.

The protests against the imprisonment of the Rye fishermen could not be brushed aside as lightly, and Barrillon had been obliged to accept a memoir from Sunderland on this subject.[4]

1 R.O. *France*, vol. 150, f. 21, to Sunderland, Feb. 13, 1686.
2 See p. 182 *post*.
3 R.O. *loc. cit.*
4 Copies in R.O. *France, Entry Book* 19, Jan. 25—Feb. 4, 1686, and A.É. *Angleterre*, vol. 158, f. 89. In behalf of Bridon and his associates.

People said the men had been seized in English waters, and James himself told Barrillon that he remembered giving passports to French fishermen when he was an admiral, permitting them to fish in that part. And if two of the three boats originally taken had been sent back, why was the third one detained at Calais?[1]

1 A.É. *loc. cit.* ff. 85–6, Barrillon to Louis XIV, Feb. 11, 1686.

CHAPTER VIII

Passports and other business

FEBRUARY

ON February 5, 1686, the public coach was getting ready to leave for Brussels. The narrow rue Saint-André des Arts was busier than usual. A lady arrived with three children. A man, an innkeeper, escorted the little party to the coach where he had engaged seats some days before. His wife and maidservant followed with two other children, who were also to go to Brussels. Two gentlemen from Poitou joined the group. One imagines that the grown-up travellers were rather subdued, even anxious, and that the lady hushed the children's excitement. Perhaps the innkeeper and his wife kept up a jovial appearance standing beside the coach. Perhaps the maid had been told to make merry, as she helped to stow away the bundles. One imagines that a little crowd had gathered as usual to see the coach go off, and that all of a sudden the spectators had to make way for some armed men who came upon the scene and arrested all the inmates of the coach, as well as those who had brought them hither. All the travellers were Huguenot fugitives, it was said—Madame Mallet and her three children, the two children of M. de l'Isle du Gast, and the gentlemen from Poitou. Two of the children, it was reported, had passports from Sir William Trumbull. The innkeeper, Louis Vion, at one time a servant to M. de Courtin when the latter was ambassador in England, was sent to the prison of le petit Châtelet, his wife, an Englishwoman, to the Bastille, and the maid to the prison de l'Abbaye. Vion was a Catholic and his wife had abjured at Saint-Sulpice, but it was a lucrative business to help the adherents of the "R.P.R." to get away.[1]

[1] B.N. MS. fr. 7052, ff. 288, 367; 7053, ff. 370, 371, 408–10 (Police reports); 17421, f. 42; A.N. O¹ 30, f. 64. Cf. Douen, *La Révocation...à Paris*, II, pp. 442–3, 471, 567. I owe my knowledge of these MS. sources to Douen.

There were also discovered in Vion's house the children of
John de Grave of Rouen whom Sir William had tried to help—
he and his wife had escaped—to London said some, to Holland
said others—and Mme Vion had undertaken to bring over the
children, but being arrested she could not keep her promise.[1]
On being examined she confessed that John de Grave and his
wife were still hidden in a house at Rouen, but they could not
be found.[2]

Sir William was to hear about this incident.

Bonrepaus had written to M. de Seignelay, as we have seen,
asking whether the court would not prefer "Savel" to "Trombal". Seignelay replied emphatically and at great length. Both
he and M. de Croissy were passionately desirous that M. Savel
should come back. They would leave no stone unturned to
facilitate his return. But unfortunately M. de Barrillon was
entirely under M. de Louvois' influence, and M. de Louvois did
not like M. Savel. The thing must therefore be done without
M. de Barrillon's participation. All the help they could give
was to reiterate the grievances against M. Trombal who gave
only too much cause for complaint by his bad behaviour—of
late he had taken to making out passports for French subjects,
passing these off as English. The King had resolved to complain
of this to the King of England. This offence joined to all the
others would oblige him to recall his envoy. "Milord Rochester"
must be made to assent to this recall. He must be made to understand that M. Savel, equally liked by the ministers and the
court of France, was better qualified to succeed in his negotiations than anyone else. M. Trombal having no intercourse with
those who could give him information concerning the affairs
of the country could not in any way enlighten the English
ministers. All the news he could impart they could see for
themselves in the Gazettes. Then, after milord Rochester had
been persuaded, Bonrepaus must use his efforts on "milord
Sonderland" who did not like Savel because of his affection for
milord Rochester. M. de Ruvigny, soon to go to England,
could give some help. Bonrepaus must never write about this

---

1 B.N. MS. fr. 7053, ff. 361-9.   2 A.N. O¹ 30, ff. 130, 137, 360.

matter except by special couriers who might be going to France.[1]

Louis XIV wrote a few days later to Barrillon. It did not seem to him that the reprimands had made "le Sieur Trumball" less zealous to take up all kinds of matters. Not only had he continued his protests concerning the Rye fishermen, but he was interposing in behalf of an Englishwoman married to a French merchant at Bordeaux, and he asked that a Miss Watson, a convert, should be handed over to an unknown young man who was to take her to England. And besides all this he was now giving out English passports to French subjects. Therefore if Barrillon by his insinuations and his skill could incline the court where he was to recall the envoy and send in his place someone less "difficile", he would accomplish an action the more agreeable in that it would contribute to a good understanding between the two crowns.[2]

Sir William went his way unconscious of these new complications. He had celebrated the anniversary of James's accession. He had inquired what he was to do on this occasion, and had heard from Whitehall: "All that can be expected on your side will be to invite as many as you think fit of the Ministers there, to give also some wine to the rabble and to trim your house and windows with what the learned call illuminations."[3] But evidently he did the thing gallantly, for a newsletter reports: "L'Envoyé d'Angleterre a fait ici de grandes réjouissances pour le jour de l'avenement à la Couronne de S.M.B. et a fait de grands festins aux dames."[4]

He also heard from Whitehall that he need not be in pain about the exceptions taken at some expressions in his memorials. "I am confident nothing more will be said of it, besides I can confirm to you the assurance of my Lord's friendship to you

1 A.É. *Angleterre*, vol. 160, f. 65, Seignelay to Bonrepaus, Feb. 9, 1686. See also vol. 160, f. 121, Bonrepaus to Seignelay, Feb. 25, 1686; f. 176, Seignelay to Bonrepaus, March 31, 1686; f. 214, Seignelay to Bonrepaus, April 9, 1686; f. 235, Bonrepaus to Seignelay, April 9, 1686.

2 *Ib.* vol. 158, f. 80, Louis XIV to Barrillon, Feb. 15, 1686.

3 *H.M.C.*, *Downshire MSS.* 1, p. 109, Dr O. Wynne to Trumbull, Jan. 28 —Feb. 7, 1686.

4 B.N. MS. fr. 10265, f. 111; cf. *Cal. Treas. Books*, 1685–9, p. 1117.

upon this occasion in particular," wrote Sunderland's secretary, "though the complaint having been made, it was to be taken notice of."[1] Sunderland himself reported that the King was satisfied by what Sir William had said in excuse to the exceptions made. His Majesty also approved very well of his last memorial concerning the affair of Orange and had ordered a copy to be sent the Prince.[2]

To the Prince of Orange, who had appealed again, Sunderland wrote a tepid letter. "His Maj^ty has done what he could possibly think fit to do in the Affaire of Orange, having spoke to the Ambassador of the French King here as warmly as his Envoy had order to speake there, and he does now desire to know what your Highness would have done further, being very intent upon doing all he can."[3] How "warmly" James had spoken on the subject of Orange to Barrillon we have seen!

As for the English wife of a Frenchman in Bordeaux, mentioned in Louis XIV's letter, hers was a sad story. Andrew Kirby, an English merchant of Bordeaux, had married one of his daughters, Elizabeth, to Thomas Lewis of Bristol, a merchant factor living in Bordeaux, and the other one, Mary, who was born in London, to Florentin Dureau, a French merchant. Dureau had abjured, but Mary, who hoped to pass for English, had not. One day in December when Mary with her husband was at her sister's house, the "jurats" came with the "soldats du guet", broke into the house, and carried both Mary and her husband to prison. Elizabeth Lewis pleaded for her sister, but the first "jurat" called her "impertinente", and threatened to carry her away also and put her into the "basse fosse", as Andrew Kirby relates. Thomas Lewis was fined for keeping his sister-in-law and her husband in his house; Florentin Dureau was released after a few days, but Mary remained in prison. After two months of captivity she renewed the appeal her father had already made. "It seemed to others, more intelligent

1 *H.M.C.*, *Downshire MSS.* I, p. 115; cf. p. 118.
2 *Ib.* p. 116, but see also R.O. *France, Entry Book* 19, Feb. 8-18, 1686.
3 R.O. *loc. cit.*, Feb. 12-22; cf. Dalrymple, *Memoirs*, II, pp. 160-1.

than herself," she concluded modestly, "that since French-women married to Englishmen could not enjoy the privileges which belonged to their husbands it ought to follow by the ordinary rule of contraries that Englishwomen married to Frenchmen should not be subjected to the same rigor as their husbands."[1] By this time Sir William doubtless realized that his intervention would be vain, for the magnificent arbitrariness of things had become very evident.

On February 19 Sir William sent his secretary to Versailles, as he often did on Tuesdays. The rest of his "goods", "furniture and household stuff", had arrived from London;[2] there had been some slight trouble with the customs officers, and the secretary was to take up this matter. Sir William, who always prided himself on having carried a point "respecting the non-payment of fees for his doctor's degree", was not the man to waste any money.

"I take ye Libertie to acquaint yor Lo^p," he wrote next day to Sunderland, "That in the Passeport which ye most Christian King gave me for my goods that came hither, there was (among ye rest) particularly express'd my Tapistry Hangings; for which notwithstanding ye Douaniers here demand the Custome, as a Right belonging (by Vertue of a Graunt) to Monsieur de Louvoy; To whome my Secretarie speaking yesterday about it, he said, It was a thing ought to be payd and would not be remitted. These Hangings being not new, but such as I had long us'd in my House in England, I would not presume to trouble yor Lo^p about so inconsiderable a matter; But that in regard of my Character I am unwilling to have any thing Introduc'd that is an Innovation, and is contrarie to what is demanded (as I thinke) either of ye French or any other Ministers when they come into England. I submitt myself wholly to y^r Lo^p^s Directions and Commands herein, and shall readily pay it, without any further Scruple, if it be thought fitt."[3]

While the secretary was at Versailles M. de Croissy, though still in bed with gout, gave him a memoir for his master which vexed the latter exceedingly.

1 H.M.C., Downshire MSS. i, pp. 76, 82, 93; R.O. France, vol. 150, ff. 35–7, M. Kirby to Trumbull, Feb. 23, 1686.
2 Cal. Treas. Books, 1685–9, p. 1117.
3 R.O. loc. cit. f. 25, to Sunderland, Feb. 20, 1686.

"I make bold allso to informe yor Lo^p," he continues, "That Monsr de Croissy complained yesterday of Notices, he said, were given him, That I had granted Passeports to ye Subjects of this King, by which meanes they had escap'd contrarie to ye Edicts. But I do assure yor Lo^p (and most humbly beg of yor Lo^{ps} Justice to beleive me That I would not affirme an Untruth) That I have not onely us'd all imaginable Precautions in every Passeport I have granted, but have constantly been so carefull as to see and speake with ye Persons coming for Passeports my self, least they might pretend onely to be English or Scotch, but be indeed French. Now, my Lord, in case any of these have made ill use, And sold or given away my Passeports to ye French (as I doubt may have happned) it is a thing I have not been able any wayes to Prevent or Remedy; And if such persons can be found, let them be punish'd as they deserve. But knowingly I am sure I have been very farr from offending."[1]

Without waiting for the Tuesday following when M. de Croissy would receive envoys Sir William wrote a long letter of justification.

Monsieur,

J'aurois attendu á Mardy prochain á vous parler sur le Memoire que vous m'aves fait l'honneur de m'envoyer, si je n'avois autant d'interest que j'en ay á me justifier de la fausse accusation qu'on me fait. Je vous diray lá-dessus, Monsieur, que je n'ay jamais songé á soustraire les Sujets du Roy Tres Chrestien de l'Obeissance qu'ils doivent á ses Edits; Ils me sont á moy-meme fort sacrés, et je serois au desespoir d'avoir fait quelque chose qui eut pû porter les Sujets de sa Maj^{té} á y faire quelque contravention. Je ne suis point venu pour cela, Et je me contente de faire les affaires ou le Roy mon Maitre a Interest, sans me mesler á celles d'autruy. Ainsi on me fait la plus grande Injustice du Monde de me croire capable de ce dont on m'accuse. Il est vray que j'ay donné des Passeports, quantité meme; Mais c'est apres avoir fait un exacte et fidel Examen, que ceux á qui je les donnois estoient Sujets du Roy mon Maitre; Et je puis vous dire, que j'ay esté si circonspect sur cette matiere, que jusques icy je n'ay pas esté trompé. Il se peut faire que quelques-uns en ont pû faire un mechant usage: Mais voudries-vous, Monsieur, me rendre responsable d'une chose qui ne depend pas de moy? Je vous crois trop equitable et trop judicieux pour vouloir m'en imputer la faute. Et pourquoy mes Passeports ne courroient-ils pas les Risques d'etre vendus ou negotiés par ceux á qui je les donne, puisque ceux du Roy meme (ainsi que j'ay appris depuis mon arrivée

[1] Ib.

en France) ont été exposés quelque fois á cet usage? Vous voyes, Monsieur, que c'est un Accident, dont je ne puis pas etre Guarand. D'ailleurs, Monsieur, mes Passeports ont eu si peu de creance aupres des officiers de sa Maj^{té} que vous scavés que je me suis plaint plusieurs fois de ce qu'on avoit arresté quelques uns des Sujets du Roy mon Maitre qui en estoient munis. Ainsi vous deves s'il vous plaist revenir de la pensée que vous avés que j'en aye favorisé quelque François pour les faire passer: Je n'avois garde, puisque je trouvois meme de la difficulté pour les Anglois. Mais sans entrer dans ce raisonnement, encore une fois, Monsieur, Je ne me mesle que de ce qui regarde mon Employ. Je ne voudrois pas pour chose au monde avoir rien fait qui eut pu deplaire á sa Maj^{té} ni qui peut en particulier vous donner quelque chagrin: Je vous prie de me faire la Justice d'en etre persuadé. Apres quoy je viens aux deux Passeports dont vous me parles.

Il est vray que je les ay donnés aux deux GentilhommesWilliamson, et l'autre á la nommé Vion. A l'egard des Premiers, j'en ay encore la memoire toute recente, me souvenant fort bien que ce sont deux Jeunes Anglois qui m'ont ete amenés par une femme Angloise chargée de leur conduite; Je les ay examinés, je les ay trouvés Anglois; Ainsi je m'inscris volontiers en faux contre les preuves qu'on pretend avoir, si elles me regardent particulierement, et c'est de quoy je vous prie de me faire part: si les Enfants ont eté meta- morphosés, je n'en sçay rien et je n'en suis pas responsable; Et je voudrois pour votre satisfaction et aussy pour la mienne tenir les autheurs de cette action, Je contribuerois de tout mon coeur á leur chatiment. Pour la Vion, c'est une Angloise qui va souvent et vien en Angleterre: Elle m'emmena trois de ses Enfans, qu'elle me dit vouloir conduire en Angleterre par le chemin de Bruxelles ou Elle me dit qu'Elle devoit achepter des Dentelles pour la Cour d'Angle- terre, Et pour m'obliger á luy faire moins de difficulté á luy accorder mon Passeport, Elle me fit voir par un certificat du Curé de sa Paroisse attesté veritable par Monsr L'Archevesque qu'elle estoit Catholique...on a grand tort de vouloir m'imputer le mechant usage qu'ils peuvent les uns et les autres avoir fait de mes Passeports. J'espere que vous aurés d'autres Sentimens que vous n'aves eu de moi, et que [vous] seres persuadé de mes Respects tres profonds pour les Ordonnances de sa Maj^{té}, Et pour vous, Monsieur, á qui je souhaitte une bonne reconvalescence."[1]

From this letter one would be inclined to think that Mme Mallet and her three children were travelling on the passport

1 R.O. *France*, vol. 150, f. 26; copy in Trumbull's hand, Feb. 21, 1686.

given to Mme Vion for herself and her three children, and that the children of M. de l'Isle du Gast had been provided with the passport made out for the young Williamsons. The English-woman who brought the young Williamsons to Sir William Trumbull was perhaps the English wife of another innkeeper, Laperle by name, for she was arrested a little later as being also implicated in this affair.[1]

M. de Croissy was probably not convinced by this letter, for ten days later his nephew Seignelay was writing to the Lieu-tenant de Police, La Reynie, "Je vous prie de m'envoyer l'Interrogatoire de la nommée Vion pour servir a faire con-noistre la mauvaise conduite du Sr Trumbol."[2] However, nothing more is heard about this matter, so it is probable that nothing more could be found.

That Sir William took into custody the property of some of the French fugitives is true,[3] that he gave shelter to some of these unfortunates he denies,[4] though on one occasion at least the police reported the presence of a French lady, hiding in his house until she could find a favourable occasion to escape.[5] From Burnet we hear of the reputation he came to have in England: "He acted a great and worthy part in harbouring many, in covering their effects, and in conveying over their jewels and plate to England which disgusted the Court of France and was not very acceptable to the court of England, though it was not then thought fit to disown him or recall him for it."[6] But Sir William was too rigidly, too pedantically attached to the conception of law and order to do anything strictly illegal. Far from embarking on an unlawful entreprise he noted with chagrin that the passports he gave his own

1 B.N. MS. fr. 7051, f. 299; 7052, ff. 288, 367.
2 A.N. O^1 30, f. 82, March 2, 1686.
3 B.N.MS.fr.7052, f. 262: "Lettre d'Estienne Chastelain marchant de dentelles du fauxbourg St Anthoine escripte de...Suisse a Estienne Chastelain son fils a Paris...21 juin 1686....Il mande aussy...qu'il a laissé un coffre ou sont ses effez chez monsieur l'ambassadeur d'Angleterre."
4 R.O. France, vol. 150, f. 99, to James II, July 9, 1686.
5 B.N. MS. fr. 7053, f. 224: "Il y a chez l'envoyé d'angleterre une dame qui n'atent qu'une bonne occasion pour partir." Desgrez to La Reynie, lieut. de police, April 25, 1686.
6 History of My Own Time, III, pp. 276–7; cf. Foxcroft Supplement, pp. 377–8.

countrymen did not always meet with recognition. The unfortunate James Bruce in acknowledging his passport remarked
that he did not feel sure it would be respected, as many Dutch
passports had been disregarded.[1] A "gentleman of polite
learning", Dr William Aglionby—later he was to be "envoy
from Queen Anne to the Swiss cantons"[2]—complained that
Sir William's passport had met with scant courtesy. He was
told that such passports could be got for 30 sous and that he
spoke French too well to be an Englishman. An Irish monk
then certified that he was English. Then it was said that he was
naturalized in France. This Aglionby disproved by his diary,
showing that he had arrived from Italy six weeks before. Then
it was said he was Italian. After being taken for examination
to a Jesuit he was released.[3]

Doubtless Sir William was often asked to stretch a point,
and doubtless some of his passports were used by others than
their owners. The Pastor Philippe de Chenevix had left two
daughters behind him in France—one was under the protection
of Spanheim, the other with a friend of her father. An acquaintance wrote from London hoping that if things came to
the worst Sir William would declare the second daughter to be
one of his family.[4] A young man who had lived for six or seven
years in England returned to France with a passport enabling
him to go back to England. With the help of another passport
obtained from Sir William he planned to take his mother out of
the country, disguised as a man.[5] A girl was caught sending
forged baptismal certificates from Guernsey to two of her
friends, directing them to go with these to Sir William's door-
keeper Le Roux, who would introduce them to the secretary
D'Ayrolle.[6]

Sunderland proved understanding in the affair of the pass-

1 H.M.C., *Downshire MSS.* 1, p. 107.
2 Chalmers, *Biogr. Dictionary*, London, 1812.
3 H.M.C., *Downshire MSS.* 1, p. 215. See pp. 226–7 for another man's experience.
4 *Ib.* p. 73; cf. p. 108. See also Douen, *La Révocation...à Paris*, ii, pp. 10
   471; Agnew, *Protestant Exiles*, ii, p. 272.
5 B.N. MS. fr. 7053, f. 161, April 30, 1686; A.N. O¹ 30, f. 158. Police reports.
6 B.N. MS. fr. 7052, ff. 185–6; cf. Douen, *op. cit.* ii, p. 437.

ports, only counselling Sir William to be very careful.[1] Barrillon wrote the same day—he had begun to work for the possible recall of the envoy, only it was a difficult affair, and the King of England would be reluctant to give his assent at first. Even though he did not think Trumbull very fit to deal with the important affairs of the first court of Europe he liked punctilious people. "Il ayme les gens exacts et formalistes qui executent ses ordres avec ponctualité et fermeté." "Milord Sonderland" had promised to do his share—he would see that some one more acceptable was sent. ("I can assure you my Lord President is as much your friend as you can desire", Sir William had just heard.)[2] Barrillon was going to try and influence Rochester next; at least he could prevent him from supporting Trumbull's claims.[3] Neither Sunderland nor Barrillon knew that there was a candidate for Sir William's succession, but that same day Bonrepaus invited Barrillon and Henry Savile for dinner.[4]

On Tuesday, February 27, Sir William went to Versailles to obtain answers to his various memorials, but received no satisfaction, in fact as far as the Orange affair went matters had taken a turn for the worse, the King being greatly incensed by the "insolent" action of the court of justice of Holland, which he attributed to the influence of the Prince of Orange. That court had extended its protection very ostentatiously to the sons of a certain M. Bosc; the boys had preceded their father to Holland and refused to return to him in France, now that he had abjured. The court had also taken into custody the sum of 25,000 francs that had been sent with the children.[5]

Monsieur de Croissy continues still indispos'd with ye Gout, and yesterday gave Audience in his Bed. Concerning ye Memorial I had presented about Orange, he told me he had represented it to ye King,

1 *H.M.C.*, *Downshire MSS.* 1, p. 120, Feb. 15–25, 1686.
2 *Ib.* p. 118.
3 A.É. *Angleterre*, vol. 158, ff. 113–14, Barrillon to Louis XIV, Feb. 25, 1686; cf. f. 107, Barrillon to Louis XIV, Feb. 21.
4 *Ib.* vol. 160, f. 121, Bonrepaus to Seignelay, Feb. 25, 1686.
5 R.O. *France*, vol. 150, f. 28: "Extract of the most Christian King's letter to Monsr Barrillon about the Prince of Orange"; ff. 30–31, "Extrait de la depesche de M. le Comte d'Avaux au Roy du 14e février 1686"; f. 32, "Extrait de la depesche du Roy a Mr le Comte D'Avaux du 21e jour de fevrier 1686". A.É. *Angleterre*, vol. 158, f. 97, Louis XIV to Barrillon, Feb. 21.

who continued still in his former Resolution, that he acknowledgd no Soveraignty of Orange to belong to ye Prince, and that although for some Reasons he did forbeare to have that Right adjudgd, yet that it was his incontestably, and that he had no other Answer to give me; Adding this late occasion of displeasure, by reason of ye Prince's refusall to deliver ye Children of one Monsr Bosc (a Counsell^r of ye Parliam^t of Tholouse, and formerly of ye Religion, but lately chang'd). Monsr Bosc had sent his Children thither, intending afterwards to escape himself, but since he made Instances by Monsr D'Avaux to have them sent back, W^ch he said ye Prince denyd, and insisted further to keepe what mony they had brought with y^m, as a Provision and Subsistence for them; He told me, The King had given Orders to stop ye Princes receiving any part of his Revenues of Orange, till he [had] given Satisfaction in this matter.

Concerning ye Fisher-boate and men detaind att Calais, I had ye same Answer allso as formerly, and that ye King would not alter ye Resolution he had taken.[1]

Barrillon had already received instructions to acquaint James II with the new shortcomings of the Prince of Orange, and James agreed readily that his attitude was most reprehensible. When Sir William's letter arrived reporting that his new memorial had met with no more success than the first James said nothing more on the subject, nor did anyone else of his council.[2]

A copy of the answer received by Trumbull concerning the principality was sent to the Prince of Orange,[3] who must have realized by this time that he would not receive the slightest satisfaction. Sir Gabriel Sylvius still read in "the Haarlem Gazettes" about Sir William Trumbull,[4] and Sir Peter Wyche in Hamburg heard that Sir William had delivered two other memorials in terms "bien fortes" about the restitution of the principality,[5] but Sir William received no further instructions to intervene. A French newsletter still refers on March 30 to the joint efforts of Trumbull and Spanheim, but comments

1 R.O. *loc. cit.* f. 39, to Sunderland, Feb. 27, 1686.
2 A.É. *Angleterre*, vol. 158, ff. 118 and 124, Barrillon to Louis XIV, Feb. 28 and March 4; cf. vol. 160, f. 80, Bonrepaus to Seignelay, March 4, 1686.
3 R.O. *France, Entry Book* 19, March 2–12, 1686.
4 H.M.C., *Downshire MSS.* I, p. 125, Feb. 27, 1686.
5 *Ib.* p. 128.

"on ne void pas que cela fasse un grand effet".[1] In April one finds Sir Gabriel Sylvius still wondering why the French King gave no satisfaction to the King of England about Orange,[2] but officially the matter was at an end and we shall hear no more about the unfortunate principality,[3] though the affair of the Rye fishermen drags on a while longer.

That nothing was accomplished was not Sir William's fault, but the services he had attempted to render the Prince of Orange were not forgotten, and when he became Secretary of State to William III one is not surprised to read: "M. Trumbull est plus lié avec les ministres hollandois que d'autres Anglois."[4]

1 B.N. MS. fr. 10265, f. 121.
2 H.M.C., op. cit. p. 146.
3 At the request of the Prince, Trumbull's successor Skelton was directed in 1687 to interpose for the liberty of M. de Lubières, President of the Parlement of Orange and of the five ministers all imprisoned. He was unsuccessful. R.O. *France, Entry Book* 19, Sunderland to Skelton, April 25—May 5, 1687; *France*, vol. 151, f. 64, Skelton to Sunderland, June 11, 1687.
4 Gigas, *Let res de divers Savants*, I, p. 494.

CHAPTER IX

Little satisfaction

MARCH

SUNDERLAND had taken up the question of the "Tapistry Hangings" with James, who was informed by Rochester that "the French ministers who came here have always been free from Customs for their household goods, amongst which Tapestry hangings are certainly included, and are accordingly exempted here, upon the minister's certificate that they are for his own use"[1]—it seemed therefore reasonable that the English ministers at the court of France should have the same exemption. Sir William felt relieved.

I have yᵉ Honʳ of yoʳ Loᵖˢ of yᵉ 15ᵗʰ of last Month and have taken yᵉ Libertie to speake to Monsʳ de Croissy (who continues still in bed, much troubled with yᵉ Gout) about my Tapistry Hangings: He has promisd me to represent yᵉ matter againe to yᵉ King. And for yᵉ granting of Passeports, I returne my most humble Thankes for yᵉ Justice yoʳ Loᵖ is pleasd to do me in beleiving That as I have hitherto been very carefull in giving them, so that I will...continue still my uttmost Endeavours, not to give any just Cause of Complaint: Yoʳ Loᵖ will before this have seen yᵉ truth of my Case, concerning Passeports, in yᵉ Letter I wrott to Monsʳ de Croissy upon that Subject, whereof I sent yᵉ Copie to Mr Bridgeman...

Besides yᵉ Suisses Deputies of Fribourg, who demanded yᵉ payment of some Arreares, there are come hither some others from yᵉ Protestant Cantons, desiring to make their Excuses for yᵉ receiving yᵉ French Huguenots that were fled thither. But these have not yet been admitted to any Audience...

I feare my Solicitʳ, Mr Robson, has not yet attended yoʳ Loᵖ about my Bill of Extraordinaries; I most humbly beg yoʳ favʳ in yᵉ Dispatch of it, having another Quarter almost readie, and having been forc'd hitherto to live upon my Credit.[2]

1 *H.M.C., Downshire MSS.* 1, pp. 119–20.
2 R.O. *France*, vol. 150, f. 41, to Sunderland, March 6, 1686.

Before Sir William had left for France the Queen had entrusted him with a letter for Louis XIV in behalf of a sister of the Duchess Mazarin, Olympia Mancini, comtesse de Soissons,[1] another of Mazarin's beautiful and restless nieces. She claimed a share of the property of her mother-in-law, the Princess of Carignano, whose death was expected shortly, but having fled from France at the time of the *affaire des poisons* she was living in disgrace at Brussels, and her son, the famous Prince Eugene, had not improved matters by joining the Imperial army. Sir William had thought it best not to deliver the letter at the time and had been praised for his discretion.[2]

Now, however, James had written to recommend her claims.[3]

"I receivd yesterday y⁰ Honʳ of his Majᵗⁱᵉˢ Letter in behalf of Madame la Comtesse de Soissons": writes Sir William on March 9, "I had not deliverd that of her Majᵗⁱᵉ, So that I shall give them both together. However, matters being much changd here in relation to that affaire, and y⁰ most Christian King being still indispos'd (though much better) I humbly beg pardon, if I take y⁰ Libertie to represent y⁰ Case."[4]

The Countess, he explains, had gone to Spain,[5] a proceeding which had displeased the court, and the conjuncture was not very favourable to solicit in her behalf—it would expose their Majesties' request to undoubted refusal. In the meantime therefore he would not present the letters.[6] Sir William's conduct again met with approval[7]—as for the two royal letters, they are to this day among Sir William Trumbull's papers at Easthampstead Park.

"I am earnestly solicited", continues Sir William, "to moove yoʳ Loᵖ in behalf of one Marie Kirby of Bourdeaux, an Englishwoman, married there to a French-man, who is putt in Prison upon y⁰ Account of her Religion: I thought yoʳ Loᵖ being fully instructed by her Letter, would represent her Case to his Majᵗⁱᵉˢ Consideration, if you should thinke it fitt. I have spoke of it to Monsʳ Croissy, who

---

1 H.M.C., *Downshire MSS.* i, p. 51.   2 *Ib.* p. 103.
3 *Ib.* p. 122; cf. Bulstrode's letter on p. 121, Caryll's letters on pp. 122, 129, and the abbé Rizzini's letter on p. 126.
4 R.O. *France*, vol. 150, f. 42, to Sunderland, March 9, 1686.
5 Cf. A. Renée, *Les Nièces de Mazarin*, pp. 210 *et seq.*
6 R.O. *loc. cit.*   7 H.M.C., *op. cit.* pp. 129–30; cf. pp. 154–5.

told me first That she being putt into Prison about a Particular affaire, must be releivd by ye Ordinarie forms of Justice; But finding that it was otherwise, She must be oblig'd to follow ye Condition of her Husband, att ye same time that French-women married to Englishmen not Naturaliz'd, are not onely not obligd to this but refus'd ye same Permission wch they desire."[1]

James II had assented to all that concerned the Principality of Orange, but the question of the Rye fishermen was not yet settled. James did not want to yield on a point that involved his rights in his waters, and Louis was equally determined not to give way. "Quelque instance qu'on vous fasse pour le relaschement des pescheurs françois ramenez des environs de la Rye dans le port de Calais, vous n'en devez donner aucune esperance, mon intention n'estant pas...de rien changer sur ce sujet", he instructed his ambassador.[2]

"Il fut parlé...comme si la raison estoit du costé des Anglois", notes Barrillon on March 4,[3] and that same day Sunderland wrote to Trumbull telling him that His Majesty did not think he ought to acquiesce in the answer that had been given.[4]

"I receivd yesterday allso ye Significations of his Maj^tys Pleasure", Sir William goes on to say in this same letter, "concerning ye Men and Boate still detaind att Calais, of wch I will speake againe to Mons. de Croissy."

And then on to his personal affairs.

Mr Bridgeman sent me inclos'd my Bill of Extraordinaries[5]... He gives me notice of 3 Articles excepted against; But I do not know whether it be meant in respect of ye Whole, or of any part of the Summes therein mentiond.

My Lord, As to ye Articles themselves, consisting of ye Plate and Bookes for my Chappell, For my Journey from Diepe to Paris, And for what was given (according to Custome) att my Publick Audience, I can onely say, These Articles have been allowd my Predecessors, As appeares by ye Copies of Mr Saviles and ye Lord Preston's Bills of Extraordinaries, wch I had then and have now before me; And I humbly hope I shall be treated upon ye same Foot.

1 R.O. *loc. cit.* f. 43.
2 A.É. *Angleterre*, vol. 158, f. 96, Louis XIV to Barrillon, Feb. 21, 1686.
3 *Ib.* f. 125, Barrillon to Louis XIV, March 4, 1686.
4 H.M.C., *Downshire MSS.* I, p. 123, Feb. 22—March 4, 1686.
5 See pp. 173-4 *post.*

As to any Excesse in y° Summes, I thinke nothing can be lyable, even to any Surmise, unlesse that of my Journey from Diepe to Paris; Which was occasiond by y° very ill Weather and Wayes that made it allmost as long againe as usuall, which was my Misfortune, but not my Fault. And I assure yo' Lo** I have' not sett downe severall Accidents of Lame Horses and Servants left by y° Way (though I find that allso has been don by others) which was a considerable Expense to me; But I wav'd it, to avoid any occasion of Exception... Without his Maj^ties gracious Support and yo' Lo** goodnesse to me, it is impossible for me to live here according to my Character without being ruin'd in my little Fortune.[1]

Sir William had also brought with him a letter from James II requesting leave for Mme de Gouvernet and her mother, Mme d'Hervart, both of them Protestants, to come to England. Mme de Gouvernet's daughter Esther had married Lord Eland, son of Lord Halifax. At first permission was refused—"The design now on foot", said Halifax bitterly of the enforced conversions, "is of too much importance to allow reason, generosity or good nature to break into it. There must be nothing done to particular persons that may weaken the general project."[2] Nevertheless in the end the ladies were allowed to go,[3] and Sir William could report on March 13, "Madame de Gouvernet, with her Mother, went hence this morning, for England by y° way of Calais."[4]

Sir William's next letter brings some news of the famous statue[5] ordered from the sculptor Desjardins—his real name was Van den Bogaert—by an adoring courtier, the maréchal de La Feuillade, and erected in what is known to-day as la place des Victoires. To-day a modern statue replaces La Feuillade's offering,

1 R.O. *loc. cit.* His predecessor, Lord Preston, once remarked: "I, having been here for almost 3 years and being now sinking under the expense which I have been obliged to make...." *H.M.C., 7th Report*, App., Part I, p. 348.

2 *H.M.C., Downshire MSS.* I, p. 104.

3 A.É. *Angleterre*, vol. 151, f. 356, Louis XIV to James II, Dec. 19, 1685; vol. 156, f. 229, Louis XIV to Barrillon, Dec. 21, 1685; f. 252, Barrillon to Louis XIV, Dec. 27, 1685; vol. 158, ff. 102-3, Barrillon to Louis XIV, Feb. 18, 1686; f. 110, Louis XIV to Barrillon, Feb. 28, 1686; vol. 160, f. 76, Bonrepaus to Seignelay, Feb. 7, 1686. *H.M.C., Downshire MSS.* I, pp. 115, 119, 136; Douen, *La Révocation...à Paris*, II, p. 426.

4 R.O. *France*, vol. 150, f. 46, to Sunderland, March 13, 1686; cf. f. 23.

5 A. de Boislisle, *La place des Victoires, passim.*

which was hacked to pieces in 1792. The monument showed
Louis XIV crowned by Victory. A vanquished Cerberus lay
underfoot. Divers triumphs were depicted on the bas-reliefs
of the pedestal, and at each corner of the pedestal was seated a
chained captive. These captives were said to symbolize Spain,
Holland, Germany and Turkey.

"The Statue of this King, which is sett up and allmost finishd in
yᵉ Place Feuillade," reports Sir William on March 16, "has caus'd
several Discourses among yᵉ Forraigne Ministers: The Envoyé of
Suede"—Sir William's friend Liljeroth—"has made his Complaints
to Monsʳ de Croissy about a Bas-Releif, wherein he thinkes an
Affront is offerd to yᵉ King his Master.[1] As soon as I am more
particularly inform'd, I will give yoʳ Loᵖ an Account."[2]

Another Tuesday. Another "Journey" to Versailles.
Another interview with M. de Croissy. Another fruitless
expedition. But what favour could be expected for the English
wife of a Frenchman? What answer but a new refusal in the case
of the Rye fishermen? Louis XIV had written once more—he
thought James had all the less reason to complain in that there
could be no greater enemies to royal authority in his dominions
than these Calvinist fugitives. "Il est mesme de sa prudence de
les en esloigner par toutes sortes de mauvais traitemens."[3]

"Having formerly spoke to Monsʳ de Croissy in behalf of Mrs
Kirbie of Bourdeaux," writes Sir William on March 20, "I thought
myself obligd yesterday (before I had receivd yᵉ Signification of his
Majᵗⁱᵉˢ Pleasure expressely[4]) to discourse with him againe upon that
Subject, and to offer to his Consideration yᵉ Reasonablenesse of this
Request according to their own Proceedings here in relation to
French Women married to English-men not Naturaliz'd (as is sett
forth in yoʳ Loᵖˢ Letter), But have not been able to prevail, he
assuring me The most Christian King will not depart from his

---

1 "La Suède...se plaignit amèrement que la figure et la couronne de son roi
Charles XI fussent reconnaissables dans une des têtes du Cerbère écrasé par
Louis XIV." Boislisle, p. 67.
2 R.O. *France*, vol. 150, f. 55, to Sunderland, March 16, 1686.
3 A.É. *Angleterre*, vol. 158, f. 135, Louis XIV to Barrillon, March 15, 1686.
4 Cf. *H.M.C., Downshire MSS.* I, p. 130: "His Majesty thinks it very strange
that she being an English subject should be obliged to follow the condition of
her husband when the same is denied to Frenchwomen married to Englishmen
not naturalised."

Versailles in 1684, after an engraving by Israël Silvestre. Colbert de Croissy received foreign envoys on Tuesdays in the wing at the extreme right of the *avant-cour*, the court beyond the first railing

(*Archives photographiques, Paris*)

Resolution to treate her and others, that come hither to settle and establish themselves, on ye same foot that he does his own Subjects.[1]

He told me allso, concerning ye Fisher Boate and men detain'd att Calais, That he had (by ye Kings Order) written into England to give his Maj^ty a full Account of ye Reasons of y^a Detention.

The Kings Indisposition continues still, and is plainly a Fistula, though all Danger is said to be over...

I..thanke yor Lo^p..for ye passing my Bill of Extraordinaries."[2]

In London Sunderland had again spoken to Barrillon about the Rye fishermen, but Barrillon contradicted him when he said that the boats had been taken in English waters. And even if it were true, added the ambassador, after all the three boats *had* been set free at Dunkirk, and if one of these boats had fallen then into the hands of his Most Christian Majesty's officers, no one could say the boat had been seized in the Rye roadstead! Finally he gave Sunderland to understand that he could write no more to France about that matter.[3]

And so, just as in the affair of the Principality of Orange, Louis XIV had his way and James yielded—for the time being. François Bridon, an English subject, was sent to the galleys,[4] and doubtless his associates too, but we do not know their names. We hear no more of these unfortunate men during Sir William's stay in France, but when Bevil Skelton had gone to take his place he received instructions to renew instances, nothing having been done in the matter "before Sir William Trumbull came away".[5] It is hardly necessary to add that Skelton met with no success.[6]

1 One imagines that Sir William obtained no protection either for the marquise de Cuignac who was English by birth. *H.M.C., Downshire MSS.* 1, p. 74.

2 R.O. *France*, vol. 150, f. 57, to Sunderland, March 20, 1686.

3 A.É. *Angleterre*, vol. 158, f. 153, Barrillon to Louis XIV, March 18, 1686.

4 Benoist, *Histoire de l'Édit de Nantes*, vol. v (a list of galley-slaves—no paging in this part of the book).

5 R.O. *France, Entry Book* 19, Dec. 23, 1686—Jan. 2, 1687.

6 *Ib.* vol. 151, f. 9:"As for the Fishermen of Rye that are imprisoned at Calais, whoe in my Instructions are said to be become his Majesty's Subjects, theire Case being layd before this King, Monsr de Croissi returned for answer, that the King cannot allow that his Subjects can by vertue of any Naturalization throw of his Government and become the Subjects of any other Prince unlesse he first consents to it, as in the case of the Lord Feversham, And therefore he cannot consider them any otherwise then as his owne Subjects, and gave me no encoragement to hope that any Interposition would doe them goode." To Sunderland, Jan. 29, 1687.

Sir William Trumbull was not happy in his office. "I suffer with you, dear Sir," Halifax wrote to him, "and sincerely condole for the discouraging circumstances that belong to your employment."[1] To Halifax Sir William seems to have unburdened his mind, but at his request all his letters were destroyed—"though if many such letters were written and then burnt one might say of the fire, as it is said of the sea, that the ship-wrecks have made it richer than the land".[2] From the answers received one gathers that Sir William drew "a scurvy map of France".[3]

"I have heard of ladies," said Halifax, "who would not believe their conquests entire, except their lovers lost their senses for them, but I never understood that God Almighty was of that mind, that one could not please him without being madmen... Whatever he (Louis XIV) thinketh fit to do to his own subjects, he might have more regard to his poor allies, and though we are his most particular friends, yet he is pleased to use us so very familiarly that I doubt his kindness may be misinterpreted and that spiteful folks may call it contempt."[4]

And taking coach for the country Halifax remarks:

"I shall not be more solitary than you are in a Court where you have so little satisfaction"...."I cannot but wonder", he muses, "that after the friendly advice I gave...you should be such a bungler as to be in the right and such a novice as to follow your instructions... I am sometimes tempted to put you amongst my prayers for the dead, it being impossible you should last long if you commit such mortal mistakes."[5]

Sir William himself seems to have felt already that he could accomplish little, and when Ruvigny, one of the few Protestants allowed to leave the country, retired to England where he had been envoy more than once, he took with him a message to Sir William's patron Rochester—Sir William wanted to return to England. Rochester could scarcely believe the news[6] which would have been most pleasing to the diplomats still

1 H.M.C., *Downshire MSS*. 1, p. 104, Jan. 23—Feb. 2, 1686.
2 *Ib.* p. 136, March 22—April 1, 1686.
3 *Ib.* p. 104.   4 *Ib.*   5 *Ib.* pp. 135-6.
6 *Ib.* p. 138, Ruvigny to Trumbull, March 22—April 1, 1686.

working for Sir William's recall. There was little prospect, Bonrepaus reported, of Henry Savile being sent in Trumbull's place, for James did not feel that he could trust him.[1] But to return to Sir William's official correspondence. "The Statue in ye Place Feuillade is now finisht", we hear on March 23, "and will be opend with some Ceremonie on Thursday next; Monseigneur, Madame la Dauphine, Monsieur and Madame and severall others of ye first Qualitie will be present."[2] The King himself, though almost recovered, was not to attend,[3] and Sir William went to Versailles to pay his respects.

"I thought my self oblig'd to waite upon ye most Christian King", he writes four days later, "and make my Complements (wch I did yesterday) upon his Recovering, and to signifie ye part I knew ye King my Master tooke in his Indisposition, with ye Wishes for his Perfect Health and ye continuance of it. He was pleas'd to receive me very kindly and to take it well that I came of my self without staying for any Orders to this purpose, and to say That all Assurances of his Maj^{ties} Friendsp were allwayes very wellcome to him. I took that Occasion of presenting his Maj^{ties} Letter in behalf of $Mons^r$ le Marquis de Sessac,[4] and to second it as well as I could: The King onely said He would read it and give an Answer."[5]

James had sent an ambassador to the Holy See, the Earl of Castlemaine, less renowned than his former wife. To his surprise James heard that Castlemaine had not waited upon Louis XIV.[6] Sir William was therefore instructed to let M. de Croissy know that his master disapproved of this omission, but that his Lordship "having never been employed in any public character before, might the easier commit this mistake."[7] Of his Lordship's stay in Paris Sir William writes discreetly.

1 A.É. *Angleterre*, vol. 160, f. 235, to Seignelay, April 11, 1686.
2 R.O. *France*, vol. 150, f. 58, to Sunderland, March 23, 1686.
3 Boislisle, *La place des Victoires*, p. 58.
4 Cf. *H.M.C., Downshire MSS.* i, p. 53: "You are to second the enclosed letters, one in favour of Monsieur de Sessac, for him to go to France for a time to settle his affairs." Sunderland to Trumbull, Nov. 9–19, 1685. Cf. p. 208. The marquis de Saissac, accused, like Mme de Soissons, of having been involved in the *affaire des poisons*, had fled to England where he spent ten years. He was allowed to return in 1690. Saint-Simon, *Mémoires*, v, p. 120, *n.* 8.
5 R.O. *loc. cit.* f. 59, to Sunderland, March 27, 1686.
6 He had arrived in Paris on Feb. 23. *Ib.* f.34.
7 *H.M.C., Downshire MSS.* i, pp. 133–4, from Sunderland, March 11–21, 1686.

Concerning my Ld Castlemain, att his Lo^ps first arrival I went to waite upon him, and expecting his Lo^p would go to Versailles and see ye most Christian King, I offerd him my Coach and Horses and Equipage and whatever else might depend upon me and my Services, which I repeated to his Lo^p severall times afterwards during his stay att Paris; But finding his Lo^ps resolutions were not to go thither, I thought it not fitt for me to enquire into his particular Reasons, nor to presse him any further. I shall not fail to represent this matter in ye best Termes I can, and doubt not but ye Excuses of ye oversight will be well taken.[1]

With Sir William's next letter came "Laces for my Lord Chancell^r[2] who was pleasd to order this way of conveyance".

"I was last night to waite on ye Dutchesse of Portsmouth[3] to take Leave," adds Sir William, "she designing this morning towards Bretagne. Her Grace desird me to give her humble Service to yor Lo^p, and to acquaint you That at last ye Settlement is made upon ye Duke of Richmond, and passd through all ye Forms, though not without very great Difficulties."[4]

We have not heard the last of "the new Statue".

The Emperours Envoyé[5] was yesterday att Versailles to presse Monsr de Croissy for some favourable Answer to ye Memorial he gave in of severall Damages don by ye French Troopes in ye Domaines of ye Emper^r, signifying ye ill consequences that might happen if ye Emper^r should be obligd to take Satisfaction upon ye new Conquests of ye French adjoyning: Adding, That ye Emper^r was not in ye Condition of a Slave with his Hands tyd in Chaines, otherwise than in ye Fancy of Monsr de la Feuillade (This he thought fitt to take notice of, upon occasion of one of ye Figures under ye new Statue, representing a Slave in Chaines, with ye Armes of ye Empire, ye Spread-Eagle by him). But this, he said, he did not forme as a Complaint, but onely to lett it be known he was not Insensible...[6]

---

1 R.O. *loc. cit.*   2 Jeffreys.

3 Louise de Kéroualle, late mistress of Charles II.

4 R.O. *France*, vol. 150, f. 61, to Sunderland, March 30, 1686. The Duchess had been granted the fief of Aubigny after the death of Charles Stuart, Duke of Richmond, in 1672; her son by Charles II, created Duke of Richmond in 1675, had now been naturalized in France, and would be able to inherit the lands of Aubigny which Louis XIV had erected into a dukedom for the Duchess and her son. Forneron, *Louise de Kéroualle*, pp. 218, 220.   5 Lobkowitz.

6 R.O. *loc. cit.* f. 62, to Sunderland, April 3, 1686. "L'effet politique du monument de Paris fut mauvais a l'extérieur et motiva en partie la ligue que conclurent à Augsburg, dès le 17 juillet suivant, l'Espagne, l'Autriche, la Bavière, les princes de l'Empire et la Suède." Boislisle, *op. cit.* p. 67.

The duc de Chartres, the future Regent, son of Monsieur, the Duke of Orleans, was now in his twelfth year and beginning to appear in public.[1]

"Monsieur Aubert, Introducteur de Monsieur," relates Sir William in this same letter of April 3, "was to see me lately, to invite me to make a Visit to Mons[r] le Duc de Chartres; W[ch] I readily accepted; But intending to waite on him in my own Coach and Equipage, he told me it must not be otherwise than in y[e] Duke's Coach and with y[e] same Ceremonie as to a Publick Audience. I have spoken with some of y[e] forreign Ministers here and find it has not been practisd by them, but that Mons[r] Aubert has been willing to introduce this Ceremonie for his own Advantage. But because I would not innovate, nor on y[e] other hand be wanting in all due Respects... I beg yo[r] Lo[ps] Directions."[2]

A sudden event provided a solution to this question.

1 Dangeau, *Journal*, 1, p. 294. 2 R.O. *loc. cit.*

CHAPTER X

Envoys and Consuls

APRIL—MAY

AT the end of March Madame, the Duchess of Orleans, had lost her mother, and the ambassadors and envoys made ready to condole. Sir William writes on April 6:

I have spoken with Monsieur Aubert, yᵉ Introducteur to Monsieur, to desire an Audience of Condoleance upon yᵉ Death of yᵉ Princesse Dowagʳ Palatin,[1] being willing to shew my Zeale in being of yᵉ first that should pay their Respects in this Kind. He told me that Monsieur would stay att St Clou till Easter, and not receive these Complements till after yᵉ Holy-dayes att yᵉ Palais Royal, which is in mourning ever since yᵉ Death of his late Majᵗⁱᵉ, So that if yoʳ Loᴾ thinks fitt to speake to their Majᵗⁱᵉˢ to command me to Deliver their Letters of Complement or any Message upon this occasion they will come to me in time before any of yᵉ Ministers will have Audience.

The most Christian King has been to Condole with Madame. His Recovery goes on but slowly. . . On Wenesday he saw yᵉ Cavaliers and yᵉ Ladies appointed for yᵉ Carrousel passe before his Window, where yᵉ Marquis d'Antin had yᵉ Misfortune to fall off his Horse and to receive a considerable hurt.[2]

With this letter came another packet for My Lord Chancellor and a new bill of "Extraordinaries". "Without yoʳ Loᴾˢ favour to me in my Extraʳⁱᵉˢ my Condition in yᵉ world cannot support yᵉ Charges of this Post."[3]

Tuesday, April 9. A "Journey" to Versailles. Sir William had instructions to take up several matterṣ. There was an English prisoner in the Bastille who went by the name of the Comte d'Alby, though he was formerly styled Sir Andrew White. He was one of the five brothers of Sir Ignatius White, better known as the Marquis of Albeville, the envoy who succeeded

---

1 Charlotte of Hesse.
2 Dangeau (*Journal*, 1, p. 319) gives another explanation of the fall.
3 R.O. *France*, vol. 150, f. 64, to Sunderland, April 6, 1686.

Bevil Skelton in the United Provinces.[1] The "Count" had been in prison since July 1678, "for loyalty to our King" said his friends,[2] for being a spy in the interests of Spain said the French ministers.[3] Sir William was to obtain permission for the "Count's" friends to visit him.[4]

Another matter concerned the succession of the late consul at Marseilles, Robert Lang, who had left his estate to his brother William Lang in England. But Robert Lang was naturalized, and according to the laws of the *droit d'aubaine* not only was the King of France entitled to the estate of any "aubain" or stranger who died in his dominions, but a naturalized subject could not leave his property to one who was not a subject of France. Various treaties between the crowns of England and France declared that the *droit d'aubaine* should not apply to the subjects of the King of England residing in France,[5] but in practice this privilege was often forgotten and the English envoys were not infrequently called upon to protest in the name of the heirs who found themselves despoiled.[6] Still Sir William might hope that some preferential treatment might be granted in this case. Lang had complicated the case, however, by leaving his property to a certain Couliatte or Couillette if at the time of his death there should be war between France and England, and this man had already appropriated part of the estate.[7]

Of his conversation with M. de Croissy Sir William writes as follows:

On Munday I had ye honr of yor Lops of ye 22nd of last Month concerning ye Count d'Alby; I represented it yesterday to Monsieur de

1 E. S. De Beer, The Marquis of Albeville and his Brothers. *English Historical Review*, July 1930, pp. 397–408, especially pp. 402, 403.
2 *H.M.C., Downshire MSS.* 1, p. 51.
3 *H.M.C., 7th Report*, App., Part 1, p. 296. See also pp. 298, 301, 337, 359.
4 *H.M.C., Downshire MSS.* 1, p. 136.
5 Treaties dated 1606, 1625, 1629, 1632, 1644, 1655, according to a memorial presented by Lord Preston to Louis XIV. *H.M.C., 7th Report*, App., Part 1, p. 331.
6 *Ib.* pp. 293, 294, 300, 301, 303, 304, 308, 331, 370, 410. As M. de Croissy explained to Preston: "This King having let those casualties to farm, the farmers were willing to make the best of them and had therefore tried if by these means they could draw anything out of the executors." *Ib.* pp. 294, 370.
7 *H.M.C., Downshire MSS.* 1, p. 130; cf. R.O. *France*, vol. 150, f. 57, Trumbull to Sunderland, March 20, 1686.

Croissy, who seem'd to be wholly unacquainted with yᵉ Case, but promis'd me to informe himselfe and speake to yᵉ King of it.

As to yᵉ succession of Lang (yᵉ late English Consul at Marseillis) Monsʳ de Croissy has taken care at yᵉ Offices of yᵉ Secretairies That yᵉ most Christian King should not be surprizd in yᵉ passing of any Grant for that Estate, as fall'n to him by yᵉ Droict d'Aubeine, Wᶜʰ I endeavourd to obtaine, Because David Couillette[1] has already had Sentence given against him at Marseilles, having undoubtedly no Right, nor any thing (as I conceive) to be feard from his Pretentions, or any others, unlesse this King does interpose upon Account of yᵉ Deceac'd being Naturaliz'd.[2]

The interview with M. de Croissy was proceeding unusually well when suddenly M. de Croissy made a disconcerting remark. Sir William had been told in his instructions that difficulty had been made hitherto to admit English consuls,[3] and he had been told to obtain their admission, but the question had not been raised so far.

He [M. de Croissy] tooke this occasion to say That they own'd no English Consuls in France, there being no French Consuls own'd in England; Wᶜʰ I yᵉ rather take notice of att this time, Because I heare his Majᵗⁱᵉ is sending over one in that Qualitie to Marseillis and humbly beg yoʳ Loᵖˢ particular Directions therein, being not fully informd whether yᵉ French did ever desire to have any Consul in England, or if they have, upon what reasons it has not been allow'd them.

Monsʳ de Croissy was pleasd to receive very well yᵉ Excuses I made for my Ld Castlemaine's omission in not going to Versailles, being in such hast to take his Journey towards Rome, and to assure me he would represent it to yᵉ King.[4]

A month earlier Sir William had been informed that the Earl of Sandwich, now living in profound retirement in France,[5] was threatened with the loss of his French servants, all of whom had served him long—some already settled in England had

---

1 Or "Daniel Couliatte".

2 R.O. *France*, vol. 150, f. 65, to Sunderland, April 10, 1686.

3 See p. 170 *post*. For this whole question see an interesting article by V. Barbour, "Consular Service in the Reign of Charles II", *American Historical Review*, vol. xxiii, April 1928, pp. 552–78.

4 R.O. *loc. cit.*

5 H.M.C., *Downshire MSS.* i, p. 157.

come over with him—and this danger had arisen in spite of promises made by Barrillon and Louvois.[1] Now the blow had fallen.

"My Lord Sandwich, who was retird into a Countrie House in Xaintonge," reports Sir William on April 13, "has had his Domestiques (being Huguenots) taken away from him by ye Intendant of ye Province and putt into Prison till they Signe. Monsieur de Lubieres, President of ye Parliam^t of Orange, is seizd and sent to ye Kings Prison at Lyons."[2]

For various reasons Sir William had not yet gone to pay his *visite de condoléance*.

I have deferrd my waiting upon Monsieur and making my Complements of Condoleance, in expectation of ye Hon^r of his Maj^ties Commands...Besides I have been oblig'd to keepe my Chamber by reason of an Indisposition (caus'd by ye Cholique) some dayes last past. I find allso severall of ye Ministers intend not to go, till they receive Orders; Because of ye Precedence, wch is intended to be given to ye Emper^rs Envoyé[3] and (next to him) to ye Envoyé of Spain,[4] upon ye pretence of ye near Alliance,[5] Though this Envoyé comes onely from ye Govern^r of ye Low Countries, and has never yett been admitted to his Publick Audience, nor any Credentials receivd to give him ye Character of Envoyé of Spain: And if he had, yet it is neither thought sufficient to give ye Precedence, nor proper for Monsieur to determine that matter. The Nuncio,[6] ye Embassad^rs of Venice[7] and Savoy[8] went yesterday to ye Palais Royal and made their Complements in Bands and long Clokes; W^ch is allso thought extraordinarie, unlesse it had been in consequence of ye like Audiences of Ceremonie begun to ye King. I shall wholly governe myself, according as I shall receive ye Significations of his Maj^ties pleasure from yor Lo^p.[9]

Sir William concludes this letter of April 17 with some news.

On Friday last there came a Courier from ye States of Holland to

1 *Ib.* p. 133.
2 R.O. *France*, vol. 150, f. 66, to Sunderland, April 13, 1686; cf. *H.M.C., Downshire MSS.* I, p. 148.
3 The Count de Lobkowitz (*Recueil des Instructions*..., I, p.105).
4 The Count del Val (*ib.* XI, p. 517).
5 Monsieur's daughter by his first marriage with Henrietta, daughter of Charles I, viz. Marie Louise d'Orleans, was Queen of Spain.
6 Cardinal Angelo Maria Ranucci or Ranuzzi.
7 Girolama Venier (thus in Immich, *Vorgeschichte*).
8 The Marquis Ferrero de la Marmora (*Recueil des Instructions*..., XV, p. 390).
9 R.O. *France*, vol. 150, f. 67, to Sunderland, April 17, 1686.

their Embassad^r att Madrid: He went to Monsr de Louvoy to desire a Passeport, wch Monsr de Louvoy refusd, unlesse he would shew him his Letters that he brought. The Courier replyd, That he had 2 Passeports, one from ye States and another from Monsr d'Avaux (wch he produc'd), but that he had no orders to shew any Letters and so insisted to have his Passeport. Mr de Louvoy told him, If he had no Orders and would not shew his Letters without, he might go back and gett Orders to that Purpose. The Courier said, since he was forc'd, He would shew them and held them in his Hand, refusing to deliver them; But Mon^r de Louvois [1] snatcht them away, and having lookt upon ye Superscriptions returnd them againe without op'ning them; and wrott a Letter (wch he seald) to ye Govern^r of Bayoune, with wch ye Courier went away. This Proceeding has occasion'd much discourse and various Conjectures, what that Order (wch if it had been an Ordinarie Passeport would not have been seal'd) to ye Govern^r of Bayoune will produce.[2]

Easter came, and Sir William remarks:

These Holy-dayes little businesse or Newes has been stirring. The Ministers who have made their Complem^{ts} of Condoleance were M. le Nonce,[3] ye Ambassad^{rs} of Venice,[4] Savoye[5] and Maltha and ye Envoyés of ye Emp^r,[6] of Spaine,[7] Brandenburgh,[8] Modena[9] and Mantua;[10] After w^{ch} (on Thursday last) Monsieur and Madame returnd to Versailles. The others have not thought fitt to go, till they receive their Orders.[11]

A few days later Sir William was able to give pleasant news.

Upon ye affaire of ye Count d'Alby, Monsieur de Croissy said, That his friends should not onely have permission to see him in ye Bastille, but allso, in case ye King my Master did desire it, That he should be sett att Libertie, upon this Condition, That he went out of France and returnd no more.[12]

---

1 The forms "Louvoy", "Louvois" are both used in this letter.
2 R.O. *loc. cit.*   3 Cardinal Ranucci.
4 Girolama Venier.
5 Ferrero de la Marmora.   6 Lobkowitz.
7 Del Val.   8 Spanheim.
9 The abbé Siri according to *Recueil des Instructions...*, xix, p. 385, but Sir William, in a letter of Sept. 4 mentions the abbé Rizzini as envoyé. See p. 157 *post.*
10 Count Camillo Balliani (*ib.* xv, p. 397).
11 R.O. *France*, vol. 150, f. 68, to Sunderland, April 20, 1686.
12 *Ib.* f. 70, to Sunderland, April 24, 1686; cf. *H.M.C., Downshire MSS.* 1, p. 131 (wrongly dated), and p. 153.

But to return to the question of precedence at Monsieur's court. Sunderland had written to say that there could be no dispute with the envoy of the Emperor, "but his Majesty will by no means allow you should yield to the Envoyé of any other Prince".[1] Sir William therefore takes the matter up again in his letter of May 1.

I did not go to make my Complem^ts of Condoleance upon occasion of ye Princesse Dowager Palatin's death, Because I found ye Precedence would be given to ye Envoyé of Spaine, who was to be Tackt to ye Envoyé of ye Emper^r (by reason of ye near Alliance) And it proovd accordingly: Which was ye Cause that ye Envoyés of other Crown'd Heads (vizt those of Sueden and Denmarke) did not go likewise, But stay for Orders from their Respective Masters, to that purpose.[2]

M. de Liljeroth and M. de Meyercron thought that Monsieur took too much upon himself.

The Ministers of Sueden and Denmarke made these other objections; That Monsieur tooke upon him to regulate ye Precedence, W^ch was a thing ye King himself never medled with (in ye like cases), but left it to ye Ministers to dispute about among themselves. That they were directed to come to this Audience to Monsr in ye strictest Mourning, (vizt Plaine Bands and long mourning Clokes) which they say they are never obligd to observe but in Consequence of ye like Ceremonies first payd att their Audiences to the King, To whome they are sent, and not to Monsieur; And then that their Coaches were not permitted to enter into ye Palais Royall (I meane ye Envoyés Coaches) Allthough in Audiences to ye King, ye Envoyés Coaches enter att Versailles immediately after ye Coach of Madame la Dauphine.... They have given an Account to their Respective Masters and expect particular Directions from them, As I humbly crave leave to do...from his Maj^tie.[3]

There was not too much love lost between M. de Croissy and Sir William Trumbull, yet M. de Croissy did him swift justice on one occasion and Sir William was not ungrateful. He ends this letter on a note of appreciation.

I must not forget to beseech yor Lo^p to acquaint his Maj^tie, That some few dayes agoe an Insult having been made upon some of my

1 *H.M.C.*, *op. cit.* p. 149.
2 R.O. *France*, vol. 150, f. 72, to Sunderland, May 1, 1686.
3 *Ib.*

Servants going to water my Horses att ye River, by 2 Mousqueteers, upon my Complaint, Monsieur de Croissy immediately gave Order to ye Officer to imprison ye Person that was discoverd (the other not being yet met with) and to make me all just satisfaction. This readinesse to do me speedy favour and Justice herein, in consideration of ye Charact^r I have ye Hon^r to serve his Maj^tie in, I would beg of yor Lo^p may be taken notice of.[1]

The new consul to Marseilles, John Burrow,[2] had been appointed and was to arrive shortly. Sir William promised to give him all possible assistance.[3] Consuls, as we have seen, had an uncertain status in France, and Sir William had tried to understand the situation. He writes on May 4:

> Being earnestly desird by Mr Burrowes (to whome his Maj^tie hath given a Patent to be ye English Consul att Marseillis) and allso having by my Original Instructions his Maj^ties Order to solicit this Affaire, I have made ye best Enquirie I can into what has formerly been don in ye like cases. But I cannot yet heare of any Patent from England allowd of att this Court, or any of our Consuls acknowledgd from hence and admitted to execute that Charge. I find my Lord Preston endeavourd to obtaine this in behalf of Mr Lang ye late Consul; but I am told he desisted without effecting any thing.[4] This matter being of some consequence and hearing further that ye English Merchants themselves are against ye having any Consul, and do what they can to oppose his Admission,[5] I would humbly intreate yor Lo^p to lett me have his Maj^ties Pleasure herein; which I take ye boldnesse to desire, Because I am tender of making use of his Maj^ties Name in a matter that will receive a certain Denyall, And that I know not how (att present) to carrie on by ye Authoritie of any Precedents, unless yor Lo^p will be pleasd to order some Search to be made in yor Office of what has formerly been don in ye like Case.[6]

Not all envoys who passed through Paris had Lord Castlemaine's lack of manners. On May 8 Sir William writes:

---

1 R.O. *France*, vol. 150, f. 72, to Sunderland, May 1, 1686.
2 *H.M.C., Downshire MSS.* 1, pp. 88, 139, 140.
3 R.O. *loc. cit.* f. 71, April 27, 1686.
4 *H.M.C., 7th Report*, App., Part 1, pp. 269, 274, 278, 330, 410 (Lord Preston's correspondence).
5 *H.M.C., Downshire MSS.* 1, pp. 39, 82 (Sir David English, Consul at Bordeaux).
6 R.O. *loc. cit.* f. 73, to Sunderland, May 4, 1686.

Mr Fanshaw, his Maj^ties Envoyé Extra^rie returning from Portugall, and desiring to make his Complem^ts to ye most Christian King, I took an opportunitie to present him yesterday; He was receivd very civilly, and will give yor Lo^p an Account, I suppose, by this Post. The King appeares very well and to walke without any Paine.[1]

The same letter brought Sunderland news concerning trade.

Among ye Edicts, wch y^r Lo^p will find inclos'd, that wch concernes us most is ye new Impost upon all Cotton Manufactures, wch were cheifly imported hither from England. The peices of Cotton formerly were tax'd but at 18 sols ye Peice wch consisted of 13 Aulnes, And is now to pay by ye new Edict 6 livres for 10 Aulnes, Which will be ye same thing, in effect, as a totall Prohibition.[2]

Sir William had not yet paid his visit of condolence to Monsieur and Madame. The precedence given the envoy of Spain seemed extraordinary to James, and he desired "a very particular account thereof", not thinking it possible that the court of France, and much less Monsieur, would pretend to regulate things of that nature to his prejudice. How had Sir William heard of this proposed order?[3]

Sir William replies on May 15:

Ye Notice I had that Precedency was intended to be given to ye Spanish Envoyé came from Monsieur Aubert ye Introducteur to Monsieur; who calling att my House on Easter Sunday and not finding me att home, left word with my Suisse and another of my Servants That on Tuesday morning Monsieur would give Audience, to ye Embassadors first and afterwards to ye Envoyés of ye Emper^r and Spaine. Upon this, ye next morning (being indisposd myself with a Fitt of ye Cholick) I sent my Secretarie to Monsr Aubert for some explanation of ye Message he had left for me, Who freely own'd, That if I should be hindred from coming by reason of my being ill, he should be glad of it, since it would avoid Competence and any Dissatisfaction I might receive from ye Envoyé of Spaine's being joynd to ye Envoyé of ye Emper^r, W^ch he said would be don because of ye Allyance between ye Emper^r, Spaine and Monsieur.

1 *Ib.* f. 74, to Sunderland, May 8, 1686.
2 *Ib.* There were 20 sols to the livre, and Sir William in his bills counts 1230 livres to £100. The aune or ell was equivalent to 1·88 metres.
3 H.M.C., *Downshire MSS.* 1, p. 158.

This being so plainly expressd, I thought myself oblig'd to take notice of it and not to go; Besides other Reasons, which having already troubled yor Lo^p with in my former Letters, I shall not repeate. The Envoyés of Swede and Denmarke have not yet gon upon this occasion: The former is departed this Day to take a Voyage into Sweden for this Summer; the Latter expects his Order.

There happned one particular, with which I was not acquainted when I wrott to yor Lo^p upon this Subject, of ye Envoyés Coaches not being permitted to enter into ye Palais Royall: vizt. That ye Emper^{rs} Envoyé finding ye Gates of ye Palais Royal open caus'd his Coach to go in; But when it was known, Orders were given to send it out againe, and after his Audience he was forc'd to take Coach in ye Streete.[1]

The future Duke of Berwick, young James Fitzjames, was about to leave for Buda to join the forces besieging this town that had been occupied by the Turks for many a year. "I have obtain'd a Passeport for Mr FitzJames Equipage;" continues Sir William, "He designs to waite upon ye King today att Versailles, and to begin his Journey tomorrow." [2] And on May 18 he reports: "Mr Fitzjames waited upon ye most Christian King to take his Leave, before he went for Hungarie, (for wch he sett out yesterday from hence). He was very kindly receivd, and was p^rsented with ye Kings Picture sett with Diamonds." [3]

In London this month the hangman burned a book which had given Louis XIV great annoyance, a book by the minister Claude which had been translated into English [4]—*Les Plaintes des Protestants cruellement opprimés dans le Royaume de France*. It was difficult, wrote Barrillon, to express the consternation of the English Protestants. "Il n'est rien arrivé depuis le regne du Roy d'Ang^{re} qui fasse plus d'impression sur les esprits et qui marque davantage que sa resolution est prise de s'attacher aux interests de V.M." [5] Louis XIV assured Barrillon that he was deeply touched by this mark of consideration, and though he could have sent his thanks through Barrillon he bestowed this

1 R.O. *France*, vol. 150, f. 77, to Sunderland, May 15, 1686. "Royal", "Royall", both forms are used. 2 *Ib.*
3 *Ib.* f. 78, to Sunderland, May 18, 1686.
4 H.M.C., *Downshire MSS.* 1, p. 162.
5 A.É. *Angleterre*, vol. 158, ff. 282–3, Barrillon to Louis XIV, May 16, 1686.

task upon Sir William Trumbull,[1] who must have found it a very uncongenial one and disposed of it as quickly as possible. He writes on May 22: "Monsr de Croissy desird me yesterday to assure his Maj^{tie} of ye Sense ye most Christian King has of his Maj^{ties} Justice and Fav^r in ye giving speedy Orders for ye burning of a Booke, complaind of by Monsr Barillon."[2]

On the other hand neither James nor Barillon nor Bonrepaus had been able to hinder the collection taken up in London in behalf of the Huguenots[3], and Sir William must have been cheered by the reports that reached him—2000 *l.* from St Martin's, 1500 *l.* from "the new parish of St James's", 1500 *l.* from St Pauls, Covent Garden, 380 *l.* from "St Lawrence's in the city", and 81 *l.* from "St Matthew's in Friday Street containing but about 116 houses".[4]

Louis XIV had announced that after Whitsuntide he would take a journey to the waters of Barège "upon ye Confines of Spaine, among ye Mountaines, 250 Leagues from hence". It was said that this would take up several months' time, and Sir William inquired whether he was to accompany the court.[5]

"The Popes Nuncio", we hear on May 25, "has been att Versailles to waite upon ye King to know his Pleasure about his following ye Court thither; ye King answerd, That he would not constraine him or any of ye Ministers, but leave y^m att Libertie, But he intended to take none along with him, but such as were absolutely necessarie to attend. I have discours'd with severall of ye forreign Ministers, who are of opinion not to undertake so troublesom and so expensive a Voyage, without receiving Orders from their respective Masters, upon businesse of great Importance.... Madame de Montespagne was very desirous to have beene of ye companie this Journey; but contrarie to her expectation (as I am inform'd) she has receivd Orders to retire."[6]

1 *Ib.* f. 284, Louis XIV to Barrillon, May 24, 1686; cf. f. 305, Barrillon to Louis XIV, May 30, 1686.

2 R.O. *France*, vol. 150, f. 81, to Sunderland, May 22, 1686.

3 A.É. *loc. cit.* f. 116, Barrillon to Louis XIV, Feb. 25, 1686; ff. 126–7, Barrillon to Louis XIV, March 4, 1686; vol. 160, f. 189, Bonrepaus to Seignelay, March 28, 1686.

4 H.M.C., *Downshire MSS.* I, pp. 160, 163, 166; cf. p. 184, where the sums quoted are smaller.

5 R.O. *loc. cit.*

6 *Ib.* f. 82, to Sunderland, May 25, 1686. Dangeau, *Journal*, I. pp. 337–9.

Greatly to the relief of the court the cure did not take place.

The Voyage to yᵉ Waters of Barrege is broke, upon a further Consultation of yᵉ Physitians and Chirurgeons, who were of opinion That yᵉ Season of yᵉ Yeare would be too farre advanc'd before they could arrive there, and that so long a Journey might be very dangerous to yᵉ King; It is said that (att last) it is resolvd to come to yᵉ great Operation.[1]

Monsʳ de Croissy is againe very ill with yᵉ Gout, wᶜʰ obligd him to keepe his Bed yesterday.[2]

On Tuesday, June 4, Sir William was at Versailles, and M. de Croissy received him well.

The Order for yᵉ inlarging of yᵉ Count d'Alby from yᵉ Bastille is expedited; and Monsieur de Croissy told me yesterday, That there was a Valet de pied appointed to accompanie him to Calais, and that he was to begin his Journey this day or to morrow.[3] The most Christian King has been pleasd allso to signe an Arrest de Conseil for yᵉ Revoking his Letters Patents, by wᶜʰ he had granted yᵉ Estate of Mr Lang[4] (his Majᵗⁱᵉˢ late Consul att Marseillis) as belonging to him by vertue of yᵉ Droict d'Aubeine; Which Revocation I hope will be of good consequence to our Merchants trading there,[5] That such of them as happen to die may have yᵉ Power to make their Wills and dispose of their Estates as they shall thinke fitt.[6]

---

1 The operation did not take place till November 18. Dangeau, *Journal*, I, p. 417.

2 R.O. *loc. cit.* f. 83, to Sunderland, May 29, 1686.

3 Cf. *ib.* f. 77, to Sunderland, May 8, 1686. See also A.É. *Angleterre*, vol. 158, f. 271, Louis XIV to Barrillon, May 17, and f. 293, Barrillon to Louis XIV, May 23—James is asking this favour at the request of the prisoner's brother, the Marquis d'Albeville: "C'est un homme dont on peut tirer quelque service et qui m'a donné de bons avis en d'autres temps."

4 Cf. R.O. *loc. cit.* f. 83, to Sunderland, May 29, 1686.

5 The English merchants were always uneasy about the *droit d'aubaine*. There were treaties exempting them, but the application of these was very uncertain. An English merchant, not naturalized, reported that an *échevin* had asked him: "What will become of your goods if you die?" The merchant replied that he had heirs and that there was no longer any *droit d'aubaine*. "I have not heard anything of that", said the Intendant who was present. (*H.M.C., Downshire MSS.* I, p. 92.) English merchants writing to Sir William from Bordeaux explained: "We took letters of naturality by reason of the *droit Daubene*." (*Ib.* p. 46.)

6 R.O. *loc. cit.* f. 86, to Sunderland, June 5, 1686. This matter was, however, far from being settled yet, for the law-courts took up the case next, and it went before the *Parlement* of Aix (*H.M.C., Downshire MSS.* I, p. 219), and six months after Sir William had announced the favourable "Revocation" the English consul at Marseilles was still writing to Sunderland in William Lang's

The newly appointed consul for Marseilles had arrived in Paris. Sir William had written to Sunderland, as we have seen, on the thorny question of consulships, asking him to make a search for precedents, but where a French ambassador would have been given explicit guidance, Sir William had received nothing but an affirmation of James's good pleasure. "His Majesty...directs me to tell you that he knows difficulty has been made in France from time to time about the admission of Consuls, which he sees no good reason for, but till such time as it can be otherwise settled, he intends Mr Burrows should exercise the Consulate in such manner as his predecessor." [1]

From his correspondence Burrow seems to have been a capable man, and he made the sensible suggestion which Sir William reports in this same letter of June 5. "Mr Burrowes is gon for Marseillis; He desird me to forbeare ye making any Applications for his being receivd as Consul there, to Monsr de Croissy, till he had been upon ye Place and receivd further Information." [2] As far as one can judge he pressed for no official recognition, but quietly assumed the office, which he was still exercising some years later as "Consul Burrow". [3]

behalf—he had obtained "not onely an Arrest from his most Christian Maj^tie, but also an Arrest from the Parliament at Aix in his favour", notwithstanding all this he was kept from possessing the estate. R.O. *loc. cit.* f. 174, J. Burrow to Sunderland, Dec. 27, 1686.

1 *H.M.C., Downshire MSS.* 1, p. 162, Sunderland to Trumbull, May 3–13, 1686.
2 R.O. *loc. cit.*
3 *H.M.C., op. cit.* pp. 195, 219, 311.

CHAPTER XI

The Jersey merchants and others

JUNE—JULY

EVER since December Sir William had endeavoured to get permission for a certain Mrs Wilkins to sell her house in Rouen and join her husband, an Englishman who had been naturalized in France, but was now living in England.[1] While she does not seem to have been molested she could not leave, and Sir William heard periodically from her or her husband, the latter suggesting naïvely on one occasion that ten louis be offered to one of M. de Croissy's servants to obtain the release of his wife and children.[2] Twice Sunderland wrote in her behalf.[3] At length, after Sir William had made another attempt in May,[4] relief came in June. "Monsieur de Croissy having spoken to yͤ most Christⁿ King to give permission to Mrs Wilkins and her Children to go for England, tells me he has now obtain it."[5]

"By your means", wrote Mrs Wilkins gratefully, "Gods great Providence hath preserved us out of all danger and peril of being forced to deny his holy name as others have done."[6]

Less reputable than Mrs Wilkins, the prisoner of the Bastille also returned to England.

The Count d'Alby, after having leave to be gon...desird Libertie to stay here for some time to settle his Affaires;[7] wᶜʰ being not granted, he went out of yͤ Bastille on Sunday last, accompanied with

---

1 See pp. 51, 65 *ante*.
2 *H.M.C., Downshire MSS.* I, p. 134; see also pp. 84, 108, 141, 165.
3 R.O. *France, Entry Book* 19, Dec. 21–31, 1685; *H.M.C., op. cit.* p. 162.
4 R.O. *France*, vol. 150, f. 81, to Sunderland, May 22, 1686.
5 R.O. *loc. cit.* f. 89, to Sunderland, June 12, 1686.
6 *H.M.C., op. cit.* I, p. 179.
7 The duc de Brissac owed him a large sum of money. *Ib.* p. 155.

a Valet de pied, who was appointed to see him putt into y⁰ Pacquet Boate att Calais, and to defray his Charges thither.[1]

Another, less fortunate, was carried struggling, tied to a ladder, to the prison of le grand Châtelet.[2] "One Mr Pye (a Son of Sʳ John Pye of Turnam Greene) falling into Distraction, as I am informd, and violent raving fitts, declar'd to several persons That he had a Designe to kill yᵉ French King; upon wᶜʰ he was immediately apprehended and putt into Prison."[3]

A deputation of Jersey and Guernsey merchants waited upon Sir William in this month of June. One of Sir William's brothers-in-law, Philip Dumaresq, "Seigneur of Saumarets", was established in the island of Jersey,[4] and they could hope for a good reception. A misfortune had overtaken them in the time of Lord Preston. They had come to France "time out of mind" to sell their manufactures, returning to their island with commodities and the remainder of their money in species. They had never been stopped under pretext of any edict forbidding the exportation of gold or silver from France, when one day in November 1682, embarking in a little vessel from Normandy with several bags of silver, they were arrested and their money seized by the officers of the *douane*.[5]

Sir William writes on June 15:

Severall Inhabitants of Jersey and Guernezy have lately been with me, to desire me to renew my Instances to yᵉ most Christian King for yᵉ Recovering of some mony (to yᵉ value of about 5097ˡˡ) being yᵉ Proceed of some Merchandises they had sold in France, and wᶜʰ was seiz'd by this Kings Officers at Coutance in November 1682. Yoʳ

1 R.O. *loc. cit.* cf. Ravaisson, *Archives de la Bastille*, VIII, pp. 171–3. A few months later there was some talk of having Alby succeed Castlemaine at Rome. Barrillon used all his influence to hinder this appointment. A.É. *Angleterre*, vol. 159, f. 176, Barrillon to Louis XIV, Sept. 26, 1686; f. 181, Louis XIV to Barrillon, Oct. 4, 1686.

2 B.N. MS. fr. 7052, f. 159: "Cette anglois sapelle Jan paye, Jan pie, John." (Police report.) The boy's mind seems to have been unhinged by the religious troubles he had witnessed.

3 R.O. *loc. cit.*; cf. *H.M.C., Downshire MSS.* I, pp. 39, 163, 174.

4 R.O. *loc. cit.* f. 61.

5 From Lord Preston's report, *H.M.C., 7th Report*, App., Part I, p. 274; see also pp. 274–9 *passim*, and 282; also *H.M.C., Downshire MSS.* I, pp. 16–18.

Lo^p knowes That Application has been formerly made in this matter, without any Effect; so that I thinke fitt not to stirre any further, unlesse his Maj^tie shall be pleas'd to send me any Orders herein.[1]

The long deferred *visite de condoléance* took place on June 22. Sir William had spent 468 livres "for trimming and new fitting the mourning equipage upon the mourning for the Princess Dowager Palatine", and bestowed 137 livres in gratuities to Monsieur's and Madame's coachmen and others.[2] The Introducteur, Monsieur Aubert, came to call for him with all the usual ceremonial.[3]

On Sat^rday I had my Audience att St Clou and deliverd ye Kings and Queenes Maj^ties Letters to Monsieur and Madame, together with ye Excuses for coming no sooner; W^ch were very civilly receivd and ye Complem^ts return^d to their Maj^ties. After wch I thought my self oblig'd to waite upon ye Duc de Chartres and Madamoiselle,[4] Because ye other forreign Ministers (upon this occasion) did the like, For wch though I had no Orders, yet I hope his Maj^tie will not be offended, having therein follow'd ye Example of so many others.

There was one circumstance, of no great moment, yet notice being taken of it, I beg leave to mention it to yor Lo^p; wch was, That both her Maj^ties Letters were directed to Monsieur and Madame, A Versailles. This (as yor Lo^p well knowes) being not very proper, will be easily rectifyd another time.[5]

On Tuesday, June 25, Sir William went to Versailles to see M. de Croissy, as he did almost weekly. At Sunderland's behest[6] he had presented a memorial a month before[7] concerning a native of Canterbury who, established in France, had been imprisoned on account of his religion. Though the man was doubtless of French descent M. de Croissy's answer leaves one confounded by its supreme arbitrariness.

Yesterday, for answer to ye Instances I had formerly made for Isaac le Maihieu (according to his Maj^ties Order in Council, together with a Certificat, wch I receivd of his being borne att Canterburie)

1 R.O. *France*, vol. 150, f. 90, to Sunderland, June 15, 1686.
2 *Cal. Treas. Books*, 1685–9, p. 1220. Cf. p. 117, n. 2.
3 *Gazette de France*, 1686, p. 322.
4 Son and daughter of Monsieur, aged 11 and 9.
5 R.O. *loc. cit.* f. 93, to Sunderland, June 26, 1686.
6 H.M.C., *Downshire MSS.* 1, p. 162.
7 R.O. *loc. cit.* ff. 78 and 81, to Sunderland, May 18 and 22, 1686.

Monsieur de Croissy told me, That ye said Maihieu having establisht himself for 20 yeares, and married himself, and driven a Trade in France, was to be lookt upon as Naturalizd here, and that ye most Christian King would treate him on ye same foot with his other Subjects. I humbly submit it to his Maj^ties consideration and pleasure, how farre this Answ^r may be thought satisfactorie.[1]

James declared himself not satisfied, Sir William was told to continue his instances;[2] the Archbishop of Canterbury interested himself in the case,[3] but no efforts were of any avail.

On this same Tuesday Sir William presented a new memoir. The story of this negotiation will show incidentally how high feeling was running in England. A Dartmouth merchant, John Whitrow by name, had sent his son, a boy of 14 or 15, to Morlaix to learn French in the family of a certain M. de Kergroas, and in exchange Kergroas had sent his young son to Whitrow that he might learn English. In December, waxing very busy "in prepareing for the Newfland ffishery", Whitrow requested that his son might be sent home.[4] The boy did not appear and finally Whitrow heard that he was going to become a Roman Catholic and had entered a monastery. In his "inexpressable trouble" the father wrote a threatening letter to Kergroas.

I have been tender of yor sone and noe way Inticed him to adhere to our Religion and little Expected soe Ill a Requitall. But seeing its soe I doe Resolve yor sone shall never Returne to you: Except you doe take Care to deliver my sone to Mr Mannory y^t hee doe come home wth him I will Imediately send yor Sone into ye Country where he shall be securely kept...and if I have not a sattisfactory ans^r... I will in a little tyme send him as a Sarvant to the West India^s."[5]

François de Kergroas confirmed this news; he was locked up in his room.

Sy Jan Ne vien pas d la Maison... Je sere Envoye hor du Royjome d angleterre dans Des hilles La Ou Je Ne vous voire James Davantage.[6]

1 R.O. *loc. cit.* f. 93, to Sunderland, June 26, 1686.
2 *H.M.C., Downshire MSS.* 1, p. 189.
3 *Ib.* p. 214.
4 R.O. *loc. cit.* f. 49, Whitrow to Kergroas (or Quergroas).
5 *Ib.* f. 51.
6 *Ib.* f. 53.

Barrillon had been told to intervene—"Vithron" had no right to confine young Kergroas, much less to dispatch him as a "servant" to the "islands".[1] Whitrow agreed to send back his charge, but petitioned that his own son be made to return home where he could continue in his new religion.[2] Because of this concession James supported this petition,[3] and Sir William promised to make his instances.[4]

"I send yor Lo^p", he continues on June 26, "a Copie of ye Memorial I gave in yesterday concerning Mr Whitrow's Son. I found that Mr de Quergroos had alreadie represented the matter to Monsieur de Croissie justifying himself for having anything to do either in endeavouring to change his Religion or persuading him to enter into ye Convent; But that it was ye voluntarie choice and resolution of ye Son, To wch I answerd, That supposing it were so (though there were good Reasons to induce his Father to beleive it to have been att ye Instigation of ye said Quergroos), Yet that I thought no Religion could take away from a Child that Obedience he owes to his Parents, Especially att his Age, Since according to ye Council of Trent (wch in this respect is receivd and accordingly practis'd in France) in case ye Son should already have made Profession and taken ye Habit, yet such Profession, before ye Age of 16 is Null and creates no Obligation... Upon wch Monsr de Croissy promisd me to speake to ye King about it, And said That if his friends would appoint any persons to speake with ye young man, they should have all Libertie of accesse to him; But (upon ye whole matter) gave me little hope to expect any Order for his being sent into England, in case he would not consent, but should still persist in his resolution to stay in ye Convent...."[5]

Sunderland had asked for further information concerning the Jersey and Guernsey merchants; accordingly Sir William's next letter, written on June 29, contains a long report on the subject.

---

1 A.É. *Angleterre*, vol. 158, f. 199, Louis XIV to Barrillon, April 16, 1686; f. 248, Barrillon to Louis XIV, April 29, 1686. R.O. *France*, vol. 150, f. 47, petition from Kergroas; f. 48, Statement from John Whitrow, the son; f. 69, Barrillon to James II, April 22, 1686.

2 *H.M.C., Downshire MSS.* 1, p. 160; cf. p. 174.

3 R.O. *France, Entry Book* 19, Sunderland to Trumbull, May 26—June 5, 1686.

4 R.O. *France*, vol. 150, f. 92, to Sunderland, June 22, 1686.

5 R.O. *loc. cit.* f. 93, to Sunderland, June 26, 1686.

I have... yᵉ honour of yoʳ Loᵖˢ of yᵉ 14ᵗʰ Instant [1], and in obedience to yoʳ Loᵖˢ Commands I shall give yoʳ Loᵖ this short Account of what is come to my Knowledge concerning yᵉ Seisure made att Coutance in 1682 of some mony belonging to yᵉ Inhabitants of Jersey and Guernezey.

First, My Lord, it appeares to me (by some publick Acts I have seen attested) That yᵉ Inhabitants of those Islands have time out of mind enjoyd a Libertie of this way of Trade in France, vizᵗ. by carrying back with them such mony in specie as they have made upon yᵉ Sale of their Stockings and other Goods they brought hither.

Secondly, they say, That this mony returnes allwayes back into France, and that yᵉ French who trade into those Islands, bringing thither Wine, Stuffes, Linnen Cloth and yᵉ like, are permitted to transport yᵉ mony they receive there as yᵉ proceed thereof.

They say allso, That if this be hindred, it will be impossible to continue their Commerce in France any longer; There being little or no convenience from Paris or any other Towns, with wᶜʰ they Trade, for Letters of Exchange into yᵉ said Islands.

They thinke it hard, after so long an Usage, to have such a Seizure made, without any previous notice or Prohibition: and hope they may have benefit by yᵉ Treatie of Commerce between yᵉ 2 Crowns in Febʳⁱᵉ 1677. The second Article whereof sayes... That they may traffique in yᵉ Times of Warr with yᵉ same Merchandises wᶜʰ they might in yᵉ time of Peace, Except in those of Contraband, Wᶜʰ (in yᵉ next Article) is explaind, That by Gold and Silver, coynd and not coynd, that sort of Merchandise is not to be understood.[2]

And as to yᵉ reciprocall way of Commerce, they crave yᵉ benefit of yᵉ 16ᵗʰ Article of yᵉ Treatie in yᵉ yeare 1606, by wᶜʰ it is declar'd, Que les Habitans des Isles de Jersey et Guernezey pourront librement et seurement traffiquer dans le Royaume de France, et jouiront en France de pareils Privileges dont les François jouissent esdites Isles.

That wᶜʰ will give some further hopes of yᵉ Restitution of this mony is, That I heare it remaines still att Coutance under Seques-tration, and has not been yet Confiscated and adjudgd to any person; Wᶜʰ if it had, I confesse I should have thought it desperate....

This businesse has been represented severall times to this Court by my Lᵈ Preston in yᵉ yeare 83, and Monsʳ Barrillon was spoken with concerning it: But no favourable answer could be obtain.... [3]

1 Cf. H.M.C., *Downshire MSS.* I, p. 183.
2 Cf. H.M.C., *loc. cit.* p. 16: "The Treaty of Commerce...doth declare silver and gold coined and uncoined to be no contreband." Sir L. Jenkins to Preston, Jan. 1-11, 1682-3.
3 R.O. *France*, vol. 150, f. 95, to Sunderland, June 29, 1686.

Sir William had learned not to engage rashly in lost causes, and cautious as he was he concludes: "I...do most humbly submitt my poor opinion to yor Lo^{ps} Judgem^t, That in case there be not a good Prospect of carrying on this businesse with successe it had much better not be stirrd any more. Yo^r Lo^p will easily find this, if it may be thought fitt to discourse with Monsr Barrillon about it...." [1]

Sunderland sent word to renew instances, [2] M. de Croissy promised to represent the matter to the King and also to write to Barrillon, but nothing was settled before Sir William left, and his successor Skelton was instructed to continue his efforts, [3] which he did with no success. [4]

Sir William was always interested in the doings of his colleagues and in this same letter of June 29 mentions the Dutch ambassador's [5] complaints concerning an action "that happned lately neare Lagos between ye French and Dutch Men of Warre".

"This discourse..occasiond some Heates between ye Dutch Ambassad^r and Monsr de Croissy."—How often Sir William's discourses had occasioned "Heates"!—"A great deale...was said wch would be too tedious to trouble yor Lo^p with, And wch I beleive were exasperated by ye Douäniers at Valenciennes, who opend ye Dutch Ambassad^{rs} Trunkes, in his presence, and tooke out some Bookes, wch he had brought with him for his own use, refusing to deliver them againe: Where of, when he complaind, Monsr de Croissy answerd with other Complaints against him, of having contributed to Monsr de Villarnout's getting out of France, who went with him att his last going into Holland; And further, That severall French Huguenots (whose Names he gave him in Writing) had found a Retreate and were still hid in his House." [6]

---

1 R.O. *France*, vol. 150, f. 95, to Sunderland, June 29, 1686.

2 *H.M.C.*, *loc. cit.* p. 189.

3 R.O. *France*, *Entry Book* 19: "Account of severall particulars...."

4 R.O. *France*, vol. 151, ff. 9 and 17, Skelton to Sunderland, Jan. 29 and Feb. 19, 1687.

5 W. Starrenburg, Baron van Wassenaer (*Recueil des Instructions*..., XXIII, viz. *Hollande*, III, pp. 447–9).

6 R.O. *France*, vol. 150, f. 96, to Sunderland, June 29, 1686; cf. *H.M.C.*, *Downshire MSS.* I, p. 193. On the role played by foreign ambassadors at the time of the Revocation of the Edict of Nantes see Douen, *La Révocation...à Paris*, vol. II, especially pp. 429–34. See also Spanheim's *Relation*.

Sir William's own house was closely watched, and no one could attend his chaplain's services without being reported.[1]

Mr Whitrow's petition received due consideration, though it is not probable that anything came of it.

Concerning Mr Whitrow's Son, Monsieur de Croissy has sent to Morlay to enquire his Age and other circumstances; ye most Christian King being desirous (as he said) to give his Maj^{tie} satisfaction, that he may be discharg'd from ye Convent and sent home to his Parents.[2]

Another intervention also met with justice.

An English vessell, ye St George, having been lately Arrested att Rochell, with ye Master and Seamen, upon pretence that they designd to favour ye escape of some French, I made my Instances for their being discharg'd; and upon Examination they being found innocent of any such attempt, Orders were given that ye Ship and men should be Releas'd.[3]

A very strict watch was kept over English boats, and one finds a young man complaining to Sir William that in spite of a passport and twenty certificates that he was English he had been imprisoned, liberated, and imprisoned again elsewhere. "The pretext is that an English master of a ship had carried French Protestants to England and that there is an order to arrest him."[4]

"I have very little, by this Ordinarie, to adde to my last", writes Sir William on July 6, and having no very serious news to give, he indulges in one of his rare anecdotes. At this time preparations were being made for the opening of the institution founded by Mme de Maintenon for the education of young gentlewomen of slender means, Saint-Cyr. Part of the endowment of the new school was to be derived from the income of the Abbaye of Saint-Denis.[5]

It happned, that ye Courier extra^{rie} who brought ye Newes of ye Brevet from Rome for ye imploying ye Revenues of ye Abbaye de S^t

1 A.N. O^1 30, Seignelay to La Reynie, Aug. 13, 1686.
2 R.O. *loc. cit.* f. 97, to Sunderland, July 3, 1686.
3 *Ib.*
4 H.M.C., *op. cit.* p. 174.
5 Cf. Dangeau, *Journal*, I, pp. 346–7.

Denis for ye new erected Monasterie of Madame de Maintenon, was met with by Monsieur de Seignelay, who tooke ye Pacquet, opend it and carried ye newes to ye King. Monsr de Croissy takes this as a great Invasion of his Province, complaines highly of it, and has causd him to expresse great Resentments ag^t Monsr de Seignelay upon this occasion.[1]

That M. de Croissy did not get on too well with his nephew was public knowledge.

Sir John Pye's request for the liberation of his son did not meet with too much sympathy from Sir William.

"I am informd from England," he continues in this letter of July 6, "That Sr John Pye and severall others have made their applications to obtaine an order directed to me to procure ye Releasing of his son, of whome I gave yor Lo^p an account formerly. It does no wayes become me to pretend to the setting any Bounds to his Maj^{ties} Goodnesse in behalf of any of his Subjects; And besides I beleive Mr Pye was highly distemperd when he spoke those wordes, and (since his being in Prison) has declard he was att that time in a Feavour; However since Fooles and Madmen may be lookt upon as dangerous and are often-times found to execute their Designes, I doubt not but yor Lo^p will reflect upon ye whole Case, and ye difficulties that must attend anyone in my Circumstances, to whome such an Order shall be sent...."[2]

John Pye was interned at the Château of Saumur,[3] and whether he was ever allowed to leave is doubtful.

There were always plenty of young Englishmen in Paris to be looked after—Henry Fitzjames at the Collège Louis le Grand who shared with Sir William some of his brother's letters from Hungary;[4] Sir Thomas Exton's son, who did not wait on Sir William as often as his father would have liked him to do;[5] Mr Charles Butler, his Grace of Ormond's grandson, to whom Sir William showed many civilities, befriending him in a long illness;[6] My Lord Orrery, who lodged rue de Seine with his Governor and servants;[7] Sir Archibald Kennedy,

---

1 R.O. *France*, vol. 150, f. 98, to Sunderland, July 6, 1686; cf. Sourches, *Mémoires*, I, pp. 442–3. Dangeau is less well informed, *Journal*, I, p. 357.
2 R.O. *loc. cit.*   3 A.N. O¹ 30, ff. 190, 200, 220, 239.
4 H.M.C., *Downshire MSS.* I, pp. 190–1, 195, 204–5, 222.
5 *Ib.* pp. 121, 167, 192.   6 *Ib.* pp. 159, 178.
7 B.N. MS. fr. 7053, f. 382.

nephew of George, Earl of Dumbarton;[1] Lord William Savile, returning from Spain—"I could fill a letter with my thanks for your kindness to my son Will. whilst he stayed in Paris", wrote Halifax;[2] the son of Thomas Windsor, Earl of Plymouth;[3] the Duke of St Albans attending "l'Académie du Sr Coulon";[4] Mr Primrose, a young Scottish gentleman of eighteen or nineteen, who, one hopes, learned a lesson in Lord Preston's day and no longer consorted with Portuguese gamblers.[5] There were doubtless others.

Many travellers, as we have seen, waited upon Sir William— "My Lord Chancell^{rs} brother Mr Jefferies his Maj^{ties} Consul at Alicant", on his way from Spain to England;[6] Mr Montague North, on his way from Constantinople,[7] "My Lord Hintchingbroke, Sr John Lydcott, allso Mr Rogers",[8] Mr St George Ashe, Fellow and later Provost of Trinity College, Dublin, an excellent preacher ("They are grown so zealous in France that it may not be fit for a man of his profession to stay there long");[9] "Mr Cottereau", who came to procure wines, plants and flowers for James II;[10] the Bishop of Ely's "Uncle Windebanke"[11] and the Bishop's wife, whom Sir William attended when she went to call on the Bishop's aunt, a nun at the Couvent des Filles du Calvaire, who prayed for the conversion of her nephew.[12]

To those who were ill Sir William seems to have been a good friend—there was Sir William Clifton, "a hopeful young gentleman", carried off by a malignant fever;[13] there was Sir

1 H.M.C., op. cit. p. 138. 2 Ib. p. 200; cf. pp. 136, 191.
3 Ib. p. 187.
4 Ib. p. 55, A.É. Angleterre, vol. 160, f. 341, La Reynie to Seignelay, Sept. 17, 1686.
5 H.M.C., 7th Report, App., Part I, p. 410; Downshire MSS. I, pp. 191, 209.
6 R.O. France, vol. 150, f. 94.
7 H.M.C., Downshire MSS. I, p. 183.
8 R.O. loc. cit., f. 86. Sir John was Secretary to Lord Castlemaine. See also H.M.C., op. cit. p. 173. 9 Ib. p. 166.
10 Ib. pp. 123–4; cf. p. 125, a mysterious letter from the Bishop of London. As Cottereau was a Protestant and was imprisoned later in the Bastille on the suspicion that he helped his French countrymen (Haag, France Protestante, IV, p. 77), one wonders whether the Bishop's letter contains a reference to some such errand.
11 Ib. p. 175. 12 Ib.
13 Ib. pp. 165, 176; R.O. France, vol. 150, f. 77.

William Stapleton, who required legal aid "during his last sicknesse";[1] there was the nephew of Sir Stephen Fox, Paymaster of the Forces, to whom Sir William extended much kindness in a mortal illness, and doubtless he carried out the family's request to have him interred as well as this sad conjuncture permitted.[2]

"I know your charity is such", the Earl of Clarendon once remarked, "that without any recommendation you would shew all kindness to your countrymen whom you meet abroad."[3]

All manner of services were requested of Sir William. The Lord Chancellor, as we have seen, ordered laces, bands and ruffles,[4] William Blathwayt, Secretary at War, required military *ordonnances* and documents that related to the Hôtel des Invalides—if Sir William could procure edicts and regulations concerning the government and economy of that place they would be of great use in the model of government for Chelsea Hospital His Majesty was now ordering to be prepared; this was not all, he would be glad to have also "an account of the rank and command in all places of the Marshals of France, Lieut.-Generals, *Maréchaux de Camp*, Lieut.-Generals of the Artillery and in short of all the considerable officers in the French Army".[5]

The Duke of Grafton desired him to arrange for the dispatch of pictures, books, hangings and cabinets, "all old".[6] Henry Baron Grey of Ruthin complained that the Intendant at Rouen had seized a box of clothes he was having forwarded to England,[7] and a certain Mr Whitley asked him to deal with a woman who opened his letters and had all his clothes in pawn, 400*l.* sterling's worth.[8] Dr James Fraser wanted some boxes of books and papers to be sent over with the Duchess of Portsmouth, to be directed two for Lord Sunderland, one for Lord Middleton, and one for Mr Bridgeman, Lord Sunderland's secretary.[9]

---

1 See p. 156 *post.*
2 H.M.C., *op. cit.* pp. 150, 170. The Index to this Report suggests that the name of this nephew was Giles Thornborro (?), King's Chaplain.
3 *Ib.* p. 166.　　4 *Ib.* pp. 135, 150.　　5 *Ib.* pp. 140, 163.　　6 *Ib.* p. 157.
7 *Ib.* p. 128.　　　8 *Ib.* pp. 180–1.　　　9 *Ib.* pp. 147–8.

Sir Robert Southwell sent him, for distribution in Paris, 200 copies of an Éclaircissement which the Jansenist Arnauld had had printed in order to correct some statements of his *Apologie des Catholiques* detrimental to Sir Robert's reputation.[1] Sir William's friend, Rupert Brown, wanted him to intercede for leave, already refused, to have the body of his Cousin Onely Vernon brought over from Blois, where he was buried, that he might lie with his ancestors in Sudbury, Derbyshire.[2]

From French Protestants came requests which Sir William had no power to fulfil. Marie du Chail, appointed laundress of the royal table linen in 1682,[3] appealed from London in behalf of her son, in prison at Fontenay, where her house had been pillaged by dragoons.[4] Marie de Drevon, a lady of Orange, wrote from her fourth prison to ask for aid for herself and Mlle Allix, sister of the former minister at Charenton.[5] "M. de Bergairolle" wanted the release of his two daughters from the convent of the Miséricorde at Arles, where they had been forcibly placed by the authority of the Bishop of Orange.[6] A minister settled in England begged him to get permission from M. de Croissy to sell his small estate in Languedoc—he was supporting three families in England.[7] A certain de Manes (?) wrote from St Malo gaol—he had been in prison at Caen for eleven months for undertaking to send three paper-makers to some works which he had with Messrs Cardonnel, Dupin and Gruchy near Southampton. Being released he wanted to go to Southampton, but had been arrested again.[8] Mme de Villeret wanted help to leave the country with an English family.[9]

Did Sir William ever do anything but "drudge at business" to use his own expression? Did he have any pastimes? Did

---

1 *Ib.* pp. 156, 158.
2 *Ib.* pp. 140–1, 151, 178; A.N. O¹ 30, f. 175, Seignelay to the Lieutenant-General of Blois, May 16, 1686, granting permission.
3 *H.M.C., 7th Report*, App., Part I, pp. 357, 372.
4 *H.M.C., Downshire MSS.* I, p. 82.
5 *Ib.* p. 119; cf. Douen, *La Révocation...à Paris*, III, pp. 2–3, 107–8.
6 *Ib.* p. 91.
7 *Ib.* pp. 82, 102, 115, 147, 148. J. J. Gachy to Trumbull.
8 *Ib.* pp. 157–8.   9 *Ib.* p. 88.

he go to the play? What of "our Lady Ambassadrice", as the Archbishop of York called her?[1]

One sees nothing of Sir William's private life except a bill for doctors and apothecaries, charged to the Treasury as one of his "extraordinaries",[2] and some evidence that he was interested in carrousels—allegorical tournaments in which ladies and cavaliers, divided into companies called quadrilles, performed various figures. On May 27 the duc de Saint-Aignan sent him two tickets for the carrousel to take place next day at the King's dinner-hour, shortly after two. The Duke would be on horseback himself and could do no more for Sir William. The scaffolding was exposed to the sun, and parasols were desirable, he said.[3] The subject was the story of Alexander and Thalestris, Queen of Amazons. Sixty rode in this carrousel, not counting the attendants, and Sir William and Lady Trumbull could admire the Dauphin as Alexander and the Duchess of Bourbon as Thalestris.[4]

In August Sir William must have reminded the Duke to send him tickets, for the Duke replies, no, he had not forgotten the places for the carrousel. As it would be in the Grande Écurie Monsieur le Grand Écuyer, le comte d'Armagnac, would settle them, but Sir William's rank and merit would be distinguished.[5]

1 H.M.C. Downshire MSS. 1, p. 48.
2 Cal. Treas. Book, 1685–9, p. 1221.
3 H.M.C., op. cit. p. 169.
4 For a description see Sourches, Mémoires, 1, pp. 387–94. Sir William sent home a copy of the "Ordre du Carrousel avec la liste des Cavaliers et des dames qui le composent". R.O. France, vol. 150, f. 56.
5 H.M.C., op. cit. p. 208.

CHAPTER XII

Another deadlock

JULY

ALL Sir William Trumbull's letters were hitherto addressed to Lord Sunderland, "my Lord President", as he came to be, but suddenly a letter was written to James II, and sent by a special courier. Sir William had received a message that left him utterly dumbfounded.

Paris, July 9, S.N. 1686

May it please yoᵣ most Excellent Majestie

Monsieur Bonneuil, yᵉ Introductᵣ of Ambassadᵣˢ, came to me just now with this Message, which I tooke in writing from him, and therefore shall deliver it to yoᵣ Majᵗⁱᵉ in his own wordes, Que le Roy ne pretend pas que les François qui sont de la Religion¹ jouissent des memes Privileges aupres des Ministres Etrangers que ceux qui n'en sont pas et qui sont á leurs Services.

I thought this of so extraordinarie a Nature that I have dispatcht a Courier with this Expresse to go to yoᵣ Majᵗⁱᵉ; to whome alone I am to submitt as my Judge, and by whose Countenance and Protection, as I have hitherto, so I hope still I may enjoy that which is due to yᵉ Character yoᵣ Majᵗⁱᵉ (out of yoᵣ owne meere goodnesse and favour) has been pleas'd to Honour me with.

I shall say but little to yoᵣ Majᵗⁱᵉ on this Subject, because I know yoᵣ Majᵗⁱᵉ is fully acquainted with that unquestionable Right, which forreign Ministers have enjoyd in respect of their Domestiques by the Lawes and Practise of all Nations, even yᵉ most Barbarous.

Onely as to my owne Case in particular I most humbly beg leave to observe,

That since my coming hither, no one has endeavourd to carrie himself with greater Respect and Submission to yᵉ most Christian King, his Ministers and his Edicts, than I have don: Having from the time that his Subjects of yᵉ Religion were lookt upon by him as Criminal never allowd them any Refuge in my House, nor granted

---

¹ Protestante.

any Passeports to favour their Escape; In a word, I have not followd the Examples of severall others of ye Publick Ministers, who thought they might extend their Priviledges upon ye like occasions.

When I came out of England, I brought as many English Servants with me, as I had any occasion for, on purpose to avoid all Cavils; And tooke no more French than were of absolute necessitie in my Family, because of ye Language.

A French Secretarie was of that indispensable use to me, that I was glad to meete with one who had servd my Lord Preston before in the same qualitie; And whome I have since found to be a person of such approov'd integritie and understanding in these affaires, that I can neither hope to dispatch my businesse without him, or to find another whome I can so much rely upon. And I have but 7 or 8 other French Servants; whome allso having found honest and fitt for my service, I shall thinke very hard to turne away and to be forc'd to take Strangers.

But, may it please yor Maj^tie, it is evident, That pursuant to this Message Orders will be given and executed to seize upon and take away these Servants perhaps as they go abroad with me, in case I do not immediately discharge them. This I durst not do; For (as I humbly offerd before) I acknowledge no Jurisdiction or Tribunal but yor Maj^ties. And therefore I would presume to hope for a speedie and a favourable Answer, That yor Maj^tie would protect me in this known and undoubted Right, which I am ye more encouragd to expect, having been informd of what yor Maj^tie lately did in behalf of Mr Stamford:[1] And allso, because the onely Colour they can give for their Proceeding here is, That Notice is to be given to all ye French Ministers in forreign Courts to submitt to ye like Orders of other Princes. Which prooves no more, than that if others will contradict ye Lawes and Practise receivd in all Nations, as well as they do, then one unjustifyable action may be warranted by another.

But because it does not become me to search into yor Maj^ties Councils, nor to presume to know wheth^r yor Maj^tie, in yor own most Excellent Wisedom and Judgment, may thinke fitt to grant my Request, Therefore I onely crave leave to throw my self att yor Maj^ties Feet and most humbly to implore yor gracious Pardon, in confessing,

That since this matter will be discoursd of in all Parts, and yor Maj^ties honour (which shall be allwayes dearer to me than my Life) may be reflected upon in ye Reproach cast upon yor poor Minister,

1 The Roman Catholic Resident of the Elector Palatine whose chapel in the city had been attacked. Cf. A.É. *Angleterre*, vol. 158, ff. 194, 320-1, Barrillon to Louis XIV, April 8 and June 6, 1686.

Since ye losse of my necessarie Servants, especiallie my Secretarie, will be so great, as to disenable me very much to serve yor Maj^tie as I ought to desire to do in this Station;

I do againe beseech yor Maj^tie with ye deepest humilitie to countenance and secure me in ye Just Possession of my Rights in point of my Domestiques;

Or if yor Maj^tie shall judge it as an Expedient, that you would be pleasd to Recall me home againe; Where I will attend yor Maj^ties Commands in any Service I may be capable of; Or else yor Leave to retire againe to my poor Profession. In what Condition soever I am, I will continue to ye last Moment of my Life,

May it please yor Maj^tie,

> Yo^r Maj^ties most dutifull, most
> loyall and most devoted Subject
> and Servant
>
> WILL: TRUMBULL.[1]

A letter to Sunderland accompanied the letter to James II.

> Paris, July 9, S.N. 1686.
> 12. att night

...My Lord, this afternoon (having been before with Monsr de Croissy) Monsieur Bonneuïl came to me, and told me That Monsr de Croissy had forgott to deliver to me a Message which he had by Order of ye most Christian King.

And repeating the message Sir William continues:

I am informd, That Monsieur de Croissy spoke ye same to ye Envoyés of Denmarke and Brandenburgh, and has expressely declard, That all their French Domestiques of ye Religion should not be lookt upon Protected by their Character during their stay in their Service: And ye wordes are very plaine to y^t purpose.

After giving the substance of his letter to James II he concludes:

I have nothing further to adde, but to beg of yor Lo^p a Speedie Answer of his Maj^ties Commands to me, Because I have reason to apprehend some of my Domestiques may be every day seizd upon, even as they go abroad with me.[2]

---

1 R.O. *France*, vol. 150, ff. 99–100, to James II, July 9, 1686.
2 *Ib.* f. 101, to Sunderland, July 9, 1686.

A few days later, on July 13, he wrote again to Sunderland. His letter demolished the one argument that might have made James yield to France.

Having since considerd of ye Account I gave yor Lo^p of ye Message receivd concerning ye French Domestiques of ye Religion, and having conferrd with severall of ye Publick Ministers, I find so many ill Consequences and Inconveniencies will follow, if this be once forc'd upon us, And besides those of ye Catholique Ministers, with whome I have spoken, being of opinion, That this is so great a Violation of ye Lawes of Nations and ye known Rights of all Ministers, And that it is by no meanes to be lookd upon as an affaire of Religion, but of ye Priviledges due to ye Character, that they are equally concernd with the Protestant Ministers in this case; And (on my owne particular) having carried myself since my being here and allso oblig'd all my Domestiques to their Duty; so as not to give ye least offence either to ye State or ye Establisht Religion of ye Countrie, I humbly crave leave to hope for his Maj^ties Protection.[1]

Sir William expected to have his chapel prohibited next,[2] and an edict was published a few days later[3] that gave him further uneasiness.

17 July 1686. ... I send yor Lo^p ye Declaration inclosd; wherein are some Articles, wch may be severely Interpreted against some English Ministers, that may alreadie be here, or may hereafter come over as Gouvern^rs to English Gentlemen.[4] But that wch cheifly concernes myself, and wherein I most humbly beg yor Lo^ps Directions, is to know what measures my Chaplain[5] ought to take, and

1 R.O. *loc. cit.* f. 103, to Sunderland, July 13, 1686.
2 *H.M.C.*, *Downshire MSS.* I, p. 229.
3 "Déclaration du Roy du 1er juillet 1686. ... Registrée en Parlement le 12 juillet 1686." Pilatte, *Édits*, pp. 291–4.
4 "I. Nous défendons à tous Ministres de la R.P.R. tant François qu'Etrangers de rentrer dans notre Royaume, Païs, et Terres de notre obéissance pour quelque raison et prétexte que ce puisse être, sans notre permission par écrit, et en cas qu'il s'en trouve, soit de ceux qui y seroient rentrez, ou qui y seroient restés au préjudice dudit Edit, voulons qu'ils soient punis de mort." *Ib.* p. 292.
5 "IV. Entendons néanmoins que les Ministres de la dite R.P.R. qui ne seront point nos sujets, lesquels sont en service des Ambassadeurs ou Envoyez des Princes Etrangers et Républiques, qui sont ou seront cy-après, près de Nous, puissent y demeurer sans aucun trouble ni empêchement tant qu'ils ne feront aucune fonction ni exortation hors l'enceinte des logemens desdits Ambassadeurs ou Envoyez." *Ib.* pp. 292–3.

whether he may not have ye Libertie to visit such of ye English as shall happen to fall sick in this Towne.[1]

Sir William gives little general news in these letters—the one thing uppermost in his mind excludes all other interest—but there is one significant remark. "Newes is brought from Marseillis of ye Death of Sr William Soames, wch I am extreamely sorrie for. I durst not, without my Ld Chancell^rs assistance, addresse my humble Petition to yor Lo^p; Which both in that and all my other concernes I shall ever submit to yor Lo^ps better Judgem^t."[2] Sir William Soames, who had died at Malta on June 12,[3] was on his way to Constantinople as Ambassador,[4] and what Sir William Trumbull means by his "Petition" will be gathered from a later letter.

Sir William refrained from going to Versailles until he should receive instructions from England. About a fortnight after he had dispatched his first letter an answer came. The King thought it best that he should come over to England for a month.

Accordingly he would have you let Monsieur de Croissy know that you have leave to make a step hither for some short time and that you intend to carry such French Protestant servants with you as you brought out of England, that his Majesty hopes and expects no interruption should be given to you herein, but that your said servants may have full liberty to come with you, his Majesty thinking it but reasonable that they should be put in the same condition they were when you took them into your service.

M. de Barrillon had been acquainted with this. James thought this the best expedient "because in the time of Oates' pretended plot it was the opinion of the lawyers here that no Foreign Minister could protect any servant who was a subject of his Majesty from the laws of the country". Finally Sir William was to manage the matter with all privacy, and so that it might be thought he came over only on his private affairs.[5] But as

---

1 R.O. *France*, vol. 150, f. 104, to Sunderland, July 17, 1686.
2 *Ib.*   3 *H.M.C., Downshire MSS.* 1, p. 196.
4 A. C. Wood, "The English Embassy at Constantinople." *English Historical Review*, October 1925, p. 544.
5 *H.M.C., op. cit.* p. 192, Sunderland to Trumbull, July 4–14, 1686.

Barrillon reported everything that had been decided there was not much privacy possible.

He had been approached in the matter, Barrillon said— James had thought it most unusual, but he, Barrillon, had replied that in the time of the Popish Plot there had been some talk of preventing ambassadors from having English servants of a religion other than the one established; this proposed restriction had not been put into force, nevertheless it was evidence of a claim that no subject should be exempt from the laws of the country—besides there was really no necessity for an English minister to have French Protestant servants. James had seemed to acquiesce—he had not yet received Sir William's later letters—he thought only that Trumbull should be allowed to return with the servants he had brought from England, otherwise his royal word would be involved, and falling back on his usual argument he invoked the inevitable harm done to the progress of Catholicism by popular resentment in England. "Cela feroit un fort grand bruit en ce pays-cy et nuiroit aux desseins qu'il a pour le restablissem^t de la Religion Catholique." Trumbull's first long letter had been read at a meeting of the Privy Council, and the Lord Chancellor had agreed that at the time of the Popish Plot the judges had declared no English subject exempt from law on the ground that he was servant to an ambassador. Trumbull was to be recalled for a month, supposedly for his private affairs. However Barrillon did not think that Trumbull would be sent back, nor would he wish to return to France—in that case a Catholic would be sent in his place. Barrillon added that Sunderland had come to see him once more with a message—people would say it was the fault of the King of England if Trumbull were not allowed to return with his servants.[1]

As soon as Sir William had received Sunderland's letter he went to Versailles, on July 22, although it was not the regular day for the reception of ambassadors. He returned discouraged—the matter promised to be as much of a deadlock as the affairs of Orange and the Rye fishermen.

[1] A.É. *Angleterre*, vol. 159, ff. 31–4, Barrillon to Louis XIV, July 15, 1686.

"I should not so soone have importun'd yor Maj[tie] againe," he wrote the next day, "if I thought the businesse of my French Protestant Servants concern'd onely my self; But having seriously considerd of this matter, and being exceedingly jealous of yo[r] Maj[ties] Honour, which will be reflected upon in case any Violence be offerd to my Domestiques, and having just reason to apprehend some Insulte may suddenly be offerd, I take y[e] boldnesse once more to implore yo[r] Maj[ties] Directions what measures I shall take herein.

According to yo[r] Maj[ties] Commands, signifyd to me by my Lord Presidents Letter of y[e] 4th Instant, I went yesterday to Versailles; And punctually observing y[e] Secrecie therein injoynd me, I acquainted Monsieur de Croissy, That I had obtaind yo[r] Maj[ties] Permission to go to England for a short time upon my owne Private affaires, and that I intended to take with me some few French Servants for y[e] Journey, such onely as I brought with me out of England; And that I was commanded to lett him know That yo[r] Maj[tie] hop'd and expected that no Interruption should be given me herein.

I took y[e] Libertie to explaine y[e] Reasons of this Request in this following method;[1]

First, That before my coming out of England I spoke of these Servants to Monsieur Barrillon and acquainted him That I intended to take but 3 or 4 along with me (according to y[e] Necessitie of my Affaires) And accordingly desird him to write for a Passeport from y[e] most Christian King for their Goods equally with my own; Which he obtaind. And this I thought amounted to a Permission, And so ought in Justice to have y[e] Effect I desird.

2[dly] I said, That some of them (naming my Secretary) had servd my Predecess[r] here, and returnd with him into England; And therefore I thought I could not be refusd y[e] same, Which I the rather made bold to insist upon, having y[e] Honour to find yo[r] Maj[ties] Opinion concurre with mine, That it is but reasonable they should be putt in y[e] same Condition they were when I tooke them into my Service.

3. Att that time there was no Prohibition from this King; but on y[e] contrarie an expresse Declaration, That those of ye Religion might freely stay in his Countrie as they did before; Provided they did not publickly exercise their Religion. For in ye same Edict, wch revokes that of Nantes, are these wordes, Pourront au surplus lesdits de la R.P.R. (en attendant qu'il plaise á Dieu les eclairer comme les autres) demeurer dans les Villes et Lieux de notre Royaume,

1 Cf. *H.M.C.*, *Downshire MSS.* 1, pp. 228–9.

Païs et Terres de notre obeïssance et y continuer leur commerce et jouir de leurs biens, sans pouvoir etre troublés ni empechés sous pretexte de ladite Religion.[1]

So that having taken them into my Service and they becomming my Domestiques sur la bonne Foy of this Kings owne Declaration, I thought I could not be obligd to turne them out, nor be forcd to it, contrarie to y⁰ Lawes of Nations, which give these Priviledges to all Forreign Ministers to Protect their Servants (who are not Criminals against y⁰ State) without considering what Religion or Countrie they are of.

4ᵗʰˡʸ I mentiond my particular Respect (ever since my being here) that I had shewn to y⁰ most Christian King, his Ministers and his Lawes (wᶜʰ he readily did me the Justice to own) and in keeping all my owne Servants within such Bounds, that no Complaint could be made against any of them for having offended against y⁰ State or y⁰ Establisht Religion of y⁰ Countrie.

And therefore (upon y⁰ whole matter) I could not but expect, That both in consideration of y⁰ Instances I made in yoʳ Majᵗⁱᵉˢ Name, and upon y⁰ Reason and Justice of y⁰ matter, and my own Circumspection in relation to my Conduct, That y⁰ most Christian King would distinguish my Circumstances and grant my Request.

He promis'd me to represent all these Particulars to y⁰ King his Master; And att last returning surpriz'd me with this Answer, That y⁰ King having made a Generall Rule, and having been troubled with matters of y⁰ like Nature from other Ministers (though att y⁰ same time he confess'd my case was different) he would not be troubled any more, nor change his Orders, nor either suffer any of my French Servants to go into England[2] with me, or to enjoy his Protection whilst they stayed here in my Service. That it would be to no purpose to trouble him any further with this; For it was his firme Resolution and he would not depart from it.

I confesse I expected something of Reason; But I met with nothing but absolute Will and Pleasure: onely he told me a Storie of his own Case"—Sir William's narrative goes back to M. de Croissy—"That when he was Ambassadʳ in England[3] he tooke butfewEnglish

---

1 Pilatte, *Édits*, pp. 244–5. For this misleading article of the edict revoking the Edict of Nantes see Lavisse, *Histoire de France*, VIII¹, p. 351, and *Bulletin de l'Histoire du Protestantisme*, 1894, pp. 172–3.

2 Foreign envoys were always suspected of wishing to pass off refugees as part of their suite. Thus Lord and Lady Preston had been accused of planning to take over French refugees disguised as their servants. Douen, *La Révocation...à Paris*, II, p. 430.

3 From 1668–74.

servants, and those were of yᵉ Religion of yᵉ Countrie: Which signifyd little to my Purpose; For besides his doing therein as he thought fitt for his own Convenience (being under no Constraint) He might much better be without English Servants in London, where all his businesse, even att Court, is done in his own Language; Than I can be here without French Servants, where all my Memorials and Affairs att this Court are to be in French."

And passing on to the argument provided unbeknown to him by Barillon he continues:

That which my Lord President mentions in his Letter, vizt. That in yᵉ time of Oates' pretended Plott it was yᵉ opinion of yᵉ Lawyers in England, That no Forreign Minister could Protect any Servant who was a Subject of yᵉ Kings by yᵉ Lawes of yᵉ Countrie, I humbly crave to answer,

(1) This was in a troublesome and tumultuous Time when yᵉ Lawyers (att least many of them) thought it would passe for merit to Persecute yᵉ Roman Catholiques right or wrong; And good Presidents do not usually come from such bad times.

(2) I cannot thinke this was yᵉ opinion of any Learned Civilians; because they must needs (upon consideration) know this to be contrarie to yᵉ Lawes of Nations.

(3) I neither thinke that Monsʳ Barillon or any other Publick Ministers then in England were forced to remoove their necessarie Domestiques hereupon: Or in case they did, That they were satisfyd with yᵉ Law and yᵉ Equitie of such Proceeding.

And lastly, Practise (wᶜʰ is yᵉ best Interpreter of all Lawes) has constantly gon along with this Priviledge, As I could easily shew (would it not be too tedious) in multitudes of Examples, And particularly, in those of yᵉ French Publick Ministers residing in severall Princes Courts, And of them (not long agoe) that were sent from this Court to Venice and Genoua, where they Protected even Criminals against those States, upon the account of being their Domestiques, And yet were sustaind by this King their Master in the doing thereof, and full Reparations made them upon yᵉ least pretence of any Insulte.

May it therefore please yoʳ most Gracious Majᵗⁱᵉ, I throw myself upon yoʳ Royall Mercie, beseeching you to permitt me to speake my Opinion: with all humble Submission to yoʳ Will and Pleasure:

According as this King Proceeds against his Subjects of the Religion (going on every day from one Severitie to another) There are so many Inconveniencies will befall any Protestant Minister yoʳ

Majtie shall send hither, that I cannot see how yor Majtie can be free from continuall Trouble and Complaints.

Instead of many, I will instance but in a few, and so conclude this tedious scribble. One is, That in case of mixture of Servants of diverse Religions, if those of ye Roman Catholiques happen to fall sick and consequentially ye Holy Sacrament be brought to them, those of ye other opinion do too often commit some Irreverence, for wch ye Master cannot be Responsable. And it so happned in ye Case of one of ye Domesticks of Sir Willm Lockhart whilst he was Ambassedr [1] here from his late Majtie who having a Roman Catholique sick and desiring ye Sacrament, his other Servants shutt ye Doores against it, And occasiond such a Tumult thereupon, as expos'd his House and his Character to ye greatest Affront imaginable.

In ye next Place, If I should take any new Converts for Servants, and they should come to my Chappell (as perhaps some of them would, not being well satisfyd in their Consciences of what they did upon Force) They would incurre ye Penalties of ye Edicts of Relapse; and so be seizd on by ye Magistrate and carried to Prison; Which must either cause an Inquisition in ones House before a Servant can be admitted, or else inevitably expose one to difficulties of ye like Nature.

Lastly, by this Kings Declaration of ye 12th Instant, all Ministers, as well Strangers as French found in this Kingdom are punisht with Death, with a reward of 5500 Livres to ye Discoverers; with a Permission notwithstanding to such Ministers as shall serve any Ambassadrs or Envoyez to be free, Tant qu'ils ne feront aucune fonction ni exhortation hors l'enceinte des Logemens desdits Ambassadeurs ou Envoyez.

So that in case my Chaplain should go out of my Precincts to visit any English lying sick in ye Towne, he is lyable to ye Penaltie. And it is very plain, That as not long since they have denyd yor Majties Protestant Subjects ye Rights of Sepulture, So by this new Declaration, all English Gentlemen and others, travelling and falling sick here, can have no Offices of Prayer or Sacraments administred to them; But they must be contented neither to Dye like Christians, nor to be Buried like Men.

I humbly implore yor Majties gracious Pardon for this boldnesse I have taken; And do with ye deepest humility assure yor Majesty, That nothing but ye serious consideration of yor Majties Reputation

1 1673–5. Firth and Lomas, *Notes on Diplomatic Relations*, pp. 22–3. See also pp. 15–16.

in sustaining ye just Rights of yor Minister, together with ye Reflexions I make upon ye little regard shown to such a Request made in yor Maj^ties Name....And ye Desire I have rather to Live in ye meanest Condition with credit, then in ye greatest with dishonour, proceeding from a Heart full of Zeal and Fidelitie to yor Maj^ties Service, could have made me thus troublesome to yor Maj^tie.[1]

A note to Sunderland accompanied this letter and explains a former allusion to Sir William Soames.

I did not thinke fitt to go to Versailles till yesterday, staying for ye coming of ye Post; that Monsr de Croissy might have Monsr Barillon's Letter deliverd to him before I moovd ye business to him.

I obeyd ye Contents of yor Lo^ps Letter; and urg'd severall Reasons to make my Request appeare very Just and Equitable (wch I have att large repeated to his Maj^tie in ye inclosd, wch yor Lo^p will be graciously pleasd to deliver) and Monsr de Croissy assurd me he represented fully to ye most Christian King, and were such, as he himself ownd, did distinguish ye case of my French Protestant Servants from that of ye other Ministers here; But it ended in an expresse denyall; For he said The most Christian King had made his generall Rules, wch he would not breake; That he was resolvd not to be troubled with such matters, as happned often upon his Subjects of ye Religion dwelling with Forreign Ministers, and that having given his Orders, he would not depart from them upon any consideration whatsoever; That he would neither lett me take over those I had brought from England with me, nor suffer them or any others to enjoy his Protection in my Service.

Hereupon, I did not thinke to take my Journey, there being no other cause for it expressd in yor Lo^ps Letter, besides ye Consideration (upon ye supposition that Leave would be granted) of my bringing them over with me; And I hope I have not mis-understood yor Lo^p. I took ye Libertie allso to send over ye same Courier againe; which I would not have don so soone, but that (upon Monsr de Croissy's discourse) I have too much reason to beleive That some of my Domestiques may be speedily seiz'd upon; And I thought it better, if it may be, by receiving his Maj^ties Commands, to know how to prevent this, than afterwards to make fruitlesse complaints, whilst ye Injurie and ye Affront is permanent.

My Lord, I most humbly beg yor Protection and Favour in this case. I confesse, as this Resolution taken seemes to me very unlikely to be alterd, so I can thinke (after many Reflexions) of no other

---

1 R.O. *France*, vol. 150, ff. 106–8, Trumbull to James II, July 23, 1686.

Expedient but my being Recalld; Att least if this may be with his Maj^ties good Liking and yor Lo^ps Approbation; For so many Inconveniencies of ye like Nature will frequently happen (as things go on here) that will occasion perpetuall Troubles to his Maj^tie, and make me looke in this Station, as if I came hither not to do any businesse for his Maj^tie, but to make some for him.

I must not pretend to be a Carver of my owne Fortune; otherwise my humble Request, wch I have formerly offerd to yor Lo^p, of succeeding Sr Willm Solmes att Constantinople, would make ye best End of this businesse, if it were not too great for me to desire. Att ye same time I do assure yor Lo^p, That if it be thought ye best way for me to be Recalld, though att present no other Imployment be thought upon for me, yet I will rest perfectly satisfyd in hopes of y^e continuance of yor Lo^ps Goodnesse to me.[1]

1 R.O. *loc. cit.* f. 105, Trumbull to Sunderland, July 23, 1686.

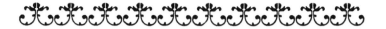

CHAPTER XIII

Sir William carries his point

JULY—AUGUST

ON the day that Sir William reported his fruitless errand at Versailles Louis XIV wrote to Barrillon. He was sure that Barrillon would have no difficulty in making the English court understand the reasonableness of his decision. It conflicted in no way with the consideration due to ambassadors and envoys who could never claim immunity for subjects of the prince to whom they were sent. As for Trumbull's contention with regard to the servants he had brought from England, it carried little weight. If his reasoning were accepted then not only people of the R.P.R., including the ministers who had taken refuge in England, Germany and Holland, could return to France as servants to an ambassador, rousing the new converts, but the worst criminals even whom the fear of just retribution kept away might come back with such ambassadors and enjoy safety. In short there were such objections to the lenience exercised hitherto that he would in future suffer none of his subjects of the R.P.R. to serve any ambassador. He had already refused a request made by Spanheim. He could not grant the request of the King of England without grave prejudice to his rulings and without renewing the cabals and intrigues of the Protestant envoys who had in the past facilitated the evasion of his subjects.[1]

Barrillon's letters written at the same time brought the pleasing news that Trumbull might be sent to Constantinople, a place for which he was much better fitted than for Paris,[2] a statement with which his Master heartily agreed.[3]

---

[1] A.É. *Angleterre*, vol. 159, ff. 40–1, Louis XIV to Barrillon, July 23, 1686.
[2] *Ib*. ff. 46 and 50, Barrillon to Louis XIV, July 22 and 25, 1686.
[3] *Ib*. f. 52, Louis XIV to Barrillon, Aug. 2, 1686.

From Barrillon's last two letters one might almost get the impression that there would be no further difficulties, but this was not to be so. Sir William's letter of July 23 roused James to obstinacy. He granted Sir William's request for the post at Constantinople, but Sir William must not leave France without the honours of war. "H.M. would have you renew your instances about your French Protestant servants, that they may be permitted to returne with you. H.M. thinks your reason for it so good and strong that he cannot see how it can be refused", replied Sunderland on the very day Sir William's courier had arrived, and he added in a kind of postscript: "The King thinks his honour so engaged in protecting your servants that his Majesty cannot be contented with anything lesse than an entire satisfaction in that particular, and will not recall you till it is given." [1]

A long letter was written by Barrillon on the next day, July 29. The King of England had spoken to him about Trumbull's servants "comme d'une affaire de la dernière importance". Barrillon had appealed to him on the ground of his master's motives, Louis XIV was acting "par un principe de piété et de religion", but James was not to be touched. "Le Roy d'Ang^re prend cette affaire fort a coeur. Il croit que sa dignité est blessée de ce qui se fait a son ministre contre le droit des gens et contre l'usage orginaire....Je ne puis assez vous expliquer combien cette affaire chagrine le Roy d'Ang^re." The incident was making a great deal of noise, and many people hoped that things would go from bad to worse. It would be most desirable, thought Barrillon, to find a compromise. [2]

Some days later Barrillon was granted a long audience. He made the most of the arguments that had been supplied to him, he invented others, but all of no avail. James would not yield. The servants that had accompanied Sir William to France must be allowed to return to England. They had gone to France on the understanding that they were to be safe. In vain Barrillon

1 R.O. *France, Entry Book* 19, July 18–28; cf. *H.M.C., Downshire MSS.* 1, pp. 197–8.
2 A.É. *Angleterre*, vol. 159, ff. 55–7, Barrillon to Louis XIV, July 29, 1686.

reminded James of the firmness and unswerving constancy his master had been obliged to exercise in order to bring about the destruction of heresy in his kingdom—the least yielding on his part would have overthrown or at least retarded this great work which James himself had witnessed with such joy. No— James thought that exceptions could be made in his case. He thought that his efforts in behalf of Catholicism and his conduct in all that concerned the interests of the King of France entitled him to a different treatment for *his* ambassador. "Sa Ma^{té} Britannique ne m'a point encore parlé avec tant de chaleur d'aucune affaire que de celle là." And Sunderland had remarked that those who had been displeased by the growing friendship of the two Kings rejoiced in this incident and had not failed to hint to James that the King of France showed him but little consideration.[1]

In France Sir William was gladdened by the return of his courier who brought him the news of his appointment to Constantinople and of the King's protection of his "domestiques". M. de Croissy was absent from Versailles, but as soon as he returned Sir William proposed to wait on him. News had come from Hungary in the meantime, and Sir William continues in this letter of August 3:

We have been exceedingly Alarm'd, by ye flying Reports in this towne, That Mr Fitzjames was killed...before Buda. But Monsr de Croissy has sent me word this morning, that ye Letters brought to ye most Christian King do mention that he is onely wounded and not mortally...I am sure his Losse would be extreamly regretted, having ye Hon^r to know him so well, and to be able to give him this Testimonie, That I was never acquainted with a Gentleman (of his Age) who gave greater Hopes than he did.[2]

Four days later, on August 7, he writes:

As soon as I had sent away my Letters by ye last Ordinarie, I went to Versailles, and represented to Monsieur de Croissy (according to my Orders) the case of my French Protestant Servants, that they might be permitted to returne, with me, acquainting him That his Maj^{tie} had expressely commanded me to renew these Instances in

1 *Ib*. ff. 58–61, Barrillon to Louis XIV, Aug. 1, 1686.
2 R.O. *France*, vol. 150, ff. 113–14, to Sunderland, Aug. 3, 1686.

his name, and y^t his Maj^{tie} was persuaded, That in consideration of ye Justice, and of his Maj^{ties} friends^p, ye Most Christian King would not refuse this.

I returnd yesterday to see if I could obtaine a Satisfactorie Answ^r; But he told me, That he expected to heare from Monsr Barrillon (who, he said, had Orders to speake to his Maj^{tie} and propose severall things to his Consideration) That he, for his part, wish'd some Expedient could be found....I perceive by this and other things, wch fell from him in discourse, That I shall have an answer according as Monsr Barrillon shall represent ye matter, after he has spoken with his Maj^{tie}.[1]

A letter from Barrillon was on the way. It came from Windsor. James had again spoken to him about the servants—they were few in number, they had passports from the King of France, permission granted to them would not necessarily entail concessions to other envoys, and besides no one could find fault if he were shown this consideration. Barrillon replied in the tones of a respectful *directeur de conscience*. He begged James to note the false zeal of those who tried to make him believe that his honour and dignity consisted in obtaining permission for his envoy to have some Frenchmen leave France because they had been in his service—it amounted to bringing back some Protestants to a place where presumably they would persist in their error. And that was what he, so zealous for the true religion, was requesting with such ardour!

James was somewhat embarrassed but avoided the issue raised. It was evident, he exclaimed, that Barrillon knew his request was not to be granted. Barrillon replied that he had no information other than that contained in the letters which he had already communicated to him.

According to Barrillon the affair continued to make a stir. In London it was commonly thought that the incident was likely to chill the good understanding between the two crowns. An amazing remark concludes this long letter—all sensible people thought Sir William a bungler; he could easily have avoided the situation by sending these servants back as "couriers". "Tous les gens sensez jugent que si le Sr Trumball

1 R.O. *France*, vol. 150, f. 115, to Sunderland, Aug. 7, 1686.

avoit esté habile il ne seroit pas tombé dans l'embarras ou il est et auroit fait repasser icy sous le pretexte d'envoyer des Courriers ceux qu'il y pretend ramener." [1] That honesty was not the best policy in the eyes of Sunderland and company scarcely needs this additional proof.

The letter that went from Louis XIV to his ambassador on August 9 was evidently the fruit of much thought and discussion —a first draft, crossed out, is based on an old argument, the second draft on a different one, an appeal to conscience. In the first one Louis declares that he had all the more cause to believe James satisfied with his reasons for hindering the return of certain subjects of the R.P.R., in that James knew he had no worse subjects, none more contrary to his authority, than French Calvinists. In the second one Louis declares he had all the more reason to believe James satisfied, in that James had shown his zeal for the Catholic religion on every occasion, and his conscience, no less than that of the King of France, was involved in putting obstacles in the way of conversion.

Yet notwithstanding, the letter went on, if James desired this mark of friendship, even after Barrillon had put the last consideration before him, Louis would grant the request. [2]

In Paris Sir William bided his time, sent the usual gazettes to Sunderland and, in a more cheerful mood, added two or three anecdotes of his own.

"This King has given Orders for y⁰ suppressing all y⁰ Publick Notaries in Normandie, without re-imbursing them anything of what they payd for those Charges, pretending they have been long enough in possession to have payd yᵐ selves; And creates 10 new Notaries in each Vicomté of that Province." [3]

"Monsʳ de Vandosme [4] had Invited y⁰ Dauphin to an Opera and other Diversions at Danet (Anet); But y⁰ King has putt it off, upon pretence of saving y⁰ Expence to Monsʳ Vandosme, Though y⁰ Opera was made and a great part of y⁰ Entertainment readie: So that tis thought some other reasons have contributed to it, wherein

---

1 A.É. *loc. cit.* ff. 69–71, Barrillon to Louis XIV, Aug. 5, 1686.
2 *Ib.* ff. 67–8, Louis XIV to Barrillon, Aug. 9, 1686.
3 R.O. *loc. cit.* f. 115, to Sunderland, Aug. 7, 1686.
4 Louis Joseph, duc de Vendôme.

Madame de Choiseul[1] has some part, who has orders to retire from ye Court, And Monsr le Marquis de Crequi,[2] St Maur,[3] Chamaranthe[4] and some others are appointed to go to their respective Regiments in ye Countrie."[5]

"The Popes Nonce[6] has of late been so Indispos'd that he receiv'd no Visits; Notwithstanding wch Monsieur de Croissy was to see him and stayd a considerable time. Severall conjectures have been made; That it was upon ye affaires of ye Palatinate; But what I have been able to learne of certainty is, That it was cheifly to make Instances to obtaine an Abbaye of Gentlewomen to be granted to Monsr de Croissy's sister (who is a Religieuse) wch cannot be effected wth out ye Popes Permission."[7]

A week after his last visit to Versailles, on one of the usual Tuesdays, on August 13, Sir William went back to see M. de Croissy, who told him that he had not yet heard from Barrillon and so could give "no further account"; he took up, however, a matter that had been pending for many months.

Some allusion has already been made to the bombarding of Genoa by France in May 1684. English merchant ships carrying goods belonging to subjects of the Republic had been seized by French men-of-war and carried into Toulon.[8] This was the case with the *Mary*, the *Hawk*, the *William and David*, and the *Fly*. The boats were released ultimately, but the cargo retained, and Sir William was directed to demand restitution,[9] which he did at various times without success.[10] An Englishman by the name of Mascall had appealed in vain for some pieces of damask taken out of the *Mary*.[11]

1 Louise Gabrielle de la Vallière, duchesse de Choiseul.
2 François Joseph, marquis de Crequy.
3 Honoré, comte de Sainte-Maure.
4 Louis d'Ornaison, comte de Chamarande.
5 R.O. *loc. cit.* f. 119, to Sunderland, Aug. 10, 1686. The passing disgrace of these courtiers is mentioned by Sourches, *Mémoires*, I, pp. 429–30; cf. Saint-Simon, *Mémoires*, I, p. 118, *n.* 3. The visit to Anet, the Opera, *Acis et Galatée*, etc. took place in Sept. Sourches, I, p. 438. Dangeau, I, p. 381.
6 Angelo Maria Ranucci or Ranuzzi.
7 R.O. *loc. cit.*; cf. *H.M.C., Downshire MSS.* I, p. 202.
8 Cf. *H.M.C., op. cit.* p. 110.   9 *Ib.* pp. 133, 189.
10 R.O. *loc. cit.* f. 79, Memorial presented on May 21; ff. 83, 89, 93, 97, to Sunderland, May 29, June 12 and 26, July 3.
11 For six months, ever since his "particular" audience with the King, Trumbull tried to get redress for Mascall. Finally he wrote on May 15: "I have in pursuance of his Maj^{ties} Orders several times solicited in behalf of Mr John

Concerning y⁰ Marchandises taken out of y⁰ 4 English Ships, during y⁰ late Troubles att Genoua, he told me, That y⁰ most Christian King had been spoke to, But that Sentences of Confiscation have been given above a Yeare agoe, and therefore he would heare no more of them. This being an expresse Denyall, and having sent yo⁰ Lo⁰ formerly a Copie of y⁰ Memoriall I presented (by which it sufficiently appeares how manifest a Contravention this is to y⁰ Marine Treatie between y⁰ 2 Crownes) I shall say no more, but humbly submitt it to his Maj^{ties} Will and Pleasure.[1]

If Sir William had not been so preoccupied with the question of his servants he would no doubt have expressed himself more forcibly.

"The Lady Stapleton", he continues in this letter of Aug 14, "(widdow of Sir Willm Stapleton[2] who lately dyd here) intending to returne into England with her Children found her 3 sons (who were att y⁰ College du Plessis) detain there and refus'd to be deliverd, contrarie to their own and their Mother's Will, upon pretence it was their Father's desire they should continue att Schoole there. She offers to leave them without any constraint to y⁰ choice of their Religion, And (in case it be thought fitt hereafter, when she has settled her affaires in England) to bring them over againe, and has sent a Petition to Mons⁰ de Croissy for their freedome."[3]

Another Tuesday came and Sir William went to Versailles. M. de Croissy again put him off. "Monsieur Barrillon had not yet had an opportunitie of discoursing fully with his Majestie about this matter; And added, Que le Roy d'Angleterre en

Mascall to obtaine Restitution of 3 peices of Damask taken out of y⁰ Ship y⁰ Mary by some fregates of y⁰ most Christian King and carried to Toulon. Att first it was pretended, that y⁰ Proofes belonging to this matter (that had been lodgd with Mons⁰ de Seignelay) had been mis-lay'd and could not be found. But having since obtain'd new Copies and renewed my Instances to obtaine Right herein, Mons⁰ de Croissy answ^d yesterday, That y⁰ said goods had been confiscated by a sentence given some time since for want of sufficient Evidence that y⁰ same belong to Mascall." *Ib.* f. 77, to Sunderland; cf. p. 49 *ante*.

1 *Ib.* f. 121, to Sunderland, Aug. 14, 1686. Trumbull's successor Skelton was directed to renew his instances in this matter. R.O. *France, Entry Book* 19: "Account of severall particulars...."

2 Governor of the Leeward Islands. He died on Aug. 2. R.O. *France*, vol. 150, f. 113, to Sunderland, Aug. 3, 1686. Cf. *H.M.C., Downshire MSS.* 1, p. 208. A letter from Lady Stapleton to Sunderland is on f. 123, Aug. 14: "My three Suns are forsably and against their wills detained from mee in plesse College."

3 R.O. *loc. cit.* f. 122, to Sunderland, Aug. 14, 1686.

seroit le maitre";[1] so Sir William returned to Paris, hoping for the best.

Barrillon had undertaken to appeal to James's conscience, but he expected no result from this argument. However he thought James would be delighted to have his request granted "et beaucoup de gens en seront fort faschez".[2]

Louis XIV wrote back stipulating that Trumbull's successor should be "better intentioned", and since he had heard that it was to be Skelton, Barrillon must see to it that he would be less interfering than his predecessor.[3]

On August 19 Barrillon wrote again. He had warned James that in permitting these servants to come back to England he was burdening his conscience with their continuing in a state of error, whereas if they remained in France they would be obliged to renounce their wrong beliefs and would return to true religion in the end. James replied eagerly that if his royal brother granted him this favour it would do a great deal of good in England—the effect would be most beneficial to Catholic interests. Then, to James's intense pleasure ("on ne scauroit s'imaginer plus de satisfaction"), Barrillon at last announced the desired permission. Trumbull might bring back the servants he had taken to France.[4]

Sir William was at once informed of this decision[5] and received his letter of revocation.[6]

"I shall accordingly attend Monsieur de Croissy", he writes on Aug 24, "to have a Day appointed for my Audience de Congé and prepare for my Returne with all convenient speed, hoping I may be ready (in case ye Indisposition[7] of ye most Christian King does not retard my Audience, as it has for some time don that of ye Ambassadᵣˢ of Siam) to come away ye latter end of ye next month or (att farthest) ye beginning of October.... Having allso formerly implord yoʳ Loᵖˢ assistance in obtaining some mony for me before I go away.... I shall

1 R.O. *loc. cit.* f. 125, to Sunderland, Aug. 21, 1686.
2 A.É. *Angleterre*, vol. 159, f. 84, Barrillon to Louis XIV, Aug. 15, 1686.
3 *Ib.* f. 73, Louis XIV to Barrillon, Aug. 16, 1686.
4 *Ib.* f. 88, Barrillon to Louis XIV, Aug. 19, 1686.
5 H.M.C., *Downshire MSS.* I, p. 207.
6 R.O. *France, Entry Book* 19, Aug. 9-19, 1686.
7 The King was suffering from a quartan ague.

adde no more, but that I am not able to furnish ye Expence of my Remoovall from hence, having not receivd any thing of my Extraordinaries of my first coming hither...." [1]

Sir William was congratulated by some on his advancement to Constantinople as to "a post of greater honour, less trouble and more profit".[2] His "patron's" brother, Clarendon, had written more dubiously: "You will forgive me if I do not advise or wish you to undertake that Embassy; it is at this time a melancholy one, and an empty one too, for the Company is at this time very low, and the trade almost gone."[3] Nevertheless Sir William must have been relieved to depart.

1 R.O. *France*, vol. 150, f. 126, to Sunderland, Aug. 24, 1686.
2 *H.M.C.*, *op. cit.* p. 206.
3 *Ib.* p. 203.

CHAPTER XIV

Homeward bound

THE remaining weeks brought little more business, and some of it of a pleasant nature.

"As soon as I had sent away my last Pacquet," writes Sir William on September 4, "yᵉ Newes came that Madame la Dauphine was Deliverd of another Son, who is to be calld Le Duc de Berrie.[1] I intend...to make my Complements hereupon to yᵉ most Christian King, when I have my Audience of Congé; About which I went yesterday to speake with Monsieur de Croissy att Versailles; But he was not yet returnd thither from yᵉ Countrie....

Concerning Sʳ William Stapletons Sons,[2] yᵉⁱʳ Mother I suppose will shortly attend yoʳ Loᵖ and give a further Account of their Fathers Will, than I can. All I know is, That during his last Sicknesse here he sent for me severall times, acquainting me That his Will was in England and desiring me to make a Codicill for him, by which he would change 2 of his Executors vizᵗ Sʳ Edmond Andros and Mr Trant (yᵉ former, because he was going upon a foreign Imployment,[3] and yᵉ other, because he did not give him Satisfaction, as he said, about a considerable Summe of mony which he had in his hands) And to appoint his Wife Executrix in their Roome; Which he sign'd, seald and publisht in my presence. He spoke to me nothing of his Intention of having his Sons bred up in France; on yᵉ contrarie I was informd by one Mr White, an Irish Preist here, That Sʳ Wᵐ Stapleton being told that Mr Trant had a designe upon yᵉ first Newes of his Death, to have his Sons detaind here, fell into a great Passion and desird yᵉ said Mr White to come to me immediately and request me (wᶜʰ he did) to make a new Will for him, That Mr Trant (under Pretence of that Will he had left in England) might

1 He was born on August 31.

2 Sunderland had written that the King remembered Sir William intended to breed up his sons in his religion: "therefore if you find my Lady intends nothing contrary thereunto you are to speak to Monsieur de Croissy that they may return into England with their mother, who submits their disposal to his Majesty." *H.M.C., Downshire MSS.* 1, p. 211.

3 He was going to New England as Governor.

have nothing to do with his Children. However I am confident it was his Desire That his Sons should be Educated in ye Religion he profess'd, And their Mother has often assurd me She designd nothing else; but she finding so great an aversion in her Children to stay in France, Especially where they complaine of ill usage and being detaind as Prisoners, she humbly Submitts y^m to his Maj^ties Pleasure....[1]

Yo^r Lo^p will find by ye Gazette á la main inclos'd, That ye Gazettier has prevented me in giving yor Lo^p a full Account of what happend last weeke att Versailles from ye Neglect of Monsr Bonneuïl ye Introducteur of Ambassad^rs; whereof I thought myself oblig'd to demand Satisfaction, and which was offerd and accepted (by myself und ye Envoyé of Genoua) by ye Mediation of Monsr L'Abbé Rizzini ye Envoyé of Modena; so y^t I need trouble yor Lo^p no further herewith."[2]

The great event that week was the magnificent picturesque reception of the three ambassadors of Siam on September 1. The place was filled, "d'une foule de courtisans et d'autres gens...jusqu'au bout de la galerie, où était le trône du roi".[3] Evidently Sir William had not been notified of this ceremony.

A postscript to this letter of September 4 brought a sad matter to Sunderland's notice. An English captain from "Cardiff near Bristol" had been found at sea with French passengers on board. His vessel and goods had been confiscated, and he himself had been condemned to perpetual slavery in the galleys; his money and effects had been seized without allowance for his subsistence and his person loaded with heavy irons. The only counsel allowed him was a Frenchman who spoke little English.[4]

1 Cf. H.M.C., op. cit. p. 202.
2 R.O. France, vol. 150, ff. 134–6, to Sunderland, Sept. 4, 1686.
3 Sourches, Mémoires, i, p. 436.
4 H.M.C., op. cit. p. 209. (The petition enclosed with Trumbull's letter.) It seems to have been assumed rather lightly that James would not object: "En 1686 [Seignelay] perd patience et fait jeter en prison pour un long temps des maîtres anglais qui avaient voulu passer cinq femmes....Comme Louis XIV est en bons termes avec le catholique Jacques II, les Anglais complices des évasions seront 'sans difficulté' condamnés aux mêmes peines que les Français." Guitard, Colbert et Seignelay, p. 118 (based on the archives of the Ministère de la Marine).
Benoist writes about one of the captains imprisoned: "Le Roi Jacques souffrit si patiemment cette injure faite à un de ses sujets qu'il étoit aisé de soupçonner qu'il étoit de l'intelligence." Histoire de l'Édit de Nantes, v, p. 963.

The captain's petition was endorsed by four English merchants of La Rochelle [1] who also said they were in hopes of retiring to England. "A noise runs here that our Sovereign King hath requested of this King 22 families. If your Honour would be so pleased to give us a word of comfort how we oft[*sic*] to act, and who the 22 persons or families may be, will be an everlasting engagement to the above named." [2]

"Having receivd ye inclosd Letters from Rochell," writes Sir William in the postscript mentioned, "I take ye Libertie to transmitt y^m to yor Lo^p. As to ye matter for which Greenefeild is imprisond, yor Lo^p will find he confesses ye Fact, vizt. That French Protestants were found on boord him, But desires Mitigation of his Punishment. The other, wch concernes ye remoovall of so many English Families from Rochell, seemes to me a matter of importance. The whole is most humbly submitted to his Maj^{ties} Consideration." [3]

Sir William evidently celebrated the arrival of the baby prince—his bill this quarter contains the item "for bonfires and other expenses upon the birth of the Duc de Berri 393 *livres*". [4] He notes another festivity in his next letter: "On Thursday ye 5^h Instant, being this King's Birthday, Bonfires were made and all other Expressions of Joy, especially in ye new Place de Victoire, where Meddals were thrown among ye People, ye Lamps burning att ye 4 Corners, [5] ye Fountaines running with Wine and ye Day concluded with Fireworkes." [6]

But in the shadow of these festivities other things were going on.

Orders have been sent from hence to ye Intendants of ye severall Provinces to disarme all ye new Converts. In Languedoc, Dauphiné and ye neighbouring Countries they have begun to putt in execution ye rasing of ye Kings Taille [7] by ye Souldiers, who are Quarterd upon such as refuse or delay to Pay; this way being found ye most Expeditious. [8]

---

1 *H.M.C. op. cit.* p. 209, "Andrew Stuckey, junior, Robert Mackerell, Henry Ranking and John Lee, English merchants, not naturalised."
2 *Ib.*　　　　　　　　　　　　　3 R.O. *loc. cit.*
4 *Cal. Treas. Books*, 1685–9, p. 1221.
5 Of the new statue.
6 R.O. *loc. cit.* f. 139, to Sunderland, Sept. 7, 1686.
7 For this tax see Lavissé, *Histoire de France*, VII^1, pp. 188–94; VIII^1, pp. 168–71.
8 R.O. *loc. cit.*

Paris. $\frac{9}{19}$ *Jan:* 1686.

My Lord,

I here send yo.ʳ Loᵖ inclos'd what Newes I have been
able to meet with since my last of yᵉ 16ᵗʰ Instant.
Among yᵉ Prints yoᵘʳ Loᵖ will find that Declaration
concerning Strangers, wᶜʰ I formerly mentiond.
I receiv'd last night a Letter from Mr Daniel of Caën
an English Merchant not Naturaliz'd, by wᶜʰ he acquaints
me, That on Munday yᵉ Intendant sent his Coach for
him to come & signe his Abjuration; Wᶜʰ he refusing to
do, he sent ten Musqueteers to carrie him to Prison &
order'd 50 Souldiers more to be Quarter'd in his House,
vpon which He imediately Signd.
        Yoᵘʳ Loᵖ will be pleas'd to deliver these Letters to
their Majᵗˢ from Monsieur, wᶜʰ I receiv'd this morning.
        I am with great truth & Respect

My Lord

                                Yoᵘʳ Loᵖˢ most obedient, most
                                faithfull & most humble servant
My Lord President.   W. Trumbull

A page of Sir William Trumbull's letters, January 9/19, 1686. Repro-
duced from R.O. State Papers, Foreign France, vol. 150, f. 5

A letter from Sunderland sent Sir William on a round of visits.

The King understanding that the Controleur Général[1] and the Abbé his son[2] have been very favourable from time to time to such Irish as study in Paris has commanded me to write the enclosed to the Controlleur. . .you are to deliver the letter yourself. The King has likewise heard from the Bishop of Laon in Ireland[3] that Monsieur Bailly,[4] Abbé de St Thierri, Monsieur Talon, Premier Valet de Chambre de la Garde Robe, and the Abbé des Marais[5] D.D. of St Sulpice have also taken great care of the said Irish, and thinks you should take some opportunity of acquainting them how sensible he is of it.[6]

Sunderland gave notice also of a petition presented in behalf of seven subjects, Irishmen to judge by their names, who were galley slaves at Marseilles. All except one had served their term and desired their release.[7] More information could be obtained from Consul Burrow.[8]

Sir William replies on September 11:

According to his Maj^ties Commands I have waited on Monsieur le Controlleur General, and deliverd ye Letter; wch he receivd with all Respect and acknowledgem^ts and will not faile to Answer it ere long. I have allso visited Monsr L'Abbé Peletier, and ye others mentiond in yor Lo^ps Letter (except Monsieur Talon, who has been for some time in ye Countrie, and is not yet return'd). They all are very sensible of his Majesties great Grace and Favour. . . .[9]
I have allso presented a Memoriall containing ye Names of those Condemn'd to ye Gallies, whose time is expir'd; I had before (of Office) spoken for some of y^m; concerning w^ch, I expect an Answer

1 Claude Le Pelletier, or le Peletier, contrôleur général des Finances.
2 Michel Le Pelletier, later Bishop of Angers, or Maurice Le Pelletier, later Superior of Saint Sulpice.
3 See R.O. *France*, vol. 150, f. 60, a letter from Louis XIV in behalf of l'evesque de Laon en Irlande.
4 Guillaume Bailly, abbé de Saint-Thierry.
5 Paul Godet des Marais, later Bishop of Chartres.
6 *H.M.C., Downshire MSS.* 1, p. 211; cf. B.N. MS. fr. 10265, f. 77 (Newsletter).
7 *Ib.*
8 R.O. *France, Entry Book* 19, Aug. 19–29. (The résumé in *H.M.C., Downshire MSS.* does not give all the facts.) See also a letter from Burrow, R.O. *France*, vol. 150, f. 117, to Sunderland, Aug. 9, 1686.
9 Cf. R.O. *loc. cit.* f. 141, Sept. 14.

from Monsieur de Seignelay. I have y⁰ Passeport for y⁰ 75 Tonns of Cahors Wine, wch Monsr de Croissy deliverd to me yesterday.[1]

It was quite true that Sir William Trumbull had already been approached in behalf of certain of these galley slaves. One of them, James Rafter, sentenced in 1676 for five years, for killing a Frenchman in self-defence, had already appealed to Lord Preston because "for want of meanes" he could not obtain his liberty.[2] He wrote again to Sir William complaining that Spaniards, Hollanders and the Duke of Savoy's subjects were released as soon as their sentence was over.[3] An Irish priest in Paris had brought Sir William a letter in behalf of a galley slave.[4] Another of the convicts mentioned by Sunderland, Nicholas Butler, serving on the galley *La Couronne*, had written desiring consideration—all strangers obtained liberty at the end of their time, but not English subjects.[5]

M. de Croissy promised Sir William to represent the matter to the King and "to obtaine a generall order in the like case, other forrain Ministers having made the same instances",[6] but Sir William leaving shortly thereafter his successor Skelton was told to insist for satisfaction.[7]

At the risk of interrupting the account of Sir William's proceedings the incredible answer received by Skelton must be quoted here.

Monsr de Croissy...has given me noe encouragement to hope for the discharge of those Prisoners in the Gallys whose time is expired. Hee sayes that it is not a thing practised, it being to be supposed that such as are condemned thither are soe criminall as not to deserve his Maj^ty or his Ministers intercession for them, And besides, should they permit all such to come out whose time was expired, there would not be enough remaining to doe the King

1 R.O. *loc. cit.* ff. 143–4, to Sunderland, Sept. 11, 1686. The 75 tons of Cahors wine were for the use of James II. Cf. f. 128 and *H.M.C., Downshire MSS.* 1, p. 207.

2 *H.M.C., 7th Report*, App., Part 1, p. 411.

3 *H.M.C., Downshire MSS.* 1, p. 93: "Marseilles, on board the galley Captain Royal." In this letter Rafter said he had been condemned to the galleys for 3 years.

4 *Ib.* p. 149. Probably refers to Rafter.

5 *Ib.* p. 183.

6 R.O. *France, Entry Book* 19: "Account of severall particulars...."

7 *Ib.*

Service, Especially since all the other Forreign Ministers have desired the same for the Subjects of theire Masters. And therefore whenever there was a discharge of any, it would be of such as had been longest there and for the lesser offences.[1]

It must not be thought, however, that foreigners only were kept in the galleys indefinitely—it was equally difficult for a French galley slave to recover his liberty.[2]

"I was in hopes to have had a Day appointed for my Audience of Congé by this time"; writes Sir William on September 14, "But yᵉ most Christian King has been pleas'd to deferre it till after his returne from Maintenon, whither he goes this day."[3]

A little news completes the letter:

> The Count de Roye,[4] having sent an Expresse hither to informe this King of yᵉ Reasons of his leaving yᵉ Service of yᵉ King of Denmarke, had his Courier dispatcht back yesterday with this Answer, That his Majᵗⁱᵉ gave him leave to retire whether he thought fitt, and to enter into any Imployment, excepting onely that of Holland. It is reported That here will be made Cent Secretaires du Roy, wᶜʰ will produce a considerable Summe of Mony.[5]

Four days later Sir William announced the expected summons: "Yesterday in yᵉ Evning yᵉ most Christian King returnd from Maintenon; And I receivd notice from yᵉ Introductʳ of Ambassadʳˢ That he has appointed tomorrow morning for my Audience of Congé."[6]

What might have been a rather serious piece of news followed.

1 R.O. *France*, vol. 151, f. 9, Skelton to Sunderland, Jan. 29, 1687. On Nov. 19, 1687, however, Skelton writes, "All the Galley Slaves and Prisoners of his Maʸᵃ Subjects for whose release I have long interceded, are now actually at Liberty except one Letherington." *Ib.* f. 114; yet judging from Skelton's correspondence this may possibly refer only to those condemned to the galleys for conveying Protestants. On the other hand it happened occasionally that after M. de Croissy had refused a thing point blank it was suddenly granted.

2 Cf. Lavisse, *Histoire de France*, VII², p. 258, "Comment les galériens étaient libérés".

3 R.O. *France*, vol. 150, f. 141, to Sunderland, Sept. 14, 1686.

4 Frédéric Charles de la Rochefoucauld, comte de Roye, later Count Lifford in Ireland. Haag, *France Protestante*, VI, pp. 354-5. Saint-Simon gives an extraordinary reason for the Count's leaving Denmark, *Mémoires*, IV, pp. 49-53, a reason not mentioned in the Danish correspondence quoted, *ib.* pp. 444-9.

5 R.O. *loc. cit.*

6 R.O. *loc. cit.* f. 145, to Sunderland, Sept. 18, 1686.

"Mr Warner, who came over with yᵉ Duke of St Albans as Chaplain, was seizd upon last night by yᵉ Commissarie of yᵉ Quarter and carried to his House; But att yᵉ request of yᵉ Duke of St Albans he obtaind Leave to returne to yᵉ Academie this morning."¹ There were no further particulars from Buda, but Sir William received "many Accounts from severall Hands, wᶜʰ agree in giving Mr Fitzjames this Testimonie, That he has signaliz'd himself all along, and in all yᵉ Actions of yᵉ greatest Danger has shewd himself among yᵉ forwardest and yᵉ bravest".²

1 R.O. *loc. cit.* The Duke's chaplain had leave to stay in France for a certain time, but leave having expired M. de Croissy had not thought fit to transmit the Duke's application for prolongation of time.

"Le Roy m'ordonne de vous avertir...que lorsque le milord St Albans vinst a Paris il fit demander a sa majesté la permission de retenir auprez de luy son ministre ce qu'elle voulust bien accorder, mais comme elle ne souffroit qu'avec peine et par la seule considération du Roy d'Angleterre le séjour dud. ministre à Paris je n'ay pas cru qu'il fust de mon devoir de parler a sa majᵗᵉ de la proroga- tion que le milord demandoit de cette permission d'autant plus qu'il disoit estre sur son depart qˡ pouvoit envoyer quelque jour devant luy ce ministre ainsi que je luy fis dire et qui d'ailleurs trouvoit chez le roy d'angleterre un libre exercice de la Religion, ainsy cette permission estant expirée, le ministre ayant donné lieu de soupçonner par sa conduite qˡ se mesloit de suborner et dogmatizer les sujets de sa matᵉ on l'avoit arresté ainsi que vous le voirez par le memoire cy-joint et sa Maᵗᵉ veut bien luy laisser la liberté de sortir incessammᵗ de son Royaume mais non pas celle d'y séjourner." A.É. *Angleterre,* vol. 159, f. 144, Colbert de Croissy to Barrillon, Sept. 20, 1686.

"Milord St Alban qui est a l'Accademie du Sʳ Coulon et que tout le monde croyoit estre party de cette ville pour aller voyager en Italie, ayant laissé un Ministre de la R.P.R. son domestique, on le faisoit observer et ceux qui le suivoient ayant eu peur de le perdre ce soir ils l'ont arresté sans ordre et l'ont conduit dans la maison du Commʳᵉ Gazon, ou peu de temps apres Milord St Alban est venu luy mesme avec son gouverneur. Il a reclamé son ministre avec beaucoup de douceur et d'honnêteté, il a dit que tout le monde croyoit en effet qu'il estoit party, parce qu'il avoit passé 7 ou 8 jours a Colombes, et il a assuré que le Roy luy avoit prorogé le temps de garder ce ministre, et que l'ordre en devoit estre expédié par Monsieur de Croissy. J'ay dit sur cela au Commʳᵉ Gazon qu'il chargeast Milord St Alban de ce ministre domestique jusqu'a nouvel ordre de sa Maᵗᵉ, n'ayant rien veu de mieux a faire en cette occasion et craignant qu'il ne fust pas convenable a son service d'exposer ce jeune Seigneur a faire quelque faute sur une telle matiere ou il croyoit voir seulement qu'il seroit deshonoré si son domestique reclamé ne luy estoit pas rendu sur sa parole." "Extrait d'une lettre de Mʳ de La Reynie du 17 Sepᵇʳᵉ 1686...on a envoyé copie de cet extrait à M. de Barrillon le 20 sept. 1686." A.É. *Angleterre,* vol. 160, f. 341. Cf. vol. 159, f. 179, Barrillon to Louis XIV, Sept. 26, 1686.

2 R.O. *loc. cit.*

The audience was once more deferred,[1] but finally tookplace.
Louis XIV, doubtless relieved to see him go, was most gracious.

The 22th [*sic*] Instant I had my Audience de Congé of ye most
Christian King; who was pleas'd to receive me with very great
favour; And after the Returne of his Complements to his Majestie
and ye assurances of ye continuation of his Friendship and readinesse
to contribute all that lyes in him towards a good Correspondence
between ye 2 Crownes, He did me y[e] Honour to declare his Satisfaction in my Conduct since my being here and to take Notice of
his Majesties having appointed me to go his Ambass[r] for Constantinople and to wishe me all good Successe in that Imployment;
And to receive very kindly y[e] Complem[ts] I made concerning y[e]
Recovery of his Health. I waited afterwards upon Monseigneur le
Dauphin. Madame la Dauphine is not yet to be seen[2]; and so I left
my Complements for her with Madame d'Arpajon: And from thence
I went to y[e] Dukes de Bourgogne, d'Anjou and Berrie. [Their
ages ranged from four years to three weeks!] Tomorrow I am to
have my Audience of Monsieur and Madame att S[t] Clou. I am
preparing to returne as soone as possibly I can: I most humbly beg
yo[r] Lo[ps] favour in considering y[e] necessarie Ceremonies and Troubles
of Remooving, That I may not be blam'd in coming no sooner,...I
have receivd from Mr Bridgeman y[e] signification of yo[r] Lo[ps] Commands concerning y[e] Ultramarine, of w[ch] I shall take care to buy y[e]
best can be gott, and bring it along with me.[3]

"On Thursday last, y[e] 26th Instant,"[1] he continues three days later,
"I waited upon Monsieur and Madame, y[e] Duke de Chartres and
Madamoiselle at St Clou, who returne their Complements to their
Majesties.[4] Monsieur gave me y[e] Inclos'd Letter for his Majestie,
with his Excuses for not sending it sooner; one w[ch] he had written
before (as he said) having been lost by some Accident.

I receivd last night y[e] honour of yo[r] Lo[ps] of y[e] 13th Instant concerning John Greenefeild, and shall not faile to obey ye Signification
of his Maj[ties] Commands in ye manner of Representing it to Monsr de

1 R.O. *France*, vol. 150, f. 148, to Sunderland, Sept. 21, 1686.

2 Sir William had asked specially to see her, but she sent him a message that
she was "dans les remèdes" and unable to receive him. *H.M.C., Downshire MSS.*
I, p. 216. A newsletter notes on Oct. 5: "Trombal Envoyé d'Ang[re] n'a point
voulu partir qu'il n'ait eu audience de congé de Madame la Dauphine qui doit
se relever un des jours de la semaine prochaine." B.N. MS. fr. 10265, f. 175. The
punctilious Sir William was probably grieved to leave any duty undone.

3 R.O. *loc. cit.* ff. 150-1, to Sunderland, Sept. 25, 1686. The *Gazette de France*,
1686, gives an account of this audience on pp. 539-40.

4 *Gazette de France*, 1686, p. 540.

Croissy....[1] The Lady Soames is dayly expected att Toulon...The Duke of St Albans fell ill (ye beginning of this weeke) of ye Small Poxe; But I heare this morning that he is thought out of Danger."[2]

As for poor Jonathan Greenfield, his case had to be handed over to Sir William's successor.[3] M. de Croissy assured the latter that the man was justly condemned,[4] and at first Louis XIV "absolutely refused" to pardon him,[5] but he was liberated in April 1687,[6] and one finds him writing 15 years later to Sir William to thank him for procuring his deliverance "out of almost unavoidable slavery".[7]

Two similar cases had also to be taken over by Bevil Skelton. A certain Bartholomew Tookey, his crew of five, and his small boat were seized at Boulogne in June, under suspicion that he had come for French Protestants,[8] while another, Jacques Lemprière by name, was imprisoned in September in the gaol of Saint-Lô for aiding Protestants to escape to Jersey.[9] Tookey was liberated after nine months[10] and Lemprière somewhat later.[11]

Sir William was busy setting his house in order. He tried to dispose of some of his property to his successor, and Skelton agreed to take over Lady Trumbull's copper, but not the coaches, unless his own successor at the Hague wanted any of the four

1 The captain condemned to the galleys for carrying Protestants. "His Matie would have you speak to Monsieur de Croissy of ye matter, acquainting him that though his Ma^ty does not think fit to interpose about the confiscation of ye Ship and Goods; yet he cannot but demand the Liberty of his Subject and that he may be free from the Condemnation of ye Gallies. You must represent this matter, so that it may appeare rather as an intercession in the petitioners behalf than otherwise." R.O. *France, Entry Book* 19, Sunderland to Trumbull, Sept. 13–23, 1686. Cf. *H.M.C., Downshire MSS.* I, p. 214.

2 R.O. *France*, vol. 150, f. 152, to Sunderland, Sept. 28, 1686.

3 R.O. *France, Entry Book* 19, "Account of severall particulars...", and a letter from Sunderland to Skelton, *ib.* March 7–17, 1686–7.

4 R.O. *France*, vol. 151, f. 9, Skelton to Sunderland, Jan. 29, 1687.

5 *Ib.* f. 15, Skelton to Sunderland, Feb. 12, 1687.

6 *Ib.* f. 40, Skelton to Sunderland, April 12, 1687. B.N. MS. fr. 17421, f. 175. Order of liberation from Seignelay for Jonatan Grinfil.

7 *H.M.C., Downshire MSS.* I, Part II, p. 812.

8 *Ib.* pp. 186, 189, 191.   9 *Ib.* p. 217.

10 R.O. *France, Entry Book* 19, "Account of severall particulars..."; *France*, vol. 151, ff. 9, 20, Skelton to Sunderland, Jan. 29 and March 8, 1687.

11 R.O. *France, Entry Book* 19, *ib.*; *France*, vol. 151, ff. 9, 114, Skelton to Sunderland, Jan. 29 and Nov. 19, 1687.

coaches there.[1] Skelton also requested help in finding a house and instructions how to govern himself.[2] Madame de Villeneuve Roussereau, whose house Sir William had rented in the rue du Bac, asked for a declaration concerning a page buried in the garden, so that there might be no difficulty when the bones were found.[3] My Lord Chancellor desired Lady Trumbull to buy and bring over with her "a night dress of Point de Paris for the head for my Lady Jeffreys".[4] Sir Richard Bulstrode wanted books on History, Geography or Morality, including *L'Espion du Grand Seigneur*,[5] also 2 lb. of the best French sealing wax and "the like quantity of sand which shines like gold to throw on letters with 3 pairs of small French scissors".[6] Lord Montague had "3 or 4 suits of hangings and a velvet bed" at Paris, and wished Sir William to bring them into England whereby the trouble of the custom could be avoided.[7] A certain M. Plegat brought samples of lead to be shown to the King.[8] The pound of ultramarine ordered by Sunderland was bought for 575 livres from M. Petitot, enamel painter to Louis XIV.[9] Sir Thomas Exton sent a message that he would like his son to come home with Sir William.[10] "Monsieur Bonneuil and Monsieur Giraut, Introducteurs des Ambassadeurs" appeared with a present from Louis XIV, the usual snuff box with the King's picture set in diamonds,[11] and they and their servants were gratified with the sum of 1035 livres.[12] The douaniers came to examine Sir William's goods.[13] Lord Arran arrived to bring congratulations on the birth of the duc de Berry.[14]

Letters to Sunderland had to be written twice a week, as usual, though there was not very much news.

The Duke de Villeroy (Gouvern[r] of Lyons) has given an Account to this Court, That ye Banke of that Cittie is in great danger of

1 *H.M.C., Downshire MSS.* 1, p. 211.   2 *Ib.* p. 202.
3 *Ib.* p. 223.   4 *Ib.* p. 219.   5 By Jean Paul Marana.
6 *Ib.* pp. 206, 221–2.   7 *Ib.* p. 220.   8 *Ib.* p. 224.
9 *Cal. Treas. Books*, 1685–9, p. 1221.   10 *H.M.C., op. cit.* p. 210.
11 A.É. *Mém. et Documents, Angleterre*, vol. 8, f. 130. The value of Trumbull's box was 5070 livres. Girault was not himself an introducteur, but "secrétaire à la conduite des ambassadeurs", Picavet, *Diplomatie française*, p. 130.
12 *Cal. Treas. Books, loc. cit.*   13 *Ib.*
14 R.O. *France*, vol. 150, f. 156, to Sunderland, Oct. 5, 1686.

Failing. The Farmers of y⁰ King there have demanded a considerable Abatement, without w^ch, they say, they are not able to subsist.[1]

I gave yor Lo^p an Account some time ago of y⁰ Complaint made by y⁰ Emperour's Envoyé here upon y⁰ Designe of Building a Fort att Huninghen; Since wch Orders have been sent from this Court to carrie on that Worke with all possible Expedition; There are now 10000 men att worke, and 'tis thought it will be finish'd in lesse than 3 weekes.

The Duke of St Albans is well recoverd of y⁰ Small-Poxe.[2]

The last letter Sir William wrote from Paris and from France on October 9 is characteristic of his disposition. Up to the end he was "troublesomely uneasy".[3]

I have receivd notice of y⁰ arrival of y⁰ Yatcht att Diepe att least a weeke before I desir'd it, and by consequence before I am readie, though I make all y⁰ hast I can. Mr Pepys wrott to me to desire me to sett a day precisely for ye coming of y⁰ Yatcht, to wch I returnd an Answer by y⁰ next Post and could not beleive y⁰ Yatcht would have been dispatcht before that came to his Hands. I will not presume to trouble yor Lo^p with severall of my Domestique affaires, especiallie y⁰ sudden sicknesse that has happned to some of my necessarie Servants, that hinders me for a few dayes. I beg yor Lo^p⁰ goodnesse in Interceding for me (if there be occasion) with his Majestie, That I may not be blamd, in these Circumstances for making y⁰ Yatcht stay a few dayes....[4]

Servants, coaches and goods were finally dispatched home via Rouen and Dieppe.[5] The Swedish Ambassador, at least, regretted Sir William's departure which, he said, deprived him of his best friend,[6] and perhaps there were others sorry too to see him go. On October 12–22 Sir William returned to the King's presence.[7] Doubtless he was glad to be back at Elm Grove, his "little house" at Ealing, the house which Halifax used to pass with a sigh when Sir William was abroad,[8] but six months later he and Lady

1 R.O. *France*, vol. 150, f. 153, to Sunderland, Oct. 2, 1686. On Villeroy's mission see Dangeau, *Journal*, 1, p. 376 *n*.
2 R.O. *loc. cit.* f. 156, to Sunderland, Oct. 5, 1686. On July 31 Sir William had mentioned that the Emperor's Envoy had complained of the French having built a bridge across the Rhine, *ib.* f. 112.
3 As James Vernon once said of Sir William. *Correspondence of Charles Talbot, Duke of Shrewsbury* (London, 1821), pp. 504–5.
4 R.O. *loc. cit.* f. 157, to Sunderland, Oct. 9, 1686.
5 *Cal. Treas. Books, loc. cit.*   6 *H.M.C., Downshire MSS.* 1, p. 218.
7 *Cal. Treas. Books, loc. cit.* p. 1095.   8 *H.M.C., op. cit.* p. 294.

Trumbull were on their way to Constantinople. The chaplain they had in Paris, Mr Hayley, accompanied them,[1] so did the secretary Sir William liked so much, Jaques Dayrolle.[2]

Sir William continued to be interested in French refugees,[3] and one of them, Pierre Motteux, dedicated to him in 1695 his translation of Saint Olon's *Present State of the Empire of Morocco*.[4] "I have the deepest Sense imaginable of your obliging Goodness," he writes, "that singular Humanity, or rather Charity, which, as it extends to many of our unhappy *Refugiés*, has made me a sharer in the Effects of your Bounty."[5]

Michel Le Vassor, a former priest converted to Protestantism in England, dedicated to Sir William his translation of the *Lettres et Memoires de François de Vargas...et de quelques Evêques d'Espagne touchant le Concile de Trente*.[6]

Qu'il étoit digne de vous, Monsieur, de fournir à la vérité cruellement persécutée en tant d'endroits, de quoi fermer la bouche

1 *H.M.C., op. cit.* p. 363, etc.

2 *Ib.* pp. 317, 375. Dayrolle, as his name came to be written, later entered the service of William III, was captured at sea in 1692 and put into the Bastille. After he was liberated he found no employment for some time and thought he would have to be porter at Easthampstead, Sir William's property, or plant cabbages in Ireland, but he received appointment as secretary to the Embassy at the Hague and was naturalized in 1696 as James Teissoniere D'Ayrolle. He was sent as Resident to Geneva in 1714, but returned to the Hague two years later where he was for many years at the Embassy. He died at the Hague on Jan. 2, 1739. His nephew and heir Solomon Dayrolle was godson of Lord Chesterfield. *Ib.* pp. 394, 430, Part II, pp. 763, 908; Douen, *La Révocation...à Paris*, III, p. 12; Agnew, *Protestant Exiles*, III, p. 56; *Recueil des Instructions, Hollande*, III, p. 33; R.O. *Lists and Indexes*, No. XIX (1904), pp. 28–31 *passim* and p. 52. *D.N.B.* under Dayrolles, Solomon.

3 *H.M.C., op. cit.* I, pp. 462–3, Part II, pp. 499, 515, 599–600, 618, 682, 813.

4 He had originally proposed to dedicate his translation of Rabelais to Sir William. Sir Godfrey Kneller, who had painted Sir William's portrait, introduced Motteux to him as author of the *Gentleman's Journal* and remarked that Mr Motteux being a French Protestant was well acquainted with Rabelais' book which exposed the superstition of Popery and accordingly he had taken pains to discover the mysteries and hidden beauties of that work. *Ib.* p. 600, and see also R. N. Cunningham, *Peter Anthony Motteux*. Cunningham suggests that perhaps Motteux felt Saint-Olon's book to be more in keeping with the interests of a statesman experienced in foreign affairs.

5 *The Present State of the Empire of Morocco*. By Monsieur de St Olon, Ambassador there in the Year 1693. London, 1695.

6 Amsterdam, 1699. The original Spanish MSS. were in Sir William's possession. They had been acquired by his grandfather; cf. *H.M.C., Downshire MSS.* I, p. v, Part II, pp. 764, 846.

à ses plus grands ennemis! Vous l'avez courageusement defendüe dans votre Patrie: vous avez secouru et protégé autant qu'il vous a été possible dans un païs étranger de bons Chrétiens, qui abandonnaient tout pour ne pas renoncer à la pureté de l'Evangile.

Another, and a greater, Bayle, would have dedicated his monumental work to him, if it had been possible. "Si des obstacles insurmontables ne m'empeschoient pas de mettre mon nom au Dictionaire [sic] Critique, je vous eusse demandé tres humblement la permission de vous le dedier et de le mettre avec son auteur sous la protection d'un nom aussi illustre que le votre." [1]

But at least he sent Sir William a copy of his Dictionary inscribed to him, and his letter may well serve as epilogue to this book.

Mylord

Je vous demande tres humblement la Grace d'agréer un exemplaire du dictionaire Critique que ie prens la liberté de vous envoier comme un hommage que toutes les personnes de lettres, et moi plus particulierement, doivent a un seigneur qui aime et connoit les sciences parfaitement, et qui favorise ceux qui les cultivent. C'est de vous Mylord que cela se doit dire tres iustement. Le gentilhomme [2] qui aura l'honneur de vous donner cette lettre et qui a servi longtems dans les armées de sa Majesté auroit pris tres agreablement cet exemplaire avec lui pour vous le presenter de ma part, s'il n'eut été embalé deja avec plusieurs autres que le libraire envoie à Londres. Vos momens, Mylord, etant infiniment precieux, ie ne m'etendrai pas a decrire le prix incomparable de la faveur que vous me ferez en recevant de bon oeil cet exemplaire, ie me contenterai de vous asseurer de ma parfaite reconnaissance et du profond respect avec quoi je suis

My lord
Votre tres humble et
tres obeissant serviteur
BAYLE

A Rotterdam le
8 de novembre 1696 [3]

1 For the text of the letter see pp. 178–80 *post*. There seem to have been other complications.

2 M. de Bellemare, *Gigas, Lettres de divers Savants*, 1, p. 493.

3 Downshire MSS. at Easthampstead Park, vol. xxxi, No. 139 (holograph); cf. *H.M.C., Downshire MSS.* 1, Part ii, p. 699.

Sir William Trumbull's Instructions

Instructions for Our Tr. etc [Trusty and Wellbeloved] Sr William Trumbull Kn^t. Our Envoyé Extraordinary to Our good Brother the most Christian King. Given at Our Court at Windsor the 21st day of Septemb^r 1685 in the first year of Our Reigne.

James R.

Having received these Instructions and Our Letters of Credence you shall with what convenient speed you may, repaire to Paris, or where the most Christian King shall bee, and as soon as you are ready for it, ask an Audience in Our name, at which having delivered Our Credentialls, you shall declare the great value and esteem Wee have for the person and friendship of that King, and how desirous Wee shall always bee to maintain the good correspondence established between Us, and embrace all occasions of improving it to the reciprocall advantage of our Crownes; that having given leave to Our R^t Trusty and Wellbeloved Cousin Richard Viscount Preston Our late Envoyé Extraordinary there, to come home, Wee have sent you to Reside as Our Minister with that King, for the better cultivating of all occasions, which shall offer in order to those Ends.

You shall lett the Most Christian King know, that as Wee are particularly concerned for the Preservation of the Peace of Christendom, so one great end of your Residing in his Court, is to bee ready upon all opportunities to communicate Our thoughts to Him, both upon such incidents, as may tend to disturb or endanger the same, and upon the measures and meanes, that may render the Peace firme and inviolable, in order whereunto Wee shall bee ready to employ not only Our best Offices, but Our utmost endeavours, not doubting but that Hee will concurre with Us therein.

Having received advice, that the French Governors in the West Indies say, they have Orders from the most Christian King, to confiscate all Vessells which shall come and Anchor in any of their Roads (as you will see by the Copies, which will bee herewith delivered unto you) and that they have actually seized severall English Fishing Vessells on the Coast of Nova Scotia, and others elsewhere; and having also been given to understand, that the French Governors in these parts, grant Commissions to Privateers in time of Peace, Our Pleasure is that you represent these matters to the Most Christian King, desiring an answer thereupon, that Wee may likewise give such Orders to Our Governours[1], as may prevent all mis-under-

---

1 Governors, Governours—both forms are used in this document.

standings, contrary to the good correspondence, which Wee desire may bee maintained between the Subjects of both Crownes. And as to the Privateers, you shall propose, that they may bee obliged to give such Security before any Commissions bee granted to them, as the Treaties direct, which Wee think may in a great measure prevent and obviate the frequent complaints, Wee receive from those parts concerning them.

You shall on all occasions protect and countenance Our Subjects trading to or in any of the Territories of the Most Christian King, and use your utmost endeavours for maintaining them in the possession of such Priviledges and Immunities, as have been stipulated by any Treaties with that Crown; And whereas upon former Complaints made of Wrongs done to Our Subjects by the unjust Seizure or detention of their Ships or Goods in the French Ports, Orders have been sent to the English Ministers residing at that Court, to apply themselves to procure Satisfaction to such, as were so injured, Wee do in like manner require you, that in cases of that or the like nature, which shall appear to you to bee yett un-relieved, or in any other Suits or just pretensions, which Our Subjects may from time to time have depending there, you use your beast endeavours to obtain speedy justice and satisfaction for them; yet for Our Honour you must not engage your self in any Complaint, but such, as being well grounded, may deserve the interposition of Our name. And whereas difficulty hath been hitherto made to admitt Our Consuls, Wee do particularly recommend it to you, to obtain admission of Our Consuls in the respective Ports of this Kingdom, where wee have or shall think fitt to appoint them, according as application shall bee made to you by any of them.

You are to take care, that Our Subjects of the Scottish Nation bee supported and preserved entire in the severall Immunities, Exemptions and Priviledges, which they have for many ages enjoyed in the Kingdom of France, and which have been allowed in severall Charters and Grants of those Kings, and allso asserted in severall judiciall Decisions of Law there, and if any Decree or Judgement have been given to the prejudice of the said Immunities, Exemptions and Priviledges, you are to use your best endeavour to gett the same reverst, and to make fitting applications to the Most Christian King and His Ministers, that Our said Subjects may bee restored to the enjoyment of all their former Priviledges whatsoever, and maintained therein for the time to come.

You shall constantly correspond with Our Ministers in other forreigne Courts, for Our better Service, and your mutuall infor-mation and assistance in your respective Negotiations; and you shall also maintaine a good Correspondence and intercourse with all the Ambassadours, Envoyés and Ministers of Princes and States in amity with Us, and as far as you can, penetrate into the designes of their respective superiours, and of what you shall discover of this nature, you shall give Us a constant account by one of Our Principall Secretaryes of State.

You are particularly to live friendly with any Minister, who shall bee there employed from the Duke of Modena, supporting all you can the interests of that Prince in the Court of Ffrance, to manifest to the World how much the Allyance that Prince hath contracted with Us, renders him valuable to Us.

If there happen to bee any Treaty or publick Overture made there, for restoring the Duke of Lorrain to his Estates, you shall acquaint the Most Christian King with the great Esteem and Kindnesse Wee have for the said Duke, whose interests you shall in Our name recommend to that King's favourable consideration; And you shall give your best assistance, as occasion offers, to the said Duke's Ministers and friends, in order to obtain for him, what may bee most for his Honour and advantage: and Wee do in like manner direct you to do all good Offices in Our name to the Elector Palatin in the matters in difference upon account of the pretensions of the Dutchesse of Orleans, whereof you are to informe yourself as particularly as you can, and you shall as occasion offers, lett the Most Christian King and His Ministers know, how much Wee desire that that affaire should bee determined amicably.

Whereas the late King Our most dear Brother deceased, did by an order in Councill bearing date the 26ᵗʰ of August 1668 (which Wee think fitt to confirm) direct His Ambassadᵣˢ not to give the hand in their own Houses to Envoyés in pursuance of what is practised by the Ambᵣˢ of other Princes, Wee think it reasonable Our Envoyés should not pretend to bee treated differently from the treatment Our Ambᵣˢ are to give to the Envoyés of other Princes, and accordingly you are not to insist to have the hand from any Ambassadour (who may happen to bee in that Court) in his own house.

You shall diligently observe the motions and intentions of that Court, particularly as to the making Warr in any part of Europe, and upon what account? what their condition is as to Force and Treasure? and towards which of their Borders or late Conquests their Troops are commanded to march? how their Navall Forces do increase or diminish? and what designes they have for the improvement of either? of all which, as also of all other occurrences, which may bee of consequence or worthy Our knowledge, or which you may find expedient to propose to Us for the advancement of the Trade of Our Subjects, or may concerne Our Subjects, or may concerne Our interest at home or abroad, you shall give frequent accounts and advertisements by one of Our Principall Secretaryes of State, with whom you are also to correspond constantly, and from whom you shall from time to time receive such further Instructions and Directions as Wee shall think requisite to send you, which you are to observe accordingly.

At your returne from thence, Wee shall expect from you a perfect and ample Narrative of what shall have happened in that Court, during your Ministry there, with a particular account of the abilities and affections of the Ministers, their Interests, mutuall Correspondencies and differences, one with another, their dispositions to Warr or Peace; their inclinations to forreign Princes or States, together with all such observations as you shall have been able to make, which may contribute to inform Us of the State of that Government.

J. R.[1]

Sir William Trumbull's Credentials

Tres Haut, Tres Excellent et Tres Puissant Prince, Nostre Tres cher et Tres aimé Bon Frere, Cousin et Ancien Allié, comme nous desirons fort d'entretenir avec soin la bonne Correspondence establie entre Nos Couronnes, Nous avons trouvé à propos à ce fin de vous envoyer le Chevalier Trumbull en qualité de Nostre Envoyé Extraordinaire, vous priant de luy donner de temps en temps des Audiences favorables et une Creance entiere en ce qu'il vous dira de Nostre part, et particulierement quand il vous asseurera de la sincerité de Nostre amitié, dont Nous vous prions d'estre tout a fait persuadé. Et ainsy Nous vous recommendons, Tres Haut, Tres Excellent et Tres Puissant Prince, Nostre Tres Cher et Tres aimé bon Frere, Cousin et ancien Allié, à la Sainte Garde de Dieu. Escrit en Nostre Cour de Whitehall ce 20ᵐᵉ d'Octobre 1685.

Vostre bon frere Cousin et ancien Allié

JACQUES R

SUNDERLAND.[2]

---

1 R.O. *France, Entry Book* 19 (not foliated).
2 *Ib.*, where see also his letter of revocation, dated Aug. 9 (O.S.), 1686.

Sir William Trumbull's "Bills of extraordinaries"[1]

(Sir William's "ordinary" was 5*l.* a day)

I. For the period September 2 to December 2, 1685

	l.	*s.*	*d.*
charges for passing my privy seal [in the Office of the] Signet [and the] Secretary's Office and for an order from the Admiralty	26	15	6[2]
fees paid at the Exchequer on 500*l.* for equipage and [on] three months ordinary	24	2	0
fees at the Treasury for a warrant and letter to the Customs Officers	2	5	0
paid at the Custom House	2	3	0
for a large barge and boats to bring myself and servants on board the Yacht	3	6	0
for porters and boats to carry my goods on board the Yacht, and the vessel for Rouen	10	0	0
for the captain of the yacht who carried me to Dieppe .	25	0	0
for the master and seamen of the yacht . . .	7	0	0
for mourning cloth for myself, coaches and servants .	66	10	0
for Communion plate for the Chapel . . .	33	2	11
for [Prayer] books for my chapel	7	13	0
for the expense of my coach horses and servants from London to Dieppe	20	14	0
	228	10	11[3]

	Livres *Tournois*	[*sols*]	[*dens*]
for the vessel that transported my horses to Dieppe and [for] the Custom House officers there .	357	0	0
for the carriage of the goods (that came in the yacht) from Dieppe to Calais . . .	354	0	0
for my journey from Dieppe to Paris, being six days	1519	13	3
for Gazettes and intelligences to the 2nd of December	153	0	0
for the Officers of the Douane at Paris . .	64	0	0
for my expences the first day I had my audience at Versailles	118	0	0

1 Reprinted from *Cal. Treas. Books*, 1685–9, by the kind permission of the Deputy Keeper of Public Records.

2 Perhaps £26. 15*s.* 0*d.*, to give the correct total.

3 *Cal. Treas. Books*, 1685–9, p. 1116. Rochester disallowed the following items: communion plate and prayer-books.

	Livres Tournois	[sols]	[dens]
given according to custom to the Guardes des Portes, the coachmen of the King and [of] Mad[ame] la Dauphine, the Servants of Monsieur de Croissy, the Introducteur des Ambassadeurs and his Lieutenants	290	0	0
for my other journey to Versailles . . .	49	10	0
for the expence of making my mourning equipage, for myself, coaches and servants . . .	1033	13	0
for stationery ware	33	0	0
	3972	2	3

which at 1230 *Livres Tournois* to 100*l.* sterling   *l.*   *s.*   *d.*

| makes . . . . | 323 | 9 | 2 |
| Total bill . . . . | 552 | 0 | 1[1] |

II. For the period December 2, 1685 to March 2, 1686[2]

	Livres	sols
for postage of letters to Jan. 1	247	19
for new year's gifts to the officers at Court and the servants of the Introducteurs as usual	259	15
for bringing the rest of my goods, furniture and household stuff from London to Rouen	852	10
for bringing them from Rouen by water to Paris . .	582	0
for the douaniers at Paris for visiting them . .	64	0
for the right of entrie of the port of Paris . . .	75	0
for benches, pulpit and other furniture requisite for my chapel	174	0
for Gazettes, prints and intelligence	719	18
for several journeys of myself and servants to Versailles .	511	10
expences of the rejouissances on the day of his Majesty's happy coming to the Crown	358	10
interest of plate for half a year as has been formerly allowed	399	0
for stationery ware	88	9
for postage of letters from Jan 1 to April 1 . . .	445	2
	4777	13

which at the above rate of exchange (as usually allowed)   *l.*   *s.*   *d.*

| makes . . . . | 388 | 8 | 6[3] |

---

1 *Cal. Treas. Books,* 1685–9, p. 1117. One of the 'o' under sols should probably read '9', to ensure correct total.

2 But includes one item of a later date.

3 *Ib.* Rochester disallowed the following items: benches, etc. and interest on plate.

III. For the period March 2 to June 2, 1686

	Livres	sols
for postage of letters as by acquit[tance] from the Post-house	407	17
for postage of letters brought to my house from several parts	165	11
for journeys and entertainment of myself and servants at Versailles	477	0[1]
for trimming and new fitting the mourning equipage upon the mourning for the Princess Dowager Palatine .	468	0
given to Monsieur's and Madame's coachmen and other charges at my audience of condolence for the Princess Dowager Palatine	137	10
for gazettes, prints and intelligence	587	5
for stationery ware	159	0
for a courier sent into England	300	0
paid by order to an engineer	83	0
	2787	3

which being reduced into English money at the usual *l. s. d.*
rate (of 1230 *livres tournois* to 100*l.* sterling) comes to 226 8 9½[2]

IV. For the period June 2 to October 12, 1686

	Livres	sols
for an express sent into England	300	0
for bonfires and other expenses upon the birth of the Duc de Berri	393	0
paid at the Post House for letters.	511	0
for letters brought to my house and paid for there .	180	0
for doctors and apothecaries during my stay at Paris	305	0
for half a year's interest of plate	399	0
given as usual to the several officers at my audience of Congé at Versailles	290	0
given and expended at my audience of Congé at St Cloud	137	10
to the Douaniers at Paris	115	0
given to Monsieur Bonneuil and Monsieur Giraut, Introducteurs des Ambassadeurs, and their servants when they brought the present from the French King . .	1035	0

1 Given erroneously in *Cal. Treas. Books*, p. 1220 as 468 livres. Cf. R.O. *Money Book*, VIII, p. 55, 24 Feb. 1686–7, which gives the sum as 477 livres. The total should read 2785 livres 3 sols.

	Livres	sols
paid for stationery ware	345	0
paid M. Petitot for a pound of ultramarine by his Majesty's order	575	0
for intelligence	895	0
for several voyages for myself and servants to Versailles .	580	0
for prints and gazettes	784	0
for the expense of my voyage to England, with the transporting of my servants, coaches and goods by Rouen and Dieppe	3570	0
to the Douaniers at Dieppe	80	0
	10494	10

	l.	s.	d.
which reduced into sterling at the above rates makes .	853	0	9[1]

	l.	s.	d.
Paid since in English money.			
to the captain of the *Catherine* yacht and to the seamen	32	0	0
for weighing my goods and other charges at the Custom House	30	0	0
[paid] at the Admiralty Office for an order for the yacht	2	3	0
for [Exchequer] fees on [my warrant for] three months ordinary	11	1	0
for ditto on ditto	11	1	0
for ditto on 800*l.* in part of my first two bills of extraordinaries	29	16	0
for ditto on 1085*l.* due by the present bill and on 226*l.* 8*s.* 9½*d.* on a former bill of extraordinaries and on 660*l.* for my ordinary from June 2 last to the time of my coming over	66	6	0
for interest and advance of money	50	0	0
	1085	7	9½[2]

1 *Cal. Treas. Books*, 1685–9, p. 1221. '9*d*' should probably read '9½*d*.' The following items were disallowed on this bill and the preceding one: interest of plate, and several journeys to Versailles which were referred to the Treasury Lords.

2 *Ib*

Sir William Trumbull and Bayle

The suggestion of dedicating the Dictionary to Sir William Trumbull probably came from Michel Le Vassor,[1] who seems to have acted as intermediary. On August 11, 1695, one finds him telling Sir William that he has informed Bayle of Sir William's kindness to him.[2] Six months later he wrote a long letter to Bayle. M. Trumbull was very well intentioned. "J'ai peine à me persuader que vous ne sachiez rien de ce que je vous ai écrit, touchant la dédicace de votre livre. Voulez-vous m'en faire une [*sic*] mystère? Je sai la chose de M. Trumball mesme." Le Vassor had seen the letter the publisher Leers had written to Sir William[3]—Sir William was much pleased and looked upon the dedication of this book as a thing which honoured him greatly. He had already the first volume of the Dictionary, but was not showing it to anyone yet according to the request of the publisher Leers. Le Vassor only wished that Bayle would be "un peu moins philosophe" and cultivate such a friend. Let him write to Sir William and give him some news of the Republic of letters. "Au nom de Dieu, ne négligez point M. Trumball....La dédicace est engagée: il n'est plus question que de faire la chose de bonne grâce."[4]

Le Vassor urged another friend in England, Pierre Sylvestre, to write to Bayle in the same strain,[5] and Sylvestre wrote to Bayle that it was rare to find such a Maecenas. "N'allez point faire le philosophe hors de saison."[6]

Des Maizeaux however tells a story about another possible patron of Bayle. "They had so advantageous an opinion of Mr Bayle's Dictionary in England, that a person of quality there, no less distinguished by his genius than by his rank and the great posts he enjoyed [marginal note: The Duke of Shrewsbury, Secretary of State] desired that the work should be dedicated to him. He desired M. Basnage to assure Mr Bayle that he would acknowledge it by a present of two hundred guineas. Mr Bayle's friends and particularly M. Basnage pressed him very much to give this Nobleman that

---

1 See p. 167 *ante*.
2 *H.M.C.*, *Downshire MSS.* I, Part II, p. 532.
3 This letter is not among Sir William's papers at Easthampstead.
4 Gigas, *op. cit.* pp. 490–3, Feb. 3, 1696
5 *Ib.* p. 492.
6 *Ib.* p. 697.

satisfaction, but in vain. He said that he had so frequently made a jest of Dedications that he would not expose himself by making one. This however was only a pretence to give a colour to his refusal. The real ground of the long and obstinate resistance which he made upon this occasion was, that he would not flatter or praise any person who had any employment in the Court of a Prince of whom he thought he had reason to complain, and this Lord was at this time in the Ministry" [marginal note: MSS. Memoirs of Mr Basnage].[1]

Sir William also was Secretary of State at this time, and the same objection must have applied to him.[2]

On March 30, 1696, the publisher Leers sent Sir William the third volume of the Dictionary, and a fortnight later Bayle himself wrote to Sir William.

"Mylord

Jusques icy je n'ai pas eu l'honneur de vous temoigner moi meme mais seulement par l'entremise de M^r Le Vassor la reconnoissance extreme que j'ai de vos bontez infiniment obligeantes, et l'admiration que je sens pour votre rare merite avec le plaisir extraordinaire que me donne la nouvelle de votre elevation à un poste que vous remplissez si glorieusement, c'est par respect et pour menager un tems precieux que vous employez au bien public de l'Angleterre d'ou depend aujourd'hui la felicité de toute l'Europe. Je me hasarde aujourd'hui, Mylord, à vous derober quelques momens, car je craindrois qu'a force de me tenir dans un silence respectueux je ne passasse dans une extremité vicieuse. Souffrez donc je vous en coniure la liberté que je prens de vous asseurer de mes tres profonds respects et de ma gratitude tres sensible.

Si des obstacles insurmontables ne m'empeschoient pas de mettre mon nom au Dictionaire (sic) Critique[3] je vous eusse demandé tres humblement la permission de vous le dedier, et de le mettre avec son auteur sous la protection d'un nom aussi illustre que le votre tant par la connoissance des sciences, que par celles qui sont proprement de ses grands emplois, ne pouvant pas me procurer cet avantage et aiant

1 Des Maizeaux, "Life of Mr Bayle", p. lxxiv, in Bayle, Dictionary, vol. 1. London, 1734.

2 If Des Maizeaux had not had the information from Basnage, one might have wondered whether there was not some confusion between Shrewsbury and Trumbull.

3 His friends prevailed upon him in the end to put his name to the Dictionary. See Des Maizeaux's Life at the beginning of the Dictionary.

eu de fortes raisons de laisser au libraire tout le soin de la dedicace, je fus ravi d'aprendre qu'il jettoit les yeux sur vous, Mylord, mais je crains que la proposition qu'il vous en a faite n'ait pas assez —[1] et telle qu'elle eut été s'il m'eut consulté avant que de se donner l'honneur de vous en ecrire. Quoi qu'il en soit, Mylord, ie vous suplie tres humblement de me compter au nombre de ceux qui ont le plus de veneration et d'attachement pour votre personne et qui font les voeux les plus ardens pour votre conservation si utile à toute la terre, et permettez moi de vous demander votre protection avec toute sorte de respect.

Mr Le Vassor m'aiant asseuré que vous trouveriez bon que je vous fisse savoir les nouveautez literaires ie vous suplie d'agréer ce peu que j'en ai apris. Feu Mr Huygens a laissé un manuscrit sur la pluralité des mondes que l'on a commencé d'imprimer mais l'on doute si l'édition sera continuée: la famille est en suspens là dessus parce qu'elle craint de faire murmurer Mrs les Theologiens à cause que l'Auteur est entré dans un assez grand detail de conjectures sur les habitans des planetes.[2] Un Hollandois nommé Hartsoeker etabli à Paris n'a pas fait difficulté dans son Essai de dioptrique[3] d'avancer beaucoup de choses particulieres sur les habitans de la lune. Il vient de publier une Physique[4] qui contient des choses assez curieuses, quoique la methode de cet auteur soit plus d'avancer des nouveautez et des coniectures particulieres que de les prouver un peu a fond. On a imprimé en Allemagne un livre posthume de Pufendorf intitulé *ius feciale divinum sive de consensu et dissensu protestantium.*[5] Il regarde comme un dogme de tres grande importance la dispute qui est entre les luthériens et les calvinistes sur la prédestination. Cet ouvrage ne fait qu'effleurer les choses, mais il en effleure beaucoup en peu de mots et temoigne la netteté de jugement de son auteur. Mr Leti Historiographe d'Amsterdam publiera au premier jour 2 ou 3 volumes in 4° de son Teatro Gallico[6] où il enferme toutes les affaires du tems, il y ioindra le long poeme qu'il a deja fait paroitre a la louange de sa majesté Britannique. On acheve a Paris l'édition des oeuvres du pere Sirmond Jesuiste qui comprendra 3 ou 4 gros volumes in folio.[7] On y acheve aussi l'impression du premier

1 The word, very illegible, looks like "distincte"—possibly there is an omission—"je crains que la proposition...n'ait pas [été] assez distincte."
2 Christiani Hugenii *Cosmotheoros sive de Terris coelestibus earumque ornatu conjecturae....* The Hague, 1698.
3 Nicolas Hartsoeker, *Essai de dioptrique.* Paris, 1694.
4 Nicolas Hartsoeker, *Principes de physique.* Paris, 1696.
5 Lübeck, 1695.
6 Gregorio Leti, *Teatro Gallico,* 7 vols. Amsterdam, 1691-7.
7 J. Sirmond, *Opera varia,* 5 vols. Paris, 1696.

volume des hommes illustres qu'un intendant de province nommé Mr Begon[1] fait peindre et decrire.

C'est trop abuser de votre patience, je finis par la protestation sincere que ie suis avec une extreme veneration

Mylord

Votre tres humble

et tres obeissant serviteur

BAYLE"

A Amsterdam le

17 d'Avril 1696.[2]

In November of that year, 1696, Bayle sent a copy of the Dictionary to Sir William.[3] The work with Bayle's inscription is now at Easthampstead Park.[4] The letter announcing the gift has been already quoted.[5]

Sir William replied in Latin, assuring the author that he had sent him "*bibliothecam potius quam librum*".[6]

Le Vassor spoke of Sir William's kind feelings towards Bayle, "mais il faut qu'il aille plus loin",[7] and six months later he remarked "M. le Chevalier Trumbull m'a fort parlé de vous aujourd'hui; il est bien de vos amis. Mais enfin je voudrois qu'il fist quelque chose".[8] Whether Sir William lived up to Le Vassor's expectations we do not know.

Sir William Trumbull's first Memorial in behalf of the Principality of Orange[9]

Au Roy trés Chretien

Sire,

Le soubz[né] Envoyé Extraord[re] du Roy de la grande Bretagne ayant fait scavoir a sa M[te] la reponce qu'il a plu a V.M.T.Ch. luy faire donner par M[r] le Marquis de Croissy, sur l'Invasion faitte dans

1 *Les Hommes illustres qui ont paru en France pendant ce siècle.* Par M. Perrault de l'Academie françoise, Paris, 1696. "Cet ouvrage est dû principalement à l'amour que M. Begon Intendant de Justice et de Marine a pour la memoire des grans hommes...." *Journal des Savans*, pp. 3–4. Paris, 1697.

2 Downshire Manuscripts at Easthampstead Park, vol. xxxi, No. 242.

3 *H.M.C., Downshire MSS.* 1, Part 11, p. 647.   4 *Ib.* p. 699.

5 See pp. 168 *ante.*   6 Gigas, *op. cit.* p. 697.

7 *Ib.* p. 498.   8 *Ib.* p. 505.

9 From Sir William's own MS. copy at Easthampstead Park. The printed copy which circulated in Holland and was sent to France by the Ambassador d'Avaux (A.É. *Angleterre*, vol. 160, f. 297. Endorsed, "receu le 21 jan[r] 1686. D'Avaux") is slightly different in one or two places. The chief differences are indicated.

la ville et principauté d'Orange par les Trouppes de V.M. il a receu de nouveaux ordres pour renouveller ses instances et luy representer tres humblement que le Roy son maitre n'a pu apprendre qu'avec un extreme deplaisir les desordres et mauvais traittemens exercés sur les sujets de Monsieur le Prince d'Orange depuis l'entrée desd. Troupes de V.M.T.Ch. dans la Ville et principauté qui fut le 25 d'octobre.

Il est d'une notorieté publique que tant mond^t S^r le Prince d'Orange que ses predecesseurs ont toujours possedé lad. Principautté avec tous les droits, prerogatives et immunités attachés a la souverainetté; cela paroit par les traittés et par les lettres de reintegration données par les Rois vos predecesseurs, lorsqu'il est arrivé que par les desordres de la Guerre lesd. Princes ont été troublés dans la juste possession de lad. principauté et c'est ce qui est incontestable.

V.M.T.Ch. ne pouvant donc legitimement pretendre aucun droit sur lad. Principauté d'Orange et ayant au contraire lors de la paix de Nimegue retably led. Prince dans la jouissance[1] d'Icelle, dont il avoit été dépossédé pendant la Guerre, au meme Etat et en la meme maniere qu'il en avoit jouy auparavant, ainsi qu'il est porté par un article separé du traitté, le Roy son maitre se plaint, qu'il y ayt été si manifestement contrevenu et voulant en prevenir les suites facheuses dans le dessein ou il est de contribuer autant qu'il luy sera possible au maintien de la paix parmi tous les princes Chretiens il ordonne expressement aud. Envoyé de supplier V.M.T.Ch. de vouloir faire remettre dans la possession de lad. Principauté led. Prince et dans tous les droits de souverainetté qu'on ne peut justement luy denier,[2] ordonner que restitution luy soit faitte des sommes exigées des habitans de lad. Ville et Principauté avec le retablissement de toutes choses en leur entier comme elles doivent etre aux termes dud. Traitté de Nimegue,[3] ayant aussy en cela quelque consideration pour le Roy son maitre qui se plaint du peu d'egards que V.M.T.Ch. paroit avoir pour un prince, qui luy est si prochainement allié.

Led. Envoyé espere et attend de V.M.T.Ch. une reponce satisfaisante pour le Roy son maitre qui ne doutte pas qu'apres de si grandes choses qu'elle a fait pour la paix qui subsiste a pñt Elle ne

1 Printed copy: "possession".
2 Printed copy: "...souverainité dont il a esté depouillé."
3 Printed copy: "...Nymegue; et comme le Roy son Maistre ainsi qu'il y est obligé, veut tousjours employer ses soins pour le maintien dudit Traitté, dont il est guarant; il se promet que vostre Majesté voudra seconder ses bonnes intentions, et repondre favorablement aux instances, qu'il a ordonné audit Envoyé de faire en son nom sur cette affaire, ayant aussy en cela quelque esgard pour un Prince qui luy est si proche."

veuille encore faire cesser tout ce qui pourroit contribuer a la troubler.[1]

Sir William Trumbull's second Memorial in behalf of the Principality of Orange

Au Roy Tres Chretien

Le soubz^{né} Envoyé Extraord^{re} du Roy de la grande Bretagne, se trouve obligé par les ordres expres qu'il a receus de Sa Majesté par le dernier Courrier; de faire scavoir a Votre Majesté, que le Roy son Maitre n'a pu étre satisfait des responses qu'il a receües de sa part sur les affaires d'Orange et qu'il souhaitteroit que V. M^{té} voulut encore y faire quelques Reflexions et sur toutes les Raisons cy-devant alleguéés esperant qu'apres cela et en consideration de ses instances Elle pourra se relacher enfin pour donner a Monsieur le Prince d'Orange satisfaction sur ses justes et legitimes pretentions, faisant eclater en cecy une nouvelle marque de sa justice et un temoignage public de sa consideration et de son amitié pour sa Majesté. a Versailles le 12e jour de febvrier 1686.[2]

Memorial presented by Sir William Trumbull in behalf of English Merchants

Au Roy Tres Chretien.

Sire

Le soubz^{né} Envoyé Ext^{re} du Roy de la Grande Bretagne obeissant a ses ordres, represente tres humblement a V.M.T.Ch. que le Roy son Maitre a receu avec un extreme deplaisir les plaintes qui lui ont été faittes par le nommé Stukey Marchand et facteur de divers Marchands Anglois a la Rochelle et plusieurs autres de ses sujets de ce que bien que comme etrangers, ils dussent pretendre de n'etre sujets aux charges publiques de votre Royaume, neantmoins les officiers de V.M.T.Ch. n'ont pas laissé de leur donner logement de gens de Guerre et de les opprimer de telle sorte, qu'ils sont menacés d'une totale ruine et d'etre reduits a une dure necessité, si V.M.T.Ch. ne donne les ordres pour mettre fin a un tel procédé. Il est Sire si contraire a la bonne foy des Traittés qui permettent aux Sujets des

---

1 Downshire MSS. at Easthampstead Park, vol. xxiii, No. 56, undated. English résumé *H.M.C., Downshire MSS.* 1, pp. 85–6.

2 R.O. *France*, vol. 150, f. 19.

deux Couronnes d'aller et venir dans l'un et l'autre Royaume, de s'y habituer et d'exercer leur commerce sans pouvoir etre inquietés en façon quelconque; que le Roy son maitre ne sauroit croire, que V.M. en etant informée puisse souffrir plus longtemps de telles violences, si contraires a la bonne intelligence, qui subsiste a present entre les deux Couronnes que V.M.T.Ch. a temoigné en tant de rencontres vouloir conserver et qui produit de si grands avantages a l'une et a l'autre nation. S. M^{té} attend donc de la Justice de V.M.T.Chr. qu'elle voudra bien les faire cesser, ordonner la restitution des sommes exigées des susd. particuliers par les Troupes de V.M.T.C. avec reparation des dommages par eux soufferts et qu'elle donnera les ordres necessaires a ce qu'a l'avenir les officiers de V.M.T.Ch. ne commettent ces sortes d'attentats sur les sujets de S. M^{té} habitués en France. C'est ce que led. Envoyé a ordre exprès de representer a V.M.T.Chr. et que le Roy son Maitre ne doutte pas qu'elle ne reponde aux intensions qu'il a de vouloir toujours entrenir (*sic*) une bonne et parfaitte Union avec Elle.[1]

Sir William Trumbull's Memorial in behalf of the Hudson's Bay Company

Au Roy tres Chrestien

Sire

Le soubz^{gné} Envoyé extraordinaire du Roy de la grande Bretagne a receu ordre de sa Majesté de rpnter a vostre Majesté tres chrestienne qu'ayant esté donné divers memoirs par le Precedent Envoyé[2] pour demander satisfaction de la part du Roy son maistre des violences et entreprises commises au mois de juillet de l'année 1683 par les habitans françois du Canada contre les Interessez en la compagnie angloise de Hudson au nord-ouest de l'Amerique.

1 R.O. *France*, vol. 148, f. 140. [Memorial presented on Dec. 5, 1685.]

2 Lord Preston had complained of the "enterprize of the French upon Nelson's port" and had demanded justice over against Radisson, then in Paris, that curious explorer-adventurer who served now the English, now the French. He had subsequently seen Radisson join the Hudson's Bay Company once more, in May 1684, and had been set to justify Radisson's actions on his return to the Company, as well as to demand reparation against the encroachments of Charles Aubert de la Chesnaye who headed the Compagnie du Nord. *H.M.C.*, 7*th Report*, App., Part 1, pp. 261, 295, 296, 298, 302, 304, 323, 328, 332, 333, 369, R.O. *France*, *Entry Book* 19, Dec. 1–11, 1684, May 7–17, 1685; *Recueil des Instructions...Angleterre*, 11, pp. 352–9; Laut, *Conquest of the Great Northwest*, *passim*; Beckles Willson, *The great Company*.

Il[1] n'a esté fait aucune justice sur cette affaire, ce qui a donné occasion au Sr de la Barre gouverneur des Colonies françoises aud. Canada sous l'authorité duquel cette premiere hostilité avoit esté commise de delivrer de nouvelles commissions pour une seconde Invasion dans la riviere et port de Nelson, ou lad. Compagnie a une factorie et habitation. Et pour cet effet, ayant envoyé deux vaisseaux montez d'environ 60 hommes, ils y sont entrez dans le mois de septembre 1684, ont attaqué la factorie, pillé les effets que la Compagnie pouvoit y avoir, rompu entierement le commerce qu'elle avoit avec les habitans du païs et surpris tous les marchandises qui luy venoient de la traitte qu'elle fait faire avec les habitans et ont exercé ces violences et pillages pendant tout l'hiver au prejudice de plus de 40^m escus pour lad. Compagnie.

Et comme s'ils eussent eu dessein d'accabler tout a fait lad. Compagnie estant sur leur retour en Canada et ayant rencontré au mois de juillet ensuivant un vaisseau[2] appartenan a lad. Compagnie qui faisoit voile vers la riviere et port de Nelson chargé de quelques provisions et vivres pour ceux de la factorie, ils ont pris led. vaisseau et l'ont emmené au Canada avec sa cargaison, maistre, matelots et passans au nombre de quatorze.

De sorte que toutes ces choses ont donné lieu a lad. Compagnie de reclamer encore de nouveau la Royale protection de sa Ma^té afin qu'elle interpose ses Instances auprez de V. M^té T. Chr. pour faire cesser ces Insultes si souvent redoublées et ord^ner la reparation des dommages par Elle soufferts avec restitution de toutes choses, tant pour ce qui regarde cette derniere Invasion que les Precedentes. C'est ce que led. Envoyé a ordre exprez du Roy son maistre de demander a V. M^té. T. Chr. et de luy repñter que la juste possession dans laquelle est lad. riviere et port de Nelson ainsi q^l a esté pleinement justifié par les memoires precedens devroit la mettre a couvert de ces sortes d'insultes, et comme la continuation ne pourroit estre que tres prejudiciable a l'alliance et bonne correspondance qui est entre les 2 couronnes il supplie V.M.T.Chr. de donner les ordres a ce qu'a l'advenir lad. Compagnie ne soit plus troublée dans l'establisse-

---

1 This is still obviously part of the foregoing sentence.

2 The *Merchant of Perpetuana* was taken in the summer of 1685 when Lord Preston was making ready to return to England. Fourteen of the crew lost their lives, the others, with the Captain, Hume, were taken to Quebec. The ship carrying Radisson, the *Happy Return*, and another ship, the *Success*, escaped. The H.B. Company was informed on Oct. 30 (O.S.) of its loss. *Cal. St P. Col., A. and W. I.* 1681–5, pp. 368–9, 660, 662, etc.; Laut, *op. cit.* I, pp. 201 *et seq.*, 208, 209, 273; Beckles Willson, *op. cit.* I, pp. 159–60.

Two days later Sunderland wrote to Trumbull directing him to protest against the violences committed. R.O. *France, Entry Book* 19, Nov. 1–11, 1685.

ment qu'il a fait aud. port de Nelson et que le S^r De la Barre soit tenu de rendre raison de ce dernier attentat comme tendant a la violation de la parfaite intelligence.[1]

Sir William Trumbull's Memorial concerning the Confiscation of certain Ships

Au Roy tres Chretien

Sire

Le soubsigné Envoyé Extraordinaire du Roy de la Grande Bretagne obeissant a ses ordres represente tres humblement a Vostre Majesté Que le Roy son Maistre a receu plainte que ceux qui commandent dans les colonies de la domination de Vostre Majesté aux Indes occidentales sous pretexte d'avoir ses ordres, comme il paroist par le formulaire de Passeport du S^r de St Laurans son Commandant General dans les Isles ffrancoises et terre ferme d'Amerique dont copie est cy jointe, arrestent et confisquent sans autre raison tous les Vaisseaux qui vont mouiller aux Rades appartenans à V.M. et delivrent de plus aux Armateurs, quoy qu'en temps de paix, des comissions, en vertu desquelles ils exercent les memes hostilités sur les Batimens des Sujets du Roy son Maistre, que s'il y avoit une guerre ouverte, ainsi qu'il a esté pratiqué sur les cotes de la nouvelle Ecosse, ou plusieurs Anglois de la nouvelle Ampspire[2] (*sic*) ayant envoyé quelques chaloupes, pour y pescher, suivant la commission qu'en ont toujours accordé les commandans de V.M. moyennant cent sols par chaque bateau, qui leur estoit payé annuellement, le nommé Burgie[3] soy disant Gouverneur d'un petit fort dans l'Abaye (*sic*) de Comto,[4] nonobstant, et sans avoir esgard au Passeport du S^r le Vallier, Gouverneur de la nouvelle Ecosse, a enlevé lesd. Chaloupes et pris un Vaisseau appartenant auxd. Anglois qu'ils ont envoyé en France avec la plus grande partie de l'Equipage.

Et comme toutes ces choses donneroient un juste Sujet de plainte au Roy son Maistre, si elles estoient authorisées de V.M. led. Envoyé prie instamment V.M. qu'elle ayst agreable de luy faire scavoir ses intentions la dessus, afin qu'il en puisse rendre compte au Roy son Maistre qui s'attend cependant qu'elle donnera les ordres a ce que ses Sujets receussent la juste satisfaction, et dedommagement des pertes par eux soufertes, et qu'à l'advenir ils ne puissent estre

1 A.É. *Angleterre*, vol. 151, ff. 365, 366. Another copy vol. 160, f. 95 [December, 1685].
2 New Hampshire.   3 Bergier.   4 la Baie de Canso.

troublés ny inquietés dans leur commerce, et qu'il ne sera plus delivrés par vos Gouverneurs des Commissions a aucun Armateur sans auparavant avoir donné bonne et suffisante caution ainsi qu'il est expressément porté par les Traitez afin d'eviter tout ce qui pourroit troubler la bonne intelligence et correspondance qui subsiste entre les deux Couronnes.[1]

Notes on the affairs of the Palatinate

The following extracts from Sir William Trumbull's letters relate to the affairs of the Palatinate. It seemed preferable to give these separately—they would have impeded the general narrative and are more interesting when read consecutively.[2]

Some of these extracts refer to the general question—how were the claims of Madame, Duchess of Orleans, sister of the late Elector Palatine, to be settled? By the mediation of the Pope?[3]

But the majority of the extracts concern the following incident. On November 5, 1685, an inhabitant of Mannheim, Jean Cardel, who had emigrated from France some years before, was arrested near Mannheim with his companion by order of Louis XIV and taken to Vincennes.

At the same time Louis XIV asked the Elector to arrest some other citizens of Mannheim and send them to France because they were equally involved in a plot against him. All the accused were Protestants.

Out of deference to Louis XIV the Elector did not demand restitution of his subjects imprisoned at Vincennes. He arrested the other men accused, but refused to hand them over until he should have further proof of their guilt. Louis thereupon recalled his envoy, the abbé Morel.[4]

"Dec. 12, 1685....The Abbé Morel, Envoyé from this Court to yᵉ Elector Palatin, makes a Demand of all yᵉ Moveables of yᵉ late Elector deceased, Among which he pretends (in behalf of Madame d'Orleans) to all yᵉ Canon and Ammunition in all yᵉ Magazins."[5]

---

1 R.O. *France*, vol. 148, f. 142. Endorsed: "Copie of my memorial deliverd to Mʳ de Croissy yᵉ 15 Dec. 85."

2 The same remark applies to the notes on Lorraine and on the Waldensians.

3 On this point see Immich, *Zur Vorgeschichte des Orleans'schen Krieges, passim*; Pagès, *Le Grand Électeur et Louis XIV*, pp. 559–60. Also A.É. *Angleterre*, vol. 156, ff. 27, 58, 62, 70, 75. Barrillon to Louis XIV, Sept.–Oct. 1685.

4 Cf. Immich, *op. cit.* pp. 34–5; Sourches, *Mémoires*, I, p. 336; *H.M.C., Downshire MSS.* I, p. 94.

5 R.O. *France*, vol. 148, f. 137, Dec. 12, 1685. All these letters are addressed to Sunderland.

"Dec. 19, 1685....Of what is come to my Hands about ye Affaires of ye Palatinate, I take ye Liberty to sent yor Lo^p ye Copies inclosd, where yor Lo^p will see ye Memorial given in by ye Abbé Morel,[1] demanding to have ye Prisoners at Manheim deliverd out to be sent hither and Tryd here: Together with ye Electors Answer,[2] And allso a Copie of that Letter[3] wch he sent by Monsr Peyker[4], his Secretarie, as a Courier expresse, Desiring onely thereby to be informd of ye Presumptions of ye Crime whereof they are accus'd, before he delivers them. Yo^r Lo^p will hereby receive ye Detail of this affaire and therefore it is needlesse to trouble you with any further Account of it. Onely I am informd, that ye Answer[5] given to this Letter is, That ye King had Reason to beleive, That ye Elector Palatin would have had such an entire Confidence in him, as to have remaind satisfyd, That he would not have demanded these Prisoners without just Cause: But since he is not, he would speake no more of it, but instantly recall his said Envoyé, l'Abbé Morel, home."[6]

"Jan. ye 2^d, 1686....I am inform'd, That ye Emper^r has given his positive Answ^r, That he would not accept of ye Arbitrage of ye Pope about ye affaires of ye Palatinat, it being opposite to ye Lawes of the Empire and ye Intentions of ye Princes interessed therein."[7]

"23 Jan. 1686....The Abbé Morel, since his returne, speakes very openly against ye Elector Palatine; So that 'tis apprehended something may be design'd that way."[8]

"Jan. 30, 1686....The Popes Nuncio[9] here endeav^{rs} to accommodate ye Differences about ye Palatinate: He has represented ye Electors Palatine's Answer otherwise than it was given out, vizt That ye Elector did not refuse ye Pope's Arbitrage, but said, It was not in his Power to accept it; And that he would lay ye Proposition before ye Emper^r, ye Princes of ye Empire, and ye next^t Successors of his Family; whose Consent, as Persons interessed in ye matter, was absolutely necessarie. However this is still highly resented att Court, though this King declares he will not disturbe ye Peace of Christendom."[10]

"Feb. 16, 1686. On Wenesday night, Monsr Peyker, Secretarie

1 Printed in Immich, *op. cit.* pp. 36–7. Copy R.O. *loc. cit.* f. 124; cf. *H.M.C., op. cit.* p. 56.
2 Printed in Immich, *op. cit.* pp. 37–8. Copy R.O. *loc. cit.* ff. 126–7; cf. *H.M.C., op. cit.* p. 58.
3 Printed in Immich, *op. cit.* pp. 38–42. Copy R.O. *loc. cit.* ff. 131–4; cf. *H.M.C., op. cit.* pp. 62–4.
4 Peucker.
5 Printed in Immich, *op. cit.* p. 341.
6 R.O. *loc. cit.* f. 147.
7 *Ib.* f. 157.
8 R.O. *France*, vol. 150, f. 6.
9 Angelo Maria Ranucci or Ranuzzi.
10 R.O. *loc. cit.* f. 10.

to y⁰ Elector Palatin, who brought y⁰ former Expresse, arrivd here with another. On Thursday morning he went to Versailles to deliver y⁰ Letter,[1] Which was written to Monsʳ de Croissy, Because y⁰ Answer given before from this King to y⁰ Elector was in these words—J'ay ordonné á mon Envoyé de revenir Incessamment auprés de moy sans vous parler davantage sur cette matiere. The Elector therefore addressed himself to Monsʳ de Croissy, to desire him to do what good Offices he could with y⁰ most Christian King in representing his Conduct concerning y⁰ Prisonners at Mannheim, Which he had since caus'd to be Examin'd, in y⁰ presence of other Wittnesses; And although there is not the least Presumptions agᵗ them of y⁰ Crime wherewith they were accus'd, Yet y⁰ Elector (to shew all possible Respect) would not sett them att Libertie, till he had acquainted Monsʳ de Croissy with y⁰ whole proceedings, and sent y⁰ Examinations that were taken to informe this King fully of all y⁰ Matter; Desiring also that Cardel (as one of his subjects) in case he bee found Innocent, may be sett att Liberty and sent back to him. This is y⁰ Substance of y⁰ Letter, as I am inform'd. I shall obtaine a Copie by y⁰ next Ordinarie, to send to yoʳ Loᵖ.

When y⁰ Pacquet was brought to Monsʳ de Croissy's y⁰ Secretarie of y⁰ Elector was not admitted to speake with him, Because he was in Bed still indispos'd with y⁰ Gout; Whereupon he deliverd it to his Commis, who went in to Monsʳ de Croissy and after he had stayd some time brought it back againe, and orderd y⁰ Secretarie to returne with it on Sunday, when there would be a Council; And though he desird to leave y⁰ Pacquet till then, he was orderd to take it away with him.

Yesterday I am told a Council was held, where it was debated whether this Letter shall be accepted or not: This King having declar'd before That he would speake no more about y⁰ Matter, and y⁰ Secretarie being sent back after that manner, gives some Apprehension that no better Answer will be given, Wᶜʰ will cause great Alarmes, especially in Germany."[2]

"Feb 20 1686....On Sunday last the Secretarie of y⁰ Electʳ Palatin went (according to appoinᵗ) to Versailles, having first communicated the Affaire to y⁰ Popes Nuncio,[3] who tooke y⁰ opportunity of going to speake with Monsieur de Croissy that morning before; But, finding Monsieur de Croissy so high in his Resentments concerning y⁰ Electors Proceedings, as (among other expressions) to say, Que l'Electeur Palatin meritoit bien d'etre chassé de ses

1 Immich, *op. cit.* pp. 69–71.   2 R.O. *loc. cit.* f. 23.
3 Cf. Immich, *op. cit.* pp. 71–2.

Estats en vint et quatre heures, he advis'd y⁰ Secretarie to forbeare
delivering his Pacquet for that time; And in y⁰ meane while the
Nuncio found meanes to propose, That allthough the Electour had
refus'd y⁰ Popes Arbitrage, yet that he would accept of y⁰ Popes
Mediation; And it is beleivd this Expedient will be agreed to, and
putt those differences into a way of being amicably compos'd;
Though y⁰ Nuncio pressing for an Answer in Writing, that should
positively declare y⁰ Acceptance of the Mediation, Monsʳ de Croissy
onely told him, That when he knew the Kings Sentiments, he should
receive it accordingly. Next day the Secretarie went againe to Monsʳ
de Croissy, who continuing still in bed, by reason of y⁰ Gout, receivd y⁰ Pacquet from his Commis, and having opend it, sent an
Answer to y⁰ Secretarie, that as soone as he was able he would speake
to y⁰ King of it and that he should come againe and receive an
Answer. Yoʳ Loᵖ will see by y⁰ Copie of y⁰ Elector's Letter inclos'd
what his proceedings have beene in relation to y⁰ Prisonners; And
if the Mediation be accepted, upon y⁰ Principall (wᶜʰ are the Pretensions of Madame) there is no doubt, but that the Matter will be
easily determin'd." [1]

"23. Febʳⁱᵉ 1686.... Y⁰ Popes Mediation about y⁰ affaires of y⁰
Palatinat is accepted of by y⁰ most Christian King, upon this Con-
dition, That y⁰ Elector make a Declaration That this shall be no
Prejudice to y⁰ Right of Madame in her Pretensions to y⁰ Succession.
A Courier is dispatcht with this to y⁰ Diett att Ratisbon, Upon y⁰
Answer to this depends y⁰ Successe of this Accommodation." [2]

"Feb. 27, 1686.... Since my last y⁰ Elector Palatins Secretary has
been with Monsʳ de Croissy to desire an Answer to his Expresse,
who told him, That y⁰ King had forbidden him to give any Answer
att all. However he intends to stay here yet some dayes, in hopes he
may obtaine something att y⁰ Intercession of y⁰ Popes Nuncio: And
Monsieur is sending an Envoyé to Heydelberg within a few dayes,
having nominated Monsieur Moras,[3] President au Mortier au Parlement de Metz and Procureur Generall de Monsieur, to go thither
in that Qualitie." [4]

"March y⁰ 9ᵗʰ, 1686.... The affaires of y⁰ Palatinat are still in y⁰
same Condition, The Nonce was on Thursday att Versailles, to persuade Monʳ de Croissy, att his Solicitation, to use his good Offices
with y⁰ King, to obtaine an Answer to y⁰ last Letter; He spoke allso
with Monsieur, desiring him to use his Interest; But Monsieur
assur'd him He had already made some ouverture, but found y⁰

1 R.O. *loc. cit.* f. 25.   2 *Ib.* f. 34.
3 Frémyn de Morovas; cf. Immich, *op. cit.* pp. 73-4.
4 R.O. *loc. cit.* f. 39.

King so chagrin upon y⁰ Subject, That he durst proceed no further.[1] It is thought therefore that yᵉ Secretarie of yᵉ Electʳ Palatin will be obligd to go away without any Answer att all to yᵉ Letter." [2]

"March 13, 1686.... The Secretarie of yᵉ Electʳ Palatin stayes here yet, in hopes (by yᵉ Mediation of yᵉ Nonce) to obtaine an Answer to yᵉ Letter he brought to Monsieur de Croissy. I send yoʳ Loᵖ a Copie of yᵉ Memorial given to yᵉ Dyett at Ratisbon." [3]

Peucker had to leave without an answer. Further attempts to have the prisoners in France liberated remained fruitless. Cardel was still a prisoner in 1700, but the prisoners at Mannheim were liberated by the Elector.[4]

"Aug. 7, 1686.... The Affaires of yᵉ Palatinate begin to stirre againe: Monsieur hath wrott a Letter to yᵉ Pope [5] (and putt it into yᵉ Nonce's hands here) to desire him to mediate, so that he may be putt into possession of his just rights. This and yᵉ season of yᵉ yeare, causes severall apprehensions, That Monsieur, alleadging he has alreadie offerd all wayes of proceeding amicably, but in vain, will trye some other methods of taking possession." [6]

Nothing came of the proposed papal arbitration which was declined by the German princes, and, other factors contributing, the Palatinate was invaded by a French army in 1688 and devastated in 1689.[7]

Notes on Lorraine

Charles IV, Duke of Lorraine, had been deprived of his duchy in circumstances too complicated to be related here.[8] Charles V had succeeded his errant uncle in 1675, but would not accept the return of his duchy on the humiliating terms imposed by the Treaty of Nimeguen. Sir William Trumbull was instructed, as we have seen, to recommend the Duke's interests to Louis XIV, and to give him every assistance.

On November 20, 1685, the Duke wrote again to James asking him to protect his rights: "Je demeure le seul Prince dépouillé de ses Estats....L'on veut me faire croire que la France regarde mes Estats comme une partie de son Royaume...par tous les nouveaux changements que l'on continue a y faire." [9] James doubtless replied,

---

1 Cf. Immich, *op. cit.* p. 76.
2 R.O. *loc. cit.* f. 42.
3 *Ib.* f. 46.
4 Immich, *op. cit.* p. 78 *n.*
5 Printed in Immich, p. 95.
6 R.O. *loc. cit.* f. 116.
7 Cf. Lavisse, *Histoire de France*, VIII¹, pp. 5, 10, 16, 20.
8 See Parisot, *Histoire de Lorraine*, t. II, pp. 82–100.
9 R.O. *France*, vol. 148, f. 121, Charles V of Lorraine to James II, Nov. 20, 1685.

for in February the Duke thanked him for his interest.[1] A month later he wrote again, requesting James's continued intervention: "Les années s'escoulent, la France demeure dans la jouissance de mes Estats, et l'inquietude de Pere s'augmente si fort que je ne puis cesser d'agir par touttes les voyes que je puis rencontrer pour tascher de remettre les Enfans que Dieu m'a donné en la possession des biens de leurs ancestres."[2]

Sir William refers occasionally to the Duke's affairs. Thus on January 16, 1686, he reports: "The Emper[rs] Envoyé[3] had yesterday a Particular Audience.... He propos'd allso some Accommodation with ye Duke of Lorraine, and moov'd this King to accept of an Envoyé from him: to which, I thinke, no Answer was given, but time taken to consider."[4]

"Feb. 16, 1686.... The Emper[rs] Envoyé having propos'd an Accommodation with ye Duke of Lorraine (as I had ye Honour to signify to yor Lo[p] formerly) and that he might be admitted to have an Agent to Treate of his Affaires att this Court, That might be receivd and own'd to that purpose, under such a Character as ye most Christian King should approove, he press'd for an Answer severall times, and att last on Tuesday Monsr de Croissy told him, That ye King would accept of an Agent from ye Duke of Lorraine and heare his propositions, Provided he did not speake anything concerning ye Restitution of Lorraine. The Emper[rs] Envoyé was surprizd with this Answer, and said, he thought this amounting to a plaine Denyall, the Duke of Lorraine being a man of too much Honour to treate on any such Termes."[5]

"July 24, 1686.... Here has been a Report, very confidently spread, that Monsr le President Cannon[6] was arrivd att Versailles as Envoyé from ye Duke de Lorraine to treate of some Accommodation. But ye truth is this; The Emperour's Envoyé had Orders (presently after his first coming) to propose ye ending of all matters (if it might be) concerning that Duke; Which Monsr de Croissy told him the King would willingly consent to, and that a Person might be sent to this Court to treate hereof; But this upon this condition, That it might be to Propose something Equivalent, and by way of Exchange; For that ye King was firmely resolvd neither to part with Lorraine or any of its Dependancies. Upon this ye Emper[rs] Envoyé

1 R.O. *France*, vol. 150, f. 15, Charles V of Lorraine to James II, Feb. 5, 1686.
2 *Ib*. f. 44. The same to the same, March 12, 1686.
3 Lobkowitz.
4 R.O. *loc. cit*. f. 4, to Sunderland, Jan. 16, 1686.
5 *Ib*. f. 23, to Sunderland, Feb. 16, 1686.
6 Claude-François Canon, premier président de la cour souveraine de Lorraine.

giving an Account of this Answer, thought yᵉ matter would have rested here, and that yᵉ Emperʳ and yᵉ Duke of Lorraine had been determind to send no person upon these Termes. In yᵉ meane while Monsieur de Vauguy̆on, Envoyé from yᵉ most Christian King to yᵉ Emperʳ, found meanes to prevaile for yᵉ sending of yᵉ President Cannon hither, And he was accordingly dispatcht and proceeded in his way as farre as Stratsbourg, or very neare; When yᵉ Duke of Lorraine (upon further consideration) changd his mind, and sent him Orders to proceed no further. This I thinke, (upon good grounds) is all that has been hitherto don in this matter."[1]

"Sept. 14, 1686.... The Count de Lobcovitz (yᵉ Emperʳˢ Envoyé here) was yesterday att Versailles, to acquaint yᵉ King with yᵉ Taking of Buda; and Deliverd to him a Letter writt with yᵉ Emperours hand; wherein I am inform'd were very great Commendations of yᵉ conduct and merit of yᵉ Duc de Lorraine, but yet without any particular requests in his behalf."[2]

The Duke was never able to rule his titular duchy, but it was restored to his son by the Treaty of Ryswick.

Notes on the Waldensians[3] in 1686

Occasionally Sir William refers to the Waldensians in his letters, some of his information coming from the Ambassador of Savoy. In order to prevent the Waldensian Valleys becoming a place of refuge for French Huguenots Louis XIV had obliged the young Duke of Savoy, Victor Amadeus, to oppress the inhabitants. From these extracts one may see the hold that Louis had over the Duke of Savoy, the Duke's initial reluctance, and the conflicting reports that helped to mislead the unhappy people.

To SUNDERLAND

Feb. 16, 1686

The Duke of Savoy is proceeding against yᵉ Huguenots within his Dominions, according to yᵉ Tenor of an Edict he has lately Publish'd, whereof I send yoʳ Loᵖ this Copie inclos'd.[4]

---

1 R.O. *loc. cit.* f. 110, to Sunderland, July 24, 1686; cf. *H.M.C., Downshire MSS.* I, pp. 206, 223.

2 *Ib.* f. 141, to Sunderland, Sept. 14, 1686.

3 Cf. Benoist, *Histoire de l'Édit de Nantes*, v, pp. 926–31; Catinat, *Mémoires*, I, pp. 21–6 (Life by Le Bouyer de Saint-Gervais), Paris, 3 vols., 1819; Chabrand, *Vaudois et Protestants des Alpes*, pp. 227–34.

4 R.O. *France*, vol. 150, f. 23. The Edict is on ff. 11–12.

Feb. 23, 1686

The Protestants in y⁰ Valley de Lucerne receiv⁴ y⁰ Notice of y⁰ Duke of Savoyes Edict without any Opposition; But they desird y⁰ Command⁰ of y⁰ Troopes not to proceed in y⁰ Execution therof, till such time as y⁰ Deputies they had sent to y⁰ Duke were return'd.[1]

March 2, 1686

The affaires of Savoye being communicated to yo⁰ Lo⁰ in y⁰ inclos'd Papers, I have onely to adde, That there are marching from hence 6 Bataillons of Foot, 2 Regiments of Horse and 1 of Dragoons, to be commanded by y⁰ Gouver⁰ of Cazall.[2]

March 6, 1686

The Italians are apprehensive of these Forces that are going into Savoy, because they will amount to between 7 and 8000 men, wᶜʰ is more than is necessarie to reduce y⁰ Huguenots.[3]

March 13, 1686

The account from Savoy of any Action from y⁰ Huguenotes in y⁰ Valley of Lucerne is not own'd by y⁰ Ambassador of Savoy.[4]

April 3ʳᵈ, 1686

I am informd That y⁰ Duke of Savoy has given permission to y⁰ Deputies of y⁰ Suisses to go to y⁰ Valley of Lucerne and to treate with those people about some Accommodation; Att wᶜʰ this Court is much dissatisfyd, pretending this ought not to have been don without y⁰ participation of y⁰ most Christian King; This I am told was occasion'd by some Jealousy y⁰ Duke of Savoy has, that there was some further Design in y⁰ French Troopes marching thither, than barely to assist him against the Huguenots.[5]

April 10, 1686

The Embassad⁰ of Savoy assur'd me yesterday That y⁰ Deputies of y⁰ Suisses to y⁰ Valley of Lucerna have accommodated y⁰ Differences there, all possible Submissions being offerd; And so that businesse seemes to be att an end, upon wᶜʰ y⁰ French Troopes have orders to march back.[6]

---

1 R.O. *France*, vol. 150, f. 34.
2 *Ib.* f. 40.   3 *Ib.* f. 41.
4 *Ib.* f. 46. The Ambassador was the Marquis Ferrero de la Marmora. *Recueil des Instructions...*, vol. xv (*Savoie...Mantoue*, II), p. 390.
5 R.O. *loc. cit.* f. 62.
6 *Ib.* f. 65; cf. A.É. *Angleterre*, vol. 158, f. 213, Barrillon to Louis XIV, on Trumbull's report, April 18, 1686.

April 24, 1686

The affaires in Savoy with y⁰ Inhabitants of Lucerna are said to be ended; That Duke having given them Leave to sell their Estates within eight Dayes, and then to be gon out of his Territories.[1]

April 27, 1686

The Affaires in Savoye were thought Accommodated upon y⁰ Termes I signifyd to yoʳ Loᵖ by y⁰ last Post. But since I heare y⁰ Huguenots resolvd to send other Deputies to Turin, to endeavʳ y⁰ obtaining some better Conditions, They beleiving y⁰ Duke of Savoye to be willing to disengage himself out of this matter as soon as he can. This King is not satisfyd with y⁰ Dukes easinesse of yeilding so easily to them, and told y⁰ Nuncio here his opinion to that purpose.[2]

May 1ˢᵗ, 1686

The Embassadʳ of Savoy told me yesterday att Versailles, That things are farr from being accommodated there, That the Protestants having time given them to y⁰ 27ᵗʰ of last Month to dispose of their Effects and be gon out of the Countrie, and to leave Procurations to some Commissaries appointed for that Purpose to sell the rest within 3 months, upon Condition they immediately layd down their Armes; But he said this Condition not being complyd with, y⁰ French Troopes had marchd in order to joyne with those of Savoye, And that he expected continually to receive y⁰ Newes of some Action that they had attacqu'd before this time, those people in severall Places.[3]

May 4, 1686

We have newes of some Action passt in Savoye, y⁰ Deputies being return'd into Switzerland without accommodating those Affaires: The particulars are not yet come to my Knowledge.[4]

May 8, 1686

Since y⁰ Account wᶜʰ I send to yoʳ Loᵖ of y⁰ late Action in Savoye, I heare that all matters are ended there, y⁰ Protestants having submitted themselves to y⁰ Duke.[5]

May 11, 1686

The affaires in Savoye are said to be concluded by y⁰ Submission of y⁰ Protestants to y⁰ Pleasure of y⁰ Duke, and that y⁰ French Troopes have Orders to march back. This Court is dissatisfyd with y⁰ Dukes Proceeding, who upon y⁰ coming of y⁰ French Forces gave notice to his Neighbours in Italy to be upon their Guard, least there should be some further designe, after y⁰ businesse was don there.[6]

1 R.O. *loc. cit.* f. 70. 2 *Ib.* f. 71. 3 *Ib.* f. 72.
4 *Ib.* f. 73. 5 *Ib.* f. 74. 6 *Ib.* f. 76.

May 18, 1686

Yᵉ affaires of Savoye are not yet fully ended, some of those people being intrencht in yᵉ Mountaines; But a little time will oblige them to surrender themselves for want of Provisions.[1]

On May 10 Louis XIV had written to Barrillon that he could inform the English court of the overthrow of the rebellious subjects of the Duke of Savoy. No heretics would be left in the mountains, but good Catholics, faithful to their Prince. The French troops were to be withdrawn shortly.[2]

Barrillon replied: "Sa Mᵗᵉ Britannique a esté fort aise d'apprendre que les sujets rebelles de Mʳ le Duc de Savoye ayent esté entierement reduits. Cette affaire est d'un fort grand éclat icy et cause beaucoup de chagrin aux Protestans zelez. Ils se souviennent que du temps de Cromwell ces mesmes gens des vallees de Lucerne furent garentis de toute oppression par la protection qu'ils reçeurent d'Angleterre." Without the aid of the French troops this victory, it was said, could not have taken place.[3]

Sir William's bald account conveys none of the indignation to which Barrillon alludes, but then he was not apt to show his feelings in his official letters. To Halifax and to Sir Richard Bulstrode he doubtless wrote differently.

Sir William Trumbull's letters from France preserved at the Record Office

While Sir William's correspondence is not given in full nothing of any importance has been excluded. In general all obviously second-hand news has been omitted, news derived from gazettes and newsletters, especially foreign news, as, for instance, information about the siege of Buda; occasional references to Louis XIV's health which is so amply described in the memoirs of the time; unimportant court news that is supplied more fully by Dangeau and Sourches; letters in which Sir William merely acknowledges instructions received, or in which he states that he is enclosing gazettes, having little other news to give.

All these letters, unless there is some indication to the contrary, are addressed to Lord Sunderland.

1 R.O. *loc. cit.* f. 78.
2 A.É. *Angleterre*, vol. 158, f. 258, May 10, 1686.
3 *Ib.* ff. 281–2, May 16, 1686.

State Papers, Foreign, France

No.	Reference	Date (N.S.) 1685	
1	Vol. 148, f. 118	Nov. 20	Quoted[1] on p. 20
2	,, ,, f. 123[2]	,, 24	,, ,, pp. 21–2
3	,, ,, f. 119	,, 28	,, ,, pp. 22–3
4	,, ,, f. 120	,, 30	,, ,, p. 24
5	,, ,, ff. 128–9	Dec. 5	,, ,, pp. 30–31, 32–3
6	,, ,, f. 130	,, 8	Omitted
7	,, ,, ff. 136–7	,, 12	Quoted on pp. 36–9, 186
8	,, ,, f. 144	,, 15	Omitted
9	,, ,, ff. 146–7	,, 19	Quoted on pp. 43–6, 49–51, 187
10	,, ,, f. 148	,, 22	,, ,, p. 53
11	,, ,, f. 152	,, 24	,, ,, pp. 54–5
12	,, ,, f. 145[2]	,, 26	Omitted
13	,, ,, ff. 153–4	,, 29	Quoted on pp. 57–9
		1686	
14	,, ,, f. 157	Jan. 2	,, ,, pp. 60–63, 187
15	,, ,, f. 158	,, 5	,, ,, pp. 63–4
16	,, ,, ff. 161–2	,, 9	,, ,, pp. 66–9
17	Vol. 150, f. 3	,, 12	,, ,, p. 71
18	,, ,, f. 4	,, 16	,, ,, pp. 72–3, 191
19	,, ,, f. 5	,, 19	,, ,, p. 74
20	,, ,, f. 6	,, 23	,, ,, p. 187
21	,, ,, f. 7	,, 26	Omitted
22	,, ,, f. 10	,, 30	Quoted on pp. 80–81, 187
23	,, ,, f. 13	Feb. 2	,, ,, p. 78
24	,, ,, f. 14	,, 6	,, ,, pp. 83–4
25	,, ,, f. 17	,, 9	Omitted
26	,, ,, f. 21	,, 13	Quoted on pp. 85–6
27	,, ,, f. 23	,, 16	,, ,, pp. 187–8, 191, 192
28	,, ,, f. 25	,, 20	,, ,, pp. 92–3, 188–9
29	,, ,, f. 34	,, 23	,, ,, pp. 189, 193
30	,, ,, f. 39	,, 27	,, ,, pp. 97–8, 189
31	,, ,, f. 40	Mar. 2	,, ,, p. 193

[1] The term "quoted" does not necessarily mean that the whole letter has been quoted.　　[2] Out of place.

No.	Reference	Date (N.S.) 1686	
32	Vol. 150, f. 41	Mar. 6	Quoted on pp. 100, 193
33	,, ,, ff. 42–3	,, 9	,, ,, pp. 101–3, 189–90
34	,, ,, f. 46	,, 13	,, ,, pp. 103, 190, 193
35	,, ,, f. 55	,, 16	,, ,, p. 104
36	,, ,, f. 57	,, 20	,, ,, pp. 104–5
37	,, ,, f. 58	,, 23	,, ,, p. 107
38	,, ,, f. 59	,, 27	,, ,, pp. 107–8
39	,, ,, f. 61	,, 30	,, ,, p. 108
40	,, ,, f. 62	Apr. 3	,, ,, pp. 108–9, 193
41	,, ,, f. 64	,, 6	,, ,, p. 110
42	,, ,, f. 65	,, 10	,, ,, pp. 111–12, 193
43	,, ,, f. 66	,, 13	,, ,, p. 113
44	,, ,, f. 67	,, 17	,, ,, pp. 113–14
45	,, ,, f. 68	,, 20	,, ,, p. 114
46	,, ,, f. 70	,, 24	,, ,, pp. 114, 194
47	,, ,, f. 71	,, 27	,, ,, p. 194
48	,, ,, f. 72	May 1	,, ,, pp. 115–16, 194
49	,, ,, f. 73	,, 4	,, ,, pp. 116, 194
50	,, ,, f. 74	,, 8	,, ,, pp. 117, 194
51	,, ,, f. 76	,, 11	,, ,, p. 194
52	,, ,, f. 77	,, 15	,, ,, pp. 117–18
53	,, ,, f. 78	,, 18	,, ,, pp. 118, 195
54	,, ,, f. 81	,, 22	,, ,, p. 119
55	,, ,, f. 82	,, 25	,, ,, p. 119
56	,, ,, f. 83	,, 29	,, ,, p. 120
57	,, ,, f. 84	June 1	Omitted
58	,, ,, f. 86	,, 5	Quoted on pp. 120–21
59	,, ,, f. 88	,, 8	Omitted
60	,, ,, f. 89	,, 12	Quoted on pp. 122–3
61	,, ,, f. 90	,, 15	,, ,, pp. 123–4
62	,, ,, f. 91	,, 19	Omitted
63	,, ,, f. 92	,, 22	,,
64	,, ,, ff. 93–4	,, 26	Quoted on pp. 124–5, 126
65	,, ,, ff. 95–6	,, 29	,, ,, pp. 127–8
66	,, ,, f. 97	July 3	,, ,, p. 129
67	,, ,, f. 98	,, 6	,, ,, pp. 129–30
68	,, ,, ff. 99–100[1]	,, 9	,, ,, pp. 135–7
69	,, ,, f. 101	,, 9	,, ,, p. 137
70	,, ,, f. 102	,, 10	Omitted

1 To James II.

No.	Reference	Date (N.S.) 1686	
71	Vol. 150, f. 103	July 13	Quoted on p. 138
72	,, ,, f. 104	,, 17	,, ,, pp. 138–9
73	,, ,, f. 105	,, 23	,, ,, pp. 145–6
74	,, ,, ff. 106–9[1]	,, 23	,, ,, pp. 141–5
75	,, ,, f. 110	,, 24	,, ,, pp. 191–2
76	,, ,, f. 111	,, 27	Omitted
77	,, ,, f. 112	,, 31	,,
78	,, ,, ff. 113–14	Aug. 3	Quoted on p. 149
79	,, ,, ff. 115–16	,, 7	,, ,, pp. 149–50, 151, 190
80	,, ,, f. 119	,, 10	,, ,, pp. 151–2
81	,, ,, ff. 121–2	,, 14	,, ,, p. 153
82	,, ,, f. 124	,, 17	Omitted
83	,, ,, f. 125	,, 21	Quoted on pp. 153–4
84	,, ,, f. 126	,, 24	,, ,, pp. 154–5
85	,, ,, f. 128	,, 28	Omitted
86	,, ,, f. 130	,, 31	,,
87	,, ,, ff. 134–6	Sept. 4	Quoted on pp. 156–8
88	,, ,, f. 139	,, 7	,, ,, p. 158
89	,, ,, ff. 143–4[2]	,, 11	,, ,, pp. 159–60
90	,, ,, f. 141	,, 14	,, ,, pp. 161, 192
91	,, ,, f. 145	,, 18	,, ,, pp. 161–2
92	,, ,, f. 148	,, 21	Omitted
93	,, ,, ff. 150–51	,, 25	Quoted on p. 163
94	,, ,, f. 152	,, 28	,, ,, pp. 163–4
95	,, ,, f. 153	Oct. 2	,, ,, pp. 165–6
96	,, ,, f. 156	,, 5	,, ,, p. 166
97	,, ,, f. 157	,, 9	,, ,, p. 166

[1] To James II.   [2] Out of place.

Authorities

(For a list of abbreviations used in the text see p. xi *ante*)

A. MANUSCRIPT

PUBLIC RECORD OFFICE

State Papers, Foreign, France, vols. 148, 150 (these two volumes contain Sir William Trumbull's letters); 151 (Correspondence of his successor, Bevil Skelton).

Entry Books, France, vol 19. (The originals of Sunderland's letters to Trumbull are at Easthampstead Park, Berks. Abstracts are given in the Report of the Historical Manuscripts Commission on the Manuscripts of the Marquess of Downshire. When these are sufficiently detailed, reference is made to them rather than to the Entry Book, since they are more easily available to the reader.)

Newsletters, France, Bundle 22.

EASTHAMPSTEAD PARK, BERKS

Papers of Sir William Trumbull. (See also under Hist. MSS. Comm.)

ARCHIVES NATIONALES

Volumes O¹ 29, O¹ 30. (Expéditions du Secrétariat de la Maison du Roi.)

ARCHIVES DU MINISTÈRE DES AFFAIRES ÉTRANGÈRES

Correspondance politique, Angleterre, vols. 151, 155–60.

Mémoires et Documents, Angleterre, vol. 8.

France, vol. 302. (This vol. contains notes by M. de Croissy on audiences given ambassadors. Unfortunately there is a gap between Aug. 1685 and Sept. 1686, and only one of Trumbull's audiences is noted.)

BIBLIOTHÈQUE NATIONALE

Fonds français 7051–3 (Recueil de pièces concernant la Révocation de l'Édit de Nantes...et provenant de M. de la Reynie).

10265 (Gazettes historiques et anecdotiques).

17421 (Correspondance d'Achille de Harlay).

B. PRINTED SOURCES

Avaux, C. de Mesmes, Comte de. Négociations en Hollande, vol. v. Paris, 1753. 6 vols.

Benoist, E. Histoire de l'Édit de Nantes, vol. v. Delft, 1693–5. 5 vols.

Browne, Sir Thomas. Works, vol. i. London, 1836. 4 vols.

Burnet, G. History of My own Time. Oxford, 1833. 6 vols.

— A Supplement, ed. by H. C. Foxcraft. Oxford, 1902.

Calendar of Treasury Books, 1685–9, prepared by W. A. Shaw. London, 1923. 4 vols.

Calendars of State Papers, Colonial Series. America and West Indies, 1681–5, 1685–8, ed. by J. W. Fortescue. London, 1898 and 1899.

Camden Society Publications. See Savile.

Chambrun, J. Pineton de. Les Larmes...qui contiennent les persécutions arrivées aux églises de la principauté d'Orange. The Hague, 1688.

Clarendon. The Correspondence of Henry Hyde, Earl of Clarendon, and of his brother, the Earl of Rochester. London, 1828. 2 vols.

Dalrymple, Sir John. Memoirs of Great Britain and Ireland. London, 1771–3. 2 vols.

Dangeau, Marquis de. Journal, vol. i. Paris, 1854–60. 19 vols.

Gazette de France. Paris, 1685, 1686.

Gigas, E. Lettres de divers Savants, vol. i. Choix de la Correspondance inédite de Pierre Bayle. Copenhagen, 1890.

Historical Manuscripts Commission, Reports.

> Appendix to 7th Report. Part I. London, 1879. MSS. of Sir Fred. Graham, Bart.
>
> Appendix to 8th Report. Part I. London, 1881. MSS. of the Earl of Denbigh.
>
> Manuscripts of the Marquess of Downshire, vol. i (in 2 parts). Papers of Sir William Trumbull. London, 1924.

Hollandse Mercurius. Haarlem, 1686.

Mercure Galant. Paris, December 1685.

Pepys, S. Tangier Papers, ed. by E. Chappell. Printed for the Navy Records Society. [London], 1935.

Pilatte, L., ed. by. Édits, Déclarations et Arrests concernans la Religion Protestante Réformée, 1662–1751. Paris, 1885.

Pope, A. Works, ed. by Elwin and Courthope. London, 1871–89. 10 vols.

Ravaisson, F. Archives de la Bastille, vol. viii. Paris, 1866–91. 17 vols.

Recueil des Instructions données aux Ambassadeurs et Ministres de France, especially vols. XXIV and XXV, viz. Angleterre I, II,... avec une introduction et des notes par J. J. Jusserand. Paris, 1929.

Savile Correspondence. Letters to and from Henry Savile. Camden Society Publications. London, 1858.

Sourches, Marquis de. Mémoires, vol. I. Paris, 1882–93. 13 vols. Index, 1912.

Spanheim, E. Relation de la Cour de France en 1690, ed. É. Bourgeois. Paris, 1900.

C. MODERN WORKS

Adair, E. R. The Exterritoriality of Ambassadors in the sixteenth and seventeenth centuries. London, 1929.

Agnew, D. C. A. Protestant Exiles from France. London, 1871. 3 vols.

American Historical Review. See under Barbour.

André, L. Les Sources de l'Histoire de France. Dix-Septième Siècle, especially vol. VI....Histoire religieuse. Paris, 1913–35. 8 vols. (Vols. I–IV are by É. Bourgeois and L. André.)

Arnaud, E. Histoire des Protestants de Provence, du Comtat Venaissin et de la Principauté d'Orange, vol. II. Paris, 1884. 2 vols.

Barbour, V. Consular Service in the Reign of Charles II. American Historical Review, vol. XXXIII. New York, April 1928.

Beer, E. S. de. The Marquis of Albeville and his Brothers. English Historical Review, vol. XLV. London, July 1930.

Boislisle, A. de. La Place des Victoires et la Place de Vendôme. Paris, 1889.

— His edition of the Mémoires de Saint-Simon. Paris, 1879–1928. 41 vols. (For the notes only, which are a mine of reliable biographical information. Excellent index for vols. I–XXVIII. Paris, 1918. 2 vols.)

Bourilly, V. Les Protestants de Provence et d'Orange sous Louis XIV. Bulletin, Société de l'Histoire du Protestantisme français. Paris, 1922–7, a series of articles, especially 1927, pp. 166–200.

Brown, R. H. The financial relations of Louis XIV and James II. Journal of Modern History, vol. III. Chicago, 1931.

Bulletin de la Société de l'Histoire du Protestantisme français. See under Bourilly and Pascal.

Chabrand, J. A. Vaudois et Protestants des Alpes. Grenoble, 1886.

Clark, G. N. The later Stuarts. Oxford, 1934.

Courtney, W. P. Article on Sir William Trumbull, D.N.B.

Davis, G. Bibliography of British History. Stuart Period. Oxford, 1928.

Douen, O. La Révocation de l'Édit de Nantes à Paris. Paris, 1894. 3 vols.

Durand, R. Louis XIV et Jacques II à la veille de la Révolution de 1688. Les trois missions de Bonrepaus en Angleterre. Revue d'Histoire moderne et contemporaine. Vol. x. Paris, 1908.

English Historical Review. See under Beer and Wood.

Firth, C. H. and S. Lomas. Notes on the diplomatic Relations of England and France, 1603–88. Oxford, 1906.

Forneron, H. Louise de Kéroualle. Paris, 1886.

Gentleman's Magazine, vol. LX, Part I. London, 1790. Memoirs of Sir William Trumbull.

Guitard, E. Colbert et Seignelay contre la Religion réformée. Second edition. Paris, 1912.

Haag, Eugène et Émile. La France protestante. Paris, 1846–59. 10 vols.

Hanotaux, G. et A. Martineau. Histoire des Colonies françaises, vol. I. L'Amérique, by Ch. de la Roncière, J. Tramond, E. Louvrière. Paris, 1929.

Haring, C. H. The Buccaneers in the West Indies. London, 1910.

Immich, M. Zur Vorgeschichte des Orleans'schen Krieges. Heidelberg, 1898.

Journal of Modern History. See under Brown.

Jusserand, J. J. See under Recueil, in the preceding section.

Klopp, O. Der Fall des Hauses Stuart, vol. III. Vienna, 1875–88. 14 vols.

Laut, A. C. The Conquest of the Great North-west. London, 1909. 2 vols.

Lavisse, E. Histoire de France, VIII¹. Louis XIV. La fin du règne (1685–1715). By A. de Saint-Léger, A. Rébelliau, P. Sagnac and E. Lavisse. Paris, 1908.

Lodge, R. The History of England. From the Restoration to the Death of William III. Political History of England, vol. VIII. London, 1910.

Lonchay, H. La Rivalité de la France et de l'Espagne aux Pays-Bas, 1635–1700. Brussels, 1896.

Pagès, G. Le Grand Électeur et Louis XIV. Paris, 1905.

Parisot, R. Histoire de Lorraine, vol. II. Paris, 1919–24. 3 vols.

Pascal, C. Louis XIV et les réfugiés huguenots en Angleterre. Bulletin, Société de l'Histoire du Protestantisme français. Paris, 1891.

Pascal, C. Un ambassadeur désagréable à la cour de Louis XIV, Sir William Trumball. Bulletin, Société de l'Histoire du Protestantisme français. Paris, 1894. (Uses French sources only. Contains many extracts from the correspondence at the Archives du Ministère des Affaires Étrangères.)

Picavet, C. G. La diplomatie française au temps de Louis XIV. Paris, 1930.

— Les commis des Affaires Étrangères au temps de Louis XIV. Revue d'Histoire moderne, vol. I. Paris, 1926.

Pirenne, H. Histoire de Belgique, vol. V. Brussels, 1920–32. 7 vols.

Pontbriant, A. de. Histoire de la Principauté d'Orange. Avignon, 1891.

Purnell, E. K. Life of Sir William Trumbull in his Report on the MSS. of the Marquess of Downshire, vol. I. Hist. MSS. Comm. London, 1924.

Ranke, L. von. A History of England, principally in the seventeenth century. Oxford, 1875. 6 vols.

Recueil des Instructions. See preceding section.

Renée, A. Les nièces de Mazarin. Paris, 1858.

Revue d'Histoire moderne. See under Picavet.

Revue d'Histoire moderne et contemporaine. See under Durand.

Saint-Léger, A. de, et Ph. Sagnac. La Prépondérance française. Louis XIV (1661–1715). Paris, 1935.

Thomson, M. A. The Secretaries of State, 1681–1782. Oxford, 1932.

Willson, Beckles. The Great Company. London, 1900. 2 vols.

Wood, A. C. The English Embassy at Constantinople, 1660–1762. English Historical Review, vol. XL. London, 1925.

Index

For EU product safety concerns, contact us at Calle de José Abascal, 56–1°,
28003 Madrid, Spain or eugpsr@cambridge.org.